Praise for *Reasons to be Cheerful*

'This is at once Steel's memoir, a rallying battle-cry to remind like-minded thinkers that they're neither alone nor impotent, and a social history of Britain over the last twenty-five years. It's polemical, passionate and consistently funny'
Independent on Sunday

'Anyone who has ever taken part in a demo – or just wishes they had – will devour Mark Steel's book in one sitting'
Ken Loach

'Mark Steel is the funniest Marxist since Groucho. He is bolshy, belligerent and bloody hilarious'
Francis Wheen

'Hysterically funny in his demolition of the inelegant nuttiness of far-left verbiage, Mark Steel makes intelligent people laugh hopefully, a job of extraordinary value'
Independent

'One of Britain's funniest and most incisive comedians'
Time Out

'Part autobiography, part political analysis, this book is both hilarious and sobering. He is informed, uncompromising, and joyfully witty'
Arthur Smith

Also by Mark Steel

IT'S NOT A RUNNER BEAN

REASONS TO BE CHEERFUL

VIVE
la
Revolution

MARK STEEL

Scribner

First published in Great Britain by Scribner, 2003
An imprint of Simon & Schuster UK Ltd
A Viacom Company

Grateful acknowledgement is made to Universal Music
Publishing for permission to reproduce lyrics from the music
of The Clash.

1 3 5 7 9 10 8 6 4 2

Simon & Schuster UK Ltd
Africa House
64–78 Kingsway
London WC2B 6AH

www.simonsays.co.uk

Simon & Schuster Australia
Sydney

A CIP catalogue record for this book is
available from the British Library

ISBN 0-7432-0805-6

Typeset by M Rules
Printed and bound in Great Britain by
The Bath Press, Bath

This book is dedicated to the memory of Joe Strummer

CONTENTS

ACKNOWLEDGEMENTS

I would like to thank Paul Foot for plenty of discussions on the subject, and the loan of his obscure books. He once told me, 'It's worth buying a good book even if you've no idea if you'll ever read it.' By saying that, the bastard cost me about ten thousand quid. Thanks to Mike Marqusee for talking over the issue with me many times, often during a lull in the cricket. And to the bank manager at Ste. Menehould who lent me some desperately needed cash from a plastic container long after the bank had shut because 'Ah, you're the English writer who's been looking round the town.'

Thanks to the French café in Crystal Palace, where the staff kindly allowed me to sit for days at a time, spreading scrappy notes across their tables. Thanks to Ben Ball for his tireless editing skills, and exhaustive notes and questions. Thanks to Pete Sinclair, Jonny Geller and Paul McGarr for their vital and reassuring comments after reading the tatty first draft, and to Susan Ram for the stuff she sent me about India.

Thanks to Bindy, especially for looking after Elliot and Eloise during the hours I sat in that café. Many thanks to those people at Radio 4, particularly Phil Clarke, who have made my lecture series possible. Thanks to the vast numbers of people who continually create a purpose for history by defying injustice today. And thanks to everyone who lived in the eighteenth and nineteenth centuries, without whom this book would not have been possible.

PREFACE

I once heard of a history teacher who asked her class, 'Who can remember what the Vikings came in?' The kids shuffled, as bored as ever, so she barked, 'Come on, we did this last week.' Eventually someone said, 'longboats Miss' and someone else said, 'rowing boats' until the teacher said, 'No, can't you remember? The answer is *hordes*. The Vikings came in *hordes*.'

Some of the historical television documentaries that pour off the assembly line make history more accessible than she did, but most still reek of pomposity. Every programmme about the English Civil War seems to include an out-of-work Shakespearian actor as Cromwell, wandering through muddy fields in his helmet and with a huge wart on his nose. He'll gaze at the camera, pause and launch into a grand soliloquy, such as 'Fain be that from this day shall parliament rule this glorious land,' as if he's Laurence Olivier in Henry V. In fact, Cromwell was from East Anglia. So it's more likely he led troops into battle with 'I tell 'ee what, be a rum ol' do if we lose'.

Even more pompous are the majority of academic works that confront you from bookshop shelves on any subject you wish to investigate. Many of them assume you already know what happened, and concern themselves with debating an obscure point put forward by a rival academic. So you're pelted with stuff like, 'The falling corn supplies indicated in Table 24 suggest Cruickshank-Leigh has underestimated the effect of grain distribution on the great Norfolk mustard riots.' And it puzzles me why, if they really wish to argue this point that no one else has shown any interest in, they don't go round to the other bloke's cottage and have it out with him there. Most people seem to manage this. If they have a dispute with their neighbour, they don't write a book that goes 'Recent studies have confirmed the frequency with which Mr Roberts has blocked my drive,' and expect it to be published by the Fontana University Press for thirty-five quid.

All this treatment has been applied to the French Revolution. But it has also, from shortly after it began, been under constant attack from those who depict it simply as a flurry of unforgivable carnage.

As anyone who has taken part in a strike or a demonstration will know, reports of events that challenge the established order can be distorted by the next morning, never mind 200 years later. And, as is the case with plenty of those modern events, once you remove the prejudice that anyone involved was fundamentally rotten, an entirely different picture emerges. The French Revolution becomes a story of people not very different from those we know today, but who found themselves participating in an extraordinary journey. So the revolution is worth studying as a guide to, and an inspiration for, our own times. But also it's a cracking tale in which every human emotion and experience, every quirk and eccentricity, every friendship, argument, love affair, every human frailty was at its most intense, as almost every idea assumed to be eternal was swept away.

Now, as a superpower stalks the world with apparent invincibility, it may be worth re-telling a tale of a time when an apparently invincible dynasty was overturned by some washer women, some slaves and a postman.

INTRODUCTION

It seems to me that we're not supposed to like the French Revolution very much. My introduction to the subject was on an unemployed afternoon in the late 1970s, slouched in front of *Blue Peter*, when I think it was Peter Purves who introduced an item on Marie Antoinette. She loved beautiful clothes, he said, and was admired for her exquisite taste in jewellery. As a result, she was loved by the people of France.

Then the mood changed, and we were told how 'outside agitators' spread untrue stories about the Queen's greedy habits. And we were shown a silhouette of a cloaked man on a horse throwing leaflets into a cobbled street. This, apparently, led to the revolution, depicted as a shadowy crowd with pikes, while five or six actors shouted, 'Down with ze Queen.' I can't recall what followed, though presumably someone showed you how to make your own guillotine using a shoebox, an elastic band and a Stanley knife.

But *Blue Peter* was only following the generally accepted version of the event, that the French Revolution was a dreadful episode with no redeeming features. To most people in Britain, suggesting there was anything positive about it must seem as peculiar as saying there was a good side to the plague. Partly this must result from the persistent, if waning, attachment of the British to royalty, which can lead to the complete abandonment of rational thinking. For example, when the Queen Mother died we were informed from endless sources that she was gloriously talented, with one documentary insisting she was a 'great dancer' and 'tremendous wit'. I expected it to continue, 'She also invented the CD ROM and once took 8 for 37 against the West Indies.' The news seemed to be full of characters like Norman St John-Stevas making statements such as 'We'd never have won the war without her, you know. Every night she used to take out a Spitfire and engage the Luftwaffe over the English Channel. The RAF tried to stop her but she insisted. Do you know, one night she was shot down over occupied France and still managed to get back the next morning for the Changing of the Guard?'

Then up would pop one of those archetypal Cockneys to tell us, 'I'll never forget it. A bloomin' great doodlebug had knocked darn the 'ole perishin' street. I was trapped under the rubble, me leg 'ad come clean off, then someone shouted, "Stone the crows, it's the Queen." Well I turned round an' there she was and that was the happiest moment of my life.'

All of this was to deny the basic truth of royalty, that the clue to her achievements was in her name. She was the mother of the Queen. So she didn't even require exceptional parenting skills. Even the staunchest royalist can't have said to her, 'Who'd have thought it – your daughter becoming queen after starting out as just a humble princess?' Which may be why, amongst all this coverage, no one seemed able to find anything that she could genuinely *do*. Given that she lived so long with such privilege you'd think she could do something, like play the bassoon or do some trick shots on a snooker table.

And there's another side to British mistrust of the revolution, in that it fits our traditional distrust of the French in general. This was expressed by football fans who chanted, 'If it wasn't for us English you'd be Krauts,' during the World Cup in France, as if the French Resistance were cowards, whereas the Germans were driven from France by battalions of tubby sunburned blokes in shorts born in 1970. With similar logic the British government at one point claimed the war against Iraq had been caused by the French by voting against the war against Iraq.

The older generation had a different way of expressing similar feelings. My lovable but late Uncle Arthur once told me, 'The thing I remember most about the war is seeing this Frog on a train eating a chunk of raw garlic. RAW. I ask you.' Others might recall the Blitz, or the Battle of Britain, but this was the scene that lodged in the mind of Uncle Arthur, and he sounded as shell-shocked as any veteran of the Battle of El Alamein. Maybe he spent months in a wartime hospital, waking up in the night screaming, 'RAW, IT'S BLOODY RAW,' while sympathetic nurses dabbed water on his forehead and assured him it was another bad dream.

Even now, we stoically refuse to learn their language. Mind you, this applies to any language. We can meet a Dutchman who might speak thirty-four languages, but we still think we're cleverer than him because he speaks English with a slight Dutch accent. With France being within swimming distance, French does get taught in English schools, but usually as a quirky luxury, like media studies or ice sculpture. As a result, if a group of English people are in France, and one of them says to a Frenchman, 'Oh well, *merci beaucoup* then and er, *au revoir*,' the others will squeal, 'Ooooh, you've picked up the lingo, haven't you?'

Making the French even more peculiar, in many eyes, is their weird revolution, during which it seems to have become normal practice to guillotine complete strangers for no apparent reason.

As for *why* it happened, one of the most popular theories seems to be that this is just the way the French are: they like a revolution, they can't help it. It's a theory that has gained momentum over the last twenty years, as around once a month the news has shown us French lorry drivers nonchalantly drawing on their pungent fags as their twenty-ton vehicles sit astride useless motorways. You can certainly imagine French parents nervously sitting before their 12-year-old children and saying, 'Now then, son, you've come to that time in life when you'll be starting to feel certain urges. Pretty soon you'll be wanting to throw rocks at the *gendarmerie*, which is natural and perfectly safe as long as you take precautions.'

The finest exponent of this theory I ever came across was a butcher in Smithfield, about eighteen stone and wearing an overall spattered with blood. He was complaining about the damage done to small butchers by the supermarkets, but it was tricky to catch his drift as he was one of those people who swear with almost every alternate word. 'What we fucking ought to fucking do,' he told me, 'is fucking do what the fucking French would fucking do and take a fucking lorryfuckingload of fucking lambs on a cross-Channel fucking ferry and fucking tip the fucking lot in the fucking sea. See how they fucking like that.' And then he looked directly at me and said, 'Mind you, mate, don't get me fucking wrong, I fucking hate the fucking French an' all.'

An honest appraisal of the revolution hasn't been helped by the majority of accounts in novels, documentaries and films. The two most famous British films covering the period have been *The Scarlet Pimpernel* and *Carry On Don't Lose Your Head*, of which the Carry On film is by far the more realistic. In *The Scarlet Pimpernel*, set in 1792, Ian McKellen plays a lackey of the revolutionary ruler Robespierre, continuously outwitted by the foppish English Pimpernel, who organizes the escape of condemned aristocrats. For such a ruthless regime, the ruling Jacobins are surprisingly careless. In the jails that accommodate prisoners about to be guillotined, they seem to allow tradesmen to wander in and out with body-size boxes, as long as they shout something like 'Just taking these out the back, guvnor.' The McKellen character chases his adversary to England and back, and loses his final confrontation in such a way that he ends the film tied up and without his trousers. For a moment you wonder whether the original plan was to make a human version of the Roadrunner, with a scene in which McKellen pointed a musket at the Pimpernel through a hole in a tree, but it bent back up through another hole so that he shot himself.

If there really was a Pimpernel, however, he'd need to be a tad more accurate than the film's researchers, because in 1792 the Terror hadn't begun, and Robespierre didn't become ruler until the second half of 1793. By contrast, it seems more plausible that Robespierre might have spotted a woman's cleavage and sniggered, 'Cor, wouldn't mind my head rolling into THEM baskets.' (That, I feel obliged to tell you, is not a genuine line from *Carry On Don't Lose Your Head* but one I'm pathetically proud to have come up with myself.)

Novels have been a little less shrill. Probably the best-known story set in the revolution is Charles Dickens' *A Tale of Two Cities*, in which Dickens appears to warn rulers everywhere to show more concern for the poor, lest they invite the rule of the mob. Like George Orwell's *1984*, although it's become celebrated as a condemnation of revolution, it's equally vicious against the pre-revolutionary regime. The aristocrat Foulon is hung by the mob while suffocating from a mouth stuffed with grass, but only because earlier he dismisses the starving, laughing that 'If they've no bread, they can eat grass.' The grotesque Madame Defarge is responsible for the hero being sent to the guillotine, but only lacks humanity because her sister and brother were callously left to die by wealthy landowners during her childhood. Hope, Dickens appears to suggest, lies in individual acts of kindness, such as that of Sydney Carton as he does his far, far better thing.

None the less, to make his point Dickens has to stretch credibility to extremes. There may have been vengeful characters such as Mme Defarge, but it's doubtful whether they would have been allowed to overturn legal decisions to send innocuous dashing Englishmen to their deaths. In any case, the period of the Terror in which the guillotine was used in Paris with the ferocity described in the book lasted only six weeks, and was mostly directed against competing factions within the revolution, rather than the aristocracy.

Dickens might be excused his simplifications, as he was using the revolution as a backdrop to make general points about the human condition – and anyway it was a novel. But many serious historians go further up the same path of explaining the affair by saying, in effect, that everyone just went mental. Take for example the attitude towards Jean Paul Marat, one of the most prominent and popular leaders of the revolution. In *Paris in the Terror* by Stanley Cloomis, the author offers this synopsis: 'Arms flailing about in all directions, he waded into the revolution with the reckless rage of a lunatic . . . He lived like a bat or owl, always hidden from the light of day . . . It's astonishing that any woman could have fallen in love with this man . . . whose appearance was so repulsive that the wildest extremists of the left and their minions from the gutter were always careful to keep a distance of several benches between themselves and him.' To back up his point he quotes an unnamed contemporary as saying, 'He is toadlike in shape, marked by bulging eyes and a flabby mouth.' And another – 'Marat had the burning, haggard eye of a hyena.' And finally, 'By his compulsive, brusque and jerky walk, one recognised him as an assassin.' Is there any evidence, I wonder, that assassins walk more jerkily than non-assassins? Maybe this is more ammunition for conspiracy theorists – Lee Harvey Oswald

Marat: the human zoo.

walked as smoothly as you like, so it *can't* have been him. Yet *Paris in the Terror*, we're informed on the front cover, was 'Book Society Choice of the Month. Presumably the other contenders that month must have been *Mein Kampf* and the Freemans catalogue.

This isn't confined to the relatively obscure Loomis. Thomas Carlyle, who wrote one of the most celebrated histories of the revolution, describes Marat as 'one squalidest horse-leech, redolent of soot.'[1] Hilaire Belloc declares 'Marat is easily judged. He was not sane,'[2] and Simon Schama in *Citizens* tells us that Marat 'made an art form of confrontational ugliness' as 'His eyes were not quite aligned.'[3] After all, modern society would be so much fairer if we reverted to those quaint but effective eleventh-century methods of judging people as being demons and traitors if they lacked a symmetrical face. Finally, Schama informs us, 'contemporaries were divided on which kind of bird Marat most resembled'. The favourites, apparently, were an eagle or a scavenging crow.

So not only did this bloke lead a revolution, he was a veritable human zoo. If he hadn't been so busy he'd have ended up on the working-men's-club circuit as 'the Amazing Beast-man – impersonates every creature on the evolutionary scale, from crow to toad to horse-leech', for a finale becoming redolent of soot.

Maybe he was insane and unfeasibly ugly, but none of these historians addresses the problem this raises. Of every character in the revolution, Marat was the most demonstrably popular, largely because of his journalism. When he was acquitted following a trial, he was paraded through the streets by thousands. And his death was followed by almost Diana-style grief. So how did an insane unaligned-eyed soot man manage that?

The treatment of Marat is only one example of the prejudices about the revolution and its leaders. A book entitled *The French Revolution and Its Legacy*, edited by Geoffrey Best, tells us in the introduction, 'Hitler, Mussolini and Franco were themselves heirs of the French Revolution.' If only the Nazi war criminals at the Nuremberg trials had thought to say, 'It wasn't our fault – Robespierre and the Jacobins made us do it.'

In recent years, some historians have developed another angle on the revolution, that it had few lasting effects at all. The leaders in this field appear to be those now in charge of the palace at Versailles. Throughout this vast monument to royal decadence, now a major tourist attraction, there are no clues as to why the building ceased to be the home of the royal family after 1789. The 95-page guidebook that accompanies a visit makes two references to how the royals were 'forced to leave' in that year. And the only allusion to the revolution is that afterwards the estate was left 'with unkempt buildings and gardens'. At the Palace itself, gardens, bedchambers, drawing rooms and galleries are displayed with no hint as to how this came to an end. Some tourists must come away assuming that in 1789 the royals just decided to move somewhere else, perhaps because Versailles was going downhill as an area. Maybe drug dealers were moving in, or the local schools weren't up to the standards they wanted for the prince.

Something shared by both theories is the prominence of the Terror as one of history's most appalling atrocities. But around 2,650 death sentences were passed in Paris during the eighteen months of the Terror – gruesome, but not in the first division of historical blood-letting, even for the French. In the attack on the Paris Commune of 1871, an estimated 25,000 were killed. In one day of the St Bartholomew's Day Massacre there were more killed than in a year of the Terror.

In a historical corpse count, next to the bombing of Vietnam, or the massacres in Indonesia or Armenia that are rarely mentioned, the Paris Terror can only look up in awe. Boasts were made by American commanders that 2,500 were killed in one battle on one night in the war against Iraq. Over the last sixty years, in many areas of the world, such a death toll would have merited but a brief mention on the main evening news.

None of this excuses the killing. If someone murdered their neighbours, it probably wouldn't stand up in court if their defence was, 'There were only four of them, so why all the fuss? Don't forget sixty thousand died in one day at the Somme, Your Honour, so let's keep this in perspective.' But it does raise the question of why this particular period is singled out for vilification, even on children's television – unless this is a trend I've missed, and references to the atrocities of the Ottoman Empire turn up occasionally on *Live and Kicking* and *The Tweenies*.

It's especially odd when you consider that, throughout the French Revolution, masses of human beings felt they were taking part in the construction of a society based on values of fairness, equality and democracy; that the notion of what it meant to be a human being was transformed. The mass of the population, having previously been taught that their role was to serve, became capable of hope. Peasants, locksmiths and postmen, who must have assumed they played a similar role to that of a drone bee in a hive, found themselves shaping the way the world was run. If it was simply a carnival of unrestrained blood-lust, why would William Wordsworth have said of it at the time, 'Bliss was it in that dawn to be alive'? How could it have been the inspiration for the careers of Lord Byron, Percy Shelley and Beethoven? Why would Eric Hobsbawm be able to include amongst its supporters 'Blake, Coleridge, Robert Burns, Southey, Kant, Schelling, Hegel, Beethoven, Wilkinson the ironmaster, Telford the engineer, chemist Joseph Priestley and the Birmingham Lunar Society'?[4]

If it was a spat caused by toad-like madmen, how could it transform for ever the basis of philosophy, of music, politics, poetry, economics and warfare? Why would Goethe comment that 'From this day nothing will ever be the same'?

Incidentally, the guillotine, invented by Doctor Guillotin, was introduced as a liberal measure, and was considered to be more humane than the old methods of execution, of which the most common involved strapping the victim to a water wheel until his back broke. So it's almost certain that when the guillotine was introduced, a French Ann Widdecombe will have complained, 'Doesn't this show that the Jacobins are soft on crime? For if the burglar knows that if he is caught he will be merely beheaded instantly without hours of agony on a water wheel, there is no deterrent whatsoever. Proving once again that Mr Robespierre is the burglar's friend.'

1

The Ancien Régime

An' everybody's doing
Just what they're told to
An' nobody wants
To go to jail

MARIE ANTOINETTE

None of the above is to deny that Marie Antoinette was indeed one of the great figures of the revolution. She was specially selected, as a virgin of noble stock, to marry the heir to the throne, had an illicit affair with an army officer, fell out with the royal family she'd married into, spent unfeasible amounts on clothes and jewellery, became obsessed with charity and lost her life abruptly in her thirties in the middle of Paris. You simply don't get characters like that in modern times.

Marie Antoinette was the eighth daughter of the Emperor and Empress of Austria, and her fate was set at one year old, when a treaty bound the French and Austrians in a pact against Prussia. To cement this alliance, at thirteen she was selected to marry a French prince. To celebrate the signing of this deal, her father Joseph held a party. As well as several thousand guests, those present included eight hundred firemen, and a team of dentists in case of accidents. A pavilion was specially built for the dancing, because what sort of cheapskate would allow anything second-hand to be used on his daughter's big day, when she was bound to someone she'd never met?

In one respect, the future Queen was like any woman who moves in with a new boyfriend: she had to acquaint herself with his family customs. This began when she arrived at the French border, where she was stripped of her Austrian clothes and dressed in French replacements. At Versailles she had to address her future husband as 'Monsieur'. This was a privilege, as even the nobility had to call him 'Monseigneur', though occasionally 'Majesté' was preferred.

Each morning Marie Antoinette was obliged to undergo her formal *toilette*, in which she would be prepared for the day. She would begin by receiving underwear, laid out by the First Lady of

**Marie Antoinette aged twenty-eight, sporting
one of her delightful array of hats.**

the Bedchamber but presented to her by the Mistress of the Household. However, should a woman of senior rank enter the room during this point, the Mistress of the Household would relinquish the garment to her superior, who would take over the task.

On the night of the wedding, in May 1770, the marriage bed was blessed personally by the Archbishop of Rheims, following which Louis XV ceremonially handed his son the royal nightgown, while Marie Antoinette's was handed to her by the Duchesse de Chartres. The purpose of royal sex was entirely to produce further heirs. Otherwise, no doubt, at a certain point in proceedings a courtier would have leaned across to the King and said, 'Condom, *monseigneur*,' whereupon it would be applied by the First Duke of the Order of Contraception.

But no heirs arrived. It can't have helped Marie Antoinette to get aroused, knowing that even if she did get excited she'd have to shout, *'Oh oh oh, monsieur.'* But Louis' sexual technique wasn't helping. He described this to Joseph II, who then wrote in a letter, 'He has strong, perfectly satisfactory erections; he introduces the member, stays there without moving for about two minutes, withdraws without ejaculating but still erect, and bids goodnight.' It's not certain Joseph II's advice would have helped, though, as his response was, 'If only I could have been there! I could have seen to it. The King of France would have been whipped so that he would have ejaculated out of sheer rage like a donkey.'[1]

It's a mark of how embedded hierarchical values were in this society that it was assumed even ejaculation could be achieved if someone of superior rank ordered it. Whether it would actually help to have your father-in-law standing behind you, thrashing you with a belt and yelling, 'Come, damn you,' is another matter.

To counteract what must have been, in its own way, a miserable existence, Marie Antoinette spent money. Her dress allowance was 150,000 *livres*, itself three hundred times greater than the average annual income. Despite this she ran up debts of a further 500,000 *livres*, and then bought a pair of diamond bracelets for 400,000 *livres*.

She had an English garden built specially into the grounds of the palace at Versailles, complete with sheep to allow her to indulge her shepherdess fantasy.

But in 1785 came the most notorious of her extravagances: a diamond necklace, which she is alleged to have bought for 1,600,000 francs. It's often claimed the Queen didn't buy the necklace, and that the letter authorizing payment in her name was forged. A 1938 film of her life shows how this might have happened, when a salesman offers her the necklace, and she replies, 'Oh no, I couldn't possibly spend that much while my people are starving.' As if she would think, 'I don't mind running up debts of 500,000 francs and buying bracelets for a further 400,000, while my people are starving. That's legitimate expenses for any queen. But 1,600,000 – well, that would be taking the piss.'

The 1,600,000 franc necklace. But
you can't deny she'd look lovely.

THE FIRM

In modern Britain the discussion of royal expense is usually comic, for example when the *Daily Telegraph* insisted that the celebrations for the Queen Mother's hundredth birthday would be run 'on a shoestring'. It continued by informing us that the parade would include 'Spitfires, Hurricanes, a vast choir, a 25 foot high birthday cake, racehorses, Aberdeen Angus bulls and 12 Rolls Royces'. Still, that's the marvellous thing about that generation, they knew how to make a little stretch a long way. As her heyday was in the Second World War, maybe that's when she learned such thrift; in those days she had to make do with *powdered* Rolls-Royces.

The French royals were equally thrifty. In the middle of the century the royal household employed, amongst others, 300 cooks and 2,000 horses. Their palace at Versailles included 700 rooms and 20 kilometres of roads.

Unlike modern British royalty, the French monarchy weren't just expensive. The French king ruled the country, not just nominally or as 'official head of state', but actually. Louis XV had declared in 1766, 'Sovereign power rests in my person alone. To me alone belongs all legislative power. Public order in all its entirety emanates from me.' The king was formally head of the army, and of the Treasury. Louis XVI put this philosophy succinctly when he said, 'The state – that's me.'

All rivers navigable by boats or rafts belonged to the king. The king alone could grant a fishing licence. Highways were called the king's roads. The king could issue *'lettres de cachet'*, which could subject any individual to imprisonment without trial. One typical *lettre de cachet* was issued against a satirist who had poked fun at the mistress of Louis XV, and resulted in the writer being kept in a dungeon for eight years.

Amongst the king's furnishings was the *'lit de justice'*, a bed from which he was at liberty to pass any law without contradiction. Louis XVI infuriated his advisers on one occasion by retiring to this bed to recite a new law, then, in front of hundreds of magistrates and peers,

Louis XVI: 'The state – that's me'.

in a gesture worthy of Homer Simpson, falling asleep. Presumably the courtiers had to sit at the edge of the bed waiting for him to wake up and make a pronouncement. As a result, there is probably a law on the French statute that goes, 'Ay, what, bulawal ber I don't *like* custard leave me alone prrrr.'

PEASANT LIFE

In the late eighteenth century, the majority of French people lived on land owned by the nobility. They were barefooted and lived on black bread, and it was common for them to be strapped to a plough to pull a cart like an ox. Equally common was the practice of peasants spending the night swishing a stick against a pond to keep frogs away, so that their croaking wouldn't keep the landlord awake. If the harvest was below average, people starved. In the middle of the eighteenth century the writer Argenson wrote, 'The men are dying as thick as flies and the living are eating grass.'[2]

According to some, there was a healthy aspect to this level of income. Cardinal Richelieu wrote in his political testament, 'If people are too well off they happen to become unmanageable.' 'People' doesn't seem to have included himself, as there's no record of him refusing food unless it was black bread or grass, insisting, 'Don't give me too much or I'm simply unmanageable.'

Laws were designed to preserve not just the wealth but also the status of the nobility. In most regions, only the nobility were allowed to own pigeons, and throughout France they enjoyed the 'ban of the vintage', which gave them the legal right to gather their crop of grapes one day before any commoner. They were then permitted, according to the 'right of Banvin', to send their wine to market one month before the common wine.

The nobility were allowed to hunt anywhere, and would regularly chase their prey across cultivated fields, ruining some poor sod's crop. To aid the hunting fun, it was illegal for a commoner to kill a deer or wild boar; if a wild boar came on to the land they were working on, presumably the advice was to 'work round it'. For similar reasons, in some areas the penalty for killing a rabbit or a quail was death. Each area had its variations on the rights of nobles. In Burgundy the peasant was obliged to present the tongue of every ox slaughtered to the local lord. In the Vosges, he had to hand over the ox's bollocks.

Peasants were liable to be called up for military service, an unmarried man assumed to be on call until he was forty years old. Landowners however were usually exempt. The rule was explained at the head of one militia roll thus: 'Considering the meagreness of the soldier's pay, the way in which he is housed, clothed and fed, and the rigours of military discipline, it would be sheer cruelty to conscript men not belonging to the lowest class.'[3]

So the idea was noblemen would suffer from military service, but if your job was shooing noisy frogs out of your landlord's earshot, joining up would be a relief. It's as if the modern British Army wandered around the aisles of B&Q with recruitment forms, suggesting to the staff, 'Even if you end up on the wrong side of a bayonet fight, frankly we'll have done you a favour.'

But peasants must have felt their main role in life was to be taxed. Around one-tenth of their produce was handed directly to the Church. Then there was an income tax, called the '*taille*', which was only payable by commoners. The nobility didn't have to pay a thing. So the French state achieved the distinction of a tax system in which the poorer you were, the more you paid. To be fair, at least they didn't add to the insult by pretending it could make you rich and broadcasting it on BBC1 on Saturday nights, followed by the latest single from Ronan Keating.

The only tax on *owning* land, rather than living on it, was the '*vingtième*', but the nobility were often exempted from this as well. In the modern world we're well acquainted with the idea of the richest people employing elaborate schemes to avoid tax, but it would take the sharpest mind to concoct a system in which there was a tax on owning land with a clause that landowners didn't have to pay. The clergy were also exempt, but on condition that they voted a periodic 'gift' to the Crown.

One thing that also applied solely to the peasantry was the *corvée*, which involved them spending one day a week building and maintaining local roads. This system was introduced throughout France in 1737, as the desire for roads was growing. And no doubt anyone who objected was told, 'We can't go back to the days of state handouts if we expect a modern efficient transport system, so there is no alternative to a public/peasant partnership.'

Then there was the salt tax, known as the '*gabelle*'. Salt was essential for preserving food, but as one pamphlet of the time stated, 'Salt

**Taxation in France – an elderly peasant carrying
on his back a bishop and a nobleman.**

is often the only thing the poor have to put in their pot.' The *gabelle*
put the price beyond the poor, leading to smuggling, and then to
salt-tax agents, who would lurk behind hedges spying on anyone
suspected of buying illegal salt. So the scene, presumably, was one
familiar to the modern world, furtive customers looking both ways
outside the house of a dealer before tapping a pre-arranged knock on
the door, then arriving home triumphantly before complaining that
the stuff these days is cut with chemicals, and it will never be as
good as the gear you could get back in the 1750s.

Anyone suspected of smuggling was arrested and forced to pay
the tax or, if they had no money, taken to prison with no notification

for the family. A description of *gabelle* officers from the time tells us, 'If they enter a house they do so . . . not as honest men but like a band of robbers armed with sabres, hunting-knives and steel-tipped sticks. We leave you to judge what happens if a gang like this comes into a house where the woman is pregnant. Often it ends with the death of the fruit of her womb.'[4]

But somehow only those in charge of the guillotine have earned their place amongst the tyrants of history . . .

THE TOWNS

There is a common assumption that one of the chief divides in any society is between town and countryside. Partly this derives from the image many town dwellers, especially Londoners, have of rural areas. Mention you're going to a place such as Hereford or Totnes to a Londoner and we'll probably say, 'Cor, that's out in the sticks.' If you point out that it's like any modern town, full of pedestrianized shopping centres and modern offices, we think, 'Alright then, I suppose so.' But in our minds we're imagining a *countryside* office, where every few minutes someone shouts, 'Bloody hell, there's a sheep on the photocopier again.'

In truth, much of the town/countryside divide in modern society is a false distinction, as most countryside affairs are town affairs felt more sharply. The closure of a school, a disappearing bus route or boom in crack-dealing has a disproportionately disturbing effect on a village.

But in pre-revolutionary France, urban and rural dwellers really did grow up leading parallel lives with entirely separate values. In the towns, where most people worked as artisans or labourers, whatever hardship people faced, there were no tithes, and no one was expected to build their manager's road or swish away his frogs.

Inequality presented itself in different ways. Paris was a city of 650,000, for whom the average working day was sixteen hours.

Although there were several large factories, most of the population worked for small employers; typical carpenter's shops employed between three and seven people, locksmiths and joiners employed between two and five, and these employees often lived in the upstairs room of their boss's house. The royal government's attitude towards them was indicated in the 1770s by Turgot, one of Louis XVI's chancellors, in his 'Iron Law of Wages', which stated: 'A worker's wage can not exceed the very lowest level necessary for his maintenance and reproduction.'

It's been estimated that the average Parisian spent 58 per cent of their income on bread. Louis Sebastien-Mercier, a journalist writing just before the revolution, wrote, 'The Parisian poor have no store of provisions, they buy in fractions, two ounces of this, one of that, at a time. They never have a good piece of cheese in the house, nor a whole pound of sugar, nor a pint of oil. They buy their wood, too, very dear, about double what it costs the bourgeois.'[5]

The details may have changed, but the irony of food being more expensive for the poor, who buy smaller quantities, would be recognized by anyone who's been broke in modern Britain. I've never bought such expensive food as when I was on the dole in the 1980s, and the prelude to each meal was a primeval dig behind the settee and through the linings of pockets for lingering pennies. This would be followed by a gaze around the items in the corner shop, while thinking, 'seventeen p, 17p, please have something for 17p. Oh bollocks, Hula Hoops 18p.' So I'd make do with something like Bacon Frazzles, completing a deal with the worst ratio of pence to nutrition possible in British retailing.

If salt was the cause of much peasant anguish, pepper could be the bane of urban life. Mercier reported that throughout Paris 'Grocers sell ground pepper, done up in a twist of paper: and the dishonest ones make it go further by mixing in a little dog-dung, which being blackened and powdered blends perfectly with the pepper' – a technique perfected by the characters who sell small quantities of dope to passers-by in Brixton Market.

Most people in towns paid rent on a quarterly basis, and a familiar scene was acted out on countless doorsteps the day after this payment was due. According to Mercier, the rent man would say, 'Of course, if you can't find the money . . . I see you have a nice pair of mirrors, or there's that commode, my brother-in-law would make you a fair price for that.' Each quarter, between 3,000 and 4,000 Paris families were forced to leave their homes for non-payment, abandoning their possessions as they did so.

These craftsmen of Paris, including many of the small employers, were known as 'sans-culottes', meaning 'without breeches', which were only worn by the wealthier employers. The actions of Turgot, along with crooked pepper sellers, the rent man and others, were ensuring that when the time came these sans-culottes would form a fearsome army that would drive a revolution.

THE BOTTOM RUNG

However tough life was for peasants and sans-culottes, they were lucky not to be part of another group governed by royalist France, the slaves. In the seventeenth century, French buccaneers sailed to the Caribbean island of San Domingo (later renamed Haiti) and fought the British and Spanish for the island. By 1695 the western half of the island was theirs, where they cultivated a coffee crop, then sugar, and imported slaves from West Africa to pick it. By the time of the revolution, the trade of San Domingo accounted for £11 million, double the total trade of the whole of British colonies.

Once captured, slaves were forced to march to the African coast, where they were sold to French traders who shipped them as cargo to the plantations. They were bound, right hand to right leg and left hand to left leg, and attached in rows to iron bars for the journey, during which they were kept at the bottom of the ship, and twenty per cent died en route. On arrival in San Domingo, the survivors worked on sugar plantations every minute there was light.

Some slaves were compelled to wear tin masks to stop them eating the sugar. Punishment included applying burning wood to the victim's buttocks. Salt, pepper, lemon and ash were poured on to bleeding wounds as extra punishment. There were regular cases of slaves having burning wax poured on to them by their masters, of being burned alive, of being filled with gunpowder and blown up, of being buried up to their necks and covered in sugar to attract wasps. A favourite was known as the 'four-post', in which a slave would be staked out in the hot sun on all fours. When this particular penalty was administered to a pregnant woman, masters would thought-fully dig a hole to accommodate her belly.

Throughout this, slaves retained either a dehumanized outlook or a macabre sense of humour. A slave is recorded as having objected to a master's cutting off his ears because 'I would have nowhere to put my stump of cigarette.' Another, accused of stealing potatoes, insists that all he was carrying in his shirt were stones. When the master pulled his shirt and potatoes dropped to the floor, the slave is recorded as saying, 'Eh! Master. The devil is wicked. I put stones and he has turned them into potatoes.'[6]

Less humorously, one-third of slave babies were poisoned or starved to death by midwives, who believed this to be more humane than leaving them to grow up and face a life of slavery.

None of this justifies the guillotine either, but you can see why it must be annoyed at taking all the blame.

2

An Ongoing Row

Just around the corner in the English Civil War

WHY FRANCE?

These hardships by themselves can't explain why the revolution should have taken place, as history is packed with unjust regimes that *aren't* overthrown. And in some regions of Europe, conditions were even worse. In most German states, peasants were tied to the land as serfs. If a peasant ran off, he could be tracked down like a runaway slave. He needed his landlord's consent to marry, was obliged to drive the landlord's carriage and send his children to work as domestic staff in the lord's household. Yet the Germans got no revolution.

Revolution requires more than spontaneous revolt against the élite; it depends upon the existence of a section of society whose interests would be best served not just by a change of ruler or of a few laws, but by a new set of ethics governing every aspect of society from top to bottom.

In revolutions, as in normal life, sometimes a conflict can begin without the protagonists knowing what the real source of disagreement is. Couples can splutter along for ages despite a growing rift – perhaps one partner pursues all-night drinking sessions and charging down the front at Primal Scream gigs, while the other aspires to suburban domesticity – but neither party sees the underlying conflict, so instead they snarl at each other for years about who ate the last of the peanut butter and who broke the ironing board. In similar fashion, European society had endured several hundred years of spats and duels between two groups who would squabble, make up, then fight harder still, without ever fully understanding the nature of their conflict or arriving at a decisive blow.

CENTURIES OF SNARLING

The row at the heart of the revolution is the same one that drives Alexander Dumas' story *The Count of Monte Cristo*. In the aftermath of the revolution, sailor Edmond Dantes is promoted to captain, and is about to marry the beautiful Mercedes, but is betrayed by a friend, whose false evidence to a prosecutor consigns him to years in a dungeon. When Dantes asks why he is doing this the friend says, 'Because you are not meant to have more than me. I am a noble and you are the son of a clerk.'

This is more than a story of mere jealousy. For thousands of years the position of the ruling élite was assumed to be part of the natural order, as incontestable as the tides or the fact that the sun revolved around the earth. Chiefs and kings were God's appointed envoys on Earth, and the position of everyone was fixed by the creator. In his letters, Louis XVI proclaimed himself 'by the grace of God, King of France'. Following the crowning of a new king, the archbishop would pronounce, 'Be blessed and be crowned King in this kingdom which God has given you to rule over.' The next day the new king would be presented to groups of the disabled, whereupon he would touch each one, muttering, 'The King touches you, may God cure you.'

In some ways, the idea of a monarch being invested with spiritual radiance lasts to our own times. I was fascinated by the swooning of one royal correspondent as she drooled over the way the Queen Mother 'looked absolutely radiant at Ascot in her wonderful array of hats'. Well of course she did, she was worth about a hundred million trillion quid – she was hardly likely to turn up at Ascot in a bobble hat with DERBY COUNTY on the front.

The notion of a naturally superior élite rose in societies that depended on a belief in a natural order. Ancient slave societies justified their system by asserting that everything and everyone had a natural place allotted by nature. Aristotle summarized this most concisely when he wrote in *Politics*, 'It is nature's intention to distinguish even the bodies of freemen and slaves: the latter are usually endowed with strength to suit their employment, while the upright carriage of the former renders them unfit for servile work.' Which was convenient, as it allowed masters to think, 'I'd love to help out, but it's the upright carriage you see.'

Later, in feudal Europe, the aristocracy along with the Church sought to continue this tradition. So while today it's often suggested that personal ambition is the natural instinct that drives us all, for anyone outside the ruling élite in feudal society such an instinct would have been regarded as heresy. There was no point training hard in the hope that one day you'd become a Lord.

The feudal ideology had other consequences. Because the wealth of the aristocracy derived from ownership of the land, there wasn't the drive to compete with rivals by investing in scientific innovation or finding new markets that occupies the minds of modern corporations. And knowledge was seen not as a journey of discovery but as memorizing a fixed set of rules. Feudal regimes borrowed the works of Aristotle that suited their purpose and used them as the basis for education and thought.

From here, it may be best to leave France for a while and run through the ways in which this set of ideas was gradually undermined over a period of centuries.

WHAT IS CLASS?

The ideas and events that led to the French Revolution would be simpler to grasp if there wasn't such confusion over the word 'class'. For example, it's often assumed today that the working class no longer exists because few people work in manual jobs. But for people working with laptop computers and mobile phones, these inventions haven't made life more comfortable, they've meant that office workers are now expected to work on the way to and from work. Even in nineteenth-century cotton mills people weren't expected to drag a loom away with them and keep weaving all the way home. And most non-manufacturing jobs are hardly middle-class. You'd surprise the staff in Burger King if you walked up to the counter and said, 'You think you're it, don't you, you stuck-up middle-class snobs.' Class definition can revolve around lifestyle or fashion, whether you go to football or the theatre, drink filter coffee or tea with four sugars – in which case you'd be able to choose whichever class you fancied, or swap every six months or so.

Class can only have any real meaning if it's determined by the relationship someone has to the way in which society produces things. For example, if you're on the board of an insurance company, you have some influence over whether an office is opened or closed. If you answer phones at the office, or are a security guard or the bloke who comes round with a basket of sandwiches, you have no influence at all. And it's no good saying, 'You can't lay *me* off because I cook with coriander and watch *The Late Review*.'

In the centuries leading up to the French Revolution, very few people could be described as working class in the modern sense. But there were vast differences between the layers of society with conflicting interests over how society produced things. Obviously there was a conflict between peasants and the nobles who owned their land. But also, gradually, as technology such as the cannon, the compass and the printing press developed, a new class emerged whose wealth derived not from the land at all but from trade and commerce. It had gradually become possible to become wealthy, prominent or educated without coming from noble stock; someone from outside the aristocracy could have aspirations. This class, which came to have the snappy title of 'bourgeoisie', developed its own distinct outlook. In particular they believed they deserved a share of political power and positions in government to match their wealth. And they advocated the promotion of science, art and original thought in education.

The first major challenge to the aristocratic values that dominated feudal Europe took place in northern Italy, in the episode known as the Renaissance. Craftsmen, traders and bankers were developing the view that every human should think for him or herself, in an idea that became known as humanism. Men, instead of being miserable souls playing out their allotted role, were now seen as in partnership with God, an attitude represented by Michelangelo's painting on the ceiling in which God and Adam are the same size, as if working as a team. A writer called Mirandola referred to God as 'the great artisan'.

SCIENCE

As the new ideology grew, universities were established in which science and original study were encouraged, and for the first time in Europe in a thousand years, knowledge and ability challenged noble rank as a sign of status. The Polish civil servant Copernicus shocked the Catholic Church with his revelation that the Earth wasn't at the centre of the universe. You can see how controversial this was from the way Copernicus took twenty years to publish his theory, which finally came out on the day he died. (Or maybe that was just habit, from being in the civil service.) Then Galileo, having redesigned the telescope, discovered that Jupiter had several moons. This upset the Pope, as there were supposed to be seven heavenly bodies – the sun, the moon and five planets – because seven was the heavenly number.

So the Church forced Galileo to renounce his findings or be executed –
as if huge, pock-marked goons in tight suits came to his door and
said 'Oy, Galileo, you didn't see no moons tonight, all right?' To be
fair to the Pope, the Catholic Church did eventually give Galileo an
official pardon – in 1998. So by the year 2350 they'll get round to
apologizing for fiddling with half their choirboys as well.

In 1609, Kepler discovered that the orbits of the planets weren't
exactly circular. And Kepler too resisted his own findings, because
they questioned why God would have failed to make orbits that
weren't perfect circles. It made God fallible, as if after creating each
orbit he was saying, 'Right. Let's try again with Mars. No – circles
are the one thing I can't do.'

These weren't seen as just scientific discoveries: they required
huge leaps in philosophy. The idea of a naturally ordered universe in
which everything had its place was being undermined.

OLIVER'S ARMY

By the end of the sixteenth century the political conflict between
these world-views became a revolt. In 1572 an uprising began in
Holland, in opposition to their Spanish rulers and the Vatican, until,
after seven years of brutal war, an independent republic was formed.
The next major upheaval was in England.

At first glance it seems implausible that the English could ever
have had a civil war. The Americans, Spanish or Russians you can
imagine, but try to visualize the English in a civil war and you can
just see thousands of people in a field facing each other with pikes,
saying, 'Tut, and they said it would be sunny in the forecast.'

But the England of the seventeenth century was a land coming to
terms with the growing conflict festering across Europe. The Church
was the local government; it distributed relief for the poor, organized
the only entertainment and educated the children. For most people,
the weekly sermon was the only source of information and was, in

effect, the news. All English men and women were members of the Church of England: you could be fined for not attending on a Sunday, and it was an offence to attend a church outside your own parish. (Perhaps that last one was to prevent the middle classes from saying, 'I know we ought to send Nathan and Jemimah to the local church, but the one in Kensington has such marvellous facilities and it would be immoral to put our principles before our children.') In these churches, God was only accessible via the priest, which made the priest's role similar to that of an important person's secretary. The best the common man or woman could hope for was the priest saying, 'You can't speak to God right now, I'm afraid He's in a meeting at the moment.'

There was a parliament, but the King could decide when to call it, if at all, which was usually to raise a new tax. And because the bishops were appointed by the royal court, the King also controlled the Church and was seen as God's ambassador. At one point a story was circulated that a child had been cured by the King's spit. (Sadly, you can imagine if someone started a similar story now, half of Islington would be shrieking, 'We don't touch antibiotics any more, we go to the spit-o-therapy centre in Upper Street.')

Once again, the growing numbers of craftsmen, traders, merchants and shipowners whose living depended on a more rational line of thinking began to challenge this style of government. There was a boom in lay preachers, not appointed by the royal court, and most importantly a rapid growth in puritanism.

Puritans were mostly small landowners or craftsmen who believed that social status *could* change, depending on how hard you worked. So they believed in each individual shaping his own destiny and having his own relationship with God. Oliver Cromwell described how each night he would 'wrestle with God'.

The issue that ignited a social upheaval came when the King introduced a new tax called the 'ship tax' which a squire, John Hampden, refused to pay. This sparked off a mass campaign of non-payment. And probably a series of marches with people chanting 'can't payeth, won't payeth', and an attempt by the King to diffuse the situation by giving the tax another name: 'It is *not* the Ship Tax, it is the Maritime Charge.' It was parliament that led the campaign, so the King assembled an army to wind up parliament and arrest the leaders, and so, in short, the civil war began.

This is not the place to provide an account of the Civil War, but it is worth mentioning the types who made up each army. Cromwell, who grasped the nature of the conflict, said, 'I would rather have a plain russet-coated captain that knows what he fights for and loves what he knows, than that which you call a gentleman and is nothing else.' He was accused by a colleague of 'hiring men who have filled dung-carts', and his first captain was James Berry, who had been a clerk in a Shropshire ironworks. Sir Philip Warwick quotes a royalist soldier who said, 'In our army we have the sins of men, drinking and wenching, but in yours you have the sins of spiritual pride and rebellion.' Which shows how highly motivated the Parliamentary Army must have been, if they were recruiting soldiers by saying, 'Join our side, we've got spiritual pride and rebellion. All they've got on their side is drinking and wenching.'

Following the King's execution, Cromwell was forced to accept a series of compromises with the aristocracy, and was never able to install the radical regime he'd dreamed of. Then after his death came the ultimate compromise, when Charles II became King, giving the appearance that, for all the fighting, nothing had changed. But it had – before the Civil War, Parliament could only sit if it was invited by the King. At the end, the King could only be crowned if he was invited by Parliament; the natural order had been shattered.

HOW FRANCE THOUGHT

The rest of Europe was bound to feel the effects of the upheaval in England. One of the main changes was that people began to think of themselves as belonging to nations, which hadn't always been the case. There's the peculiar view that England is a piece of land with static values that have existed since the beginning of time. Certain members of the Conservative Party must think that when druids dragged the stones to Stonehenge, they were met by a chief who said, 'Thank you, good man, now here's a pound. Not a franc, or a euro, but a *pound*, because Stonehenge is *English*, part of Europe but not run by Europe.'

Similarly, the country we know as France would not have been thought of as a single country until the seventeenth century. Then the growth of towns, trade and commerce, combined with a series of wars between competing fiefdoms, led the aristocracy to favour a monarchy that ruled throughout the area we call France. A centralized state could provide a single army, and protect the ruling powers against their European rivals. But this state would adhere as closely as ever to feudal methods and ideology, incorporating the idea of the divine right of kings, and adding specialities such as the law-making bed and the *lettres de cachet*.

France was officially and legally divided into three orders: the clergy, the nobility and everyone else, known as 'the third estate'. But throughout the eighteenth century the bourgeoisie amongst this third estate grew in size, wealth and confidence. They produced clothing and beer and ships and the slave trade, or worked as lawyers, accountants and bankers servicing the businessmen. They began to outstrip the nobles in wealth, but they remained inferior in status. If they used their wealth to buy land, they had to pay tax like any commoner. You could be the richest man in Bordeaux, but if you didn't have the ear of the King, you couldn't even get a fishing licence.

Throughout the eighteenth century, the new class sought to win some political power by buying their way into the nobility. So there became two levels of nobility: nobles of the sword, there through birthright; and nobles of the robe, who'd paid their way in. Infuriatingly for the original nobility, they were often forced to borrow money from the *nouveau riche* types, which must have created the worst form of tension between old and new money. You can imagine a business noble visiting a noble of the sword to arrange a loan, and saying, 'Nice pad you've got here, mate.'

'Thank you, it was designed by a personal architect of Louis XVI.'

'Oh yeah, he done our holiday home in Nice. He's a specialist in mock Louis XVI period, ain't he?'

'Heh heh, no – he doesn't design *mock* Louis XVI period; you see, this *is* the Louis XVI period.'

'Yeah, I know what you're saying, but we prefer mock. I mean, that old stuff's always falling to bits, ain't it? That's why we're having the drawbridge pebbledashed.'

Some of these people tended to be the greatest defenders of the old order, like cabbies who become members of the golf club. But most of this class either couldn't push their way into the nobility, or found their influence limited when they did. For it wasn't just personal status they wanted, but an educational system and support for science that was geared to the growth of business. They desired an agricultural system more dynamic than one based on tithes and frog-swishing. They wanted a France that seized the opportunities of a new world. And they needed France to resemble a nation in *every* respect, rather than remain the disparate region it was. (Trading between regions was subject to internal tolls and customs barriers, by laws that varied from area to area, as did the system of weights and measures.) In 1789 France had no national bank, no national system for raising tax and a quarter of France couldn't understand French.

3

The Enlightenment

You have the right to free speech
As long as you're not dumb enough to actually try it

The Enlightenment Begins

When does a royal family lose authority? At what point do a mass of people believe the boy who shouts that the Emperor has no clothes? It's difficult enough to pinpoint this moment when you're living through it. The British Royal Family were certainly admired and respected by the wartime generation, as parodied by Alf Garnett, who idolized them. But by the time Princess Margaret died in 2002, there was more of a national outpouring of grief when one of the hamsters on *Animal Hospital* pegged it. Support for royals and the idea of royalty may still ebb and flow, but the mass adoration that accompanied the wedding of Charles and Diana seems to belong in another era. Such a change in attitude can't result just from the image of individual royals. In 1936 the monarchy as an institution remained fairly unscathed despite the King marrying a divorcée and supporting Hitler. But in the 1990s a princess went bulimic and appeared on *Panorama* and the whole thing appeared to be on the edge of collapse. Each successive scandal confirmed what many people already felt, that something was fundamentally skew-whiff about the whole idea of the monarchy.

Something similar but more far-reaching seems to have happened to the French in the middle of the eighteenth century, as resentment against the ideals of their royalty grew. In the last years of the reign of Louis XV, the old King was said to have shacked up with an ex-prostitute who had made her way into the court called Mme Du Barry. The affair became the subject for street singers, who sang verses such as

> The dean of Kings
> is on his knees before a countess
> who could have been your mistress
> for one *écu* a while ago . . .
> In the middle of the action
> he falls back limp.[1]

And a popular version of the Lord's Prayer became 'Our Father, who art in Versailles, abhorred be thy name . . . Give us back our daily bread, which Thou hast taken from us.'

This process was accelerated when a group of writers and philosophers, who became known as the Enlightenment, made criticism of the royal court legitimate. The philosopher Diderot wrote, 'Until a King is dragged to Tyburn with no more pomp than the meanest criminal, the people will have no conception of liberty.' In an extraordinary effort to assert the triumph of knowledge and reason, he wrote the world's first encyclopaedia, which came in seventeen volumes and took him twenty-two years.

Baron Charles de Montesquieu wrote that the image of God as a human proves he's the creation of human minds. He added that if a cow believed in God it would assume God was a cow, and, with a splendid sense of surrealism, that if triangles believed in God then God would have three sides. It's a shame he didn't go into this further, and work out whether the religious triangles would have had theological debates on matters such as whether hexagons had a soul. And perhaps the isosceles ones would insist that they would be the only triangles on their way to heaven as they were the chosen ones. Another revolutionary writer, Voltaire, produced *Candide* in 1758, a satire on priests and philosophers who had responded to an earthquake in Lisbon that killed thousands of people by insisting God had caused the earthquake for the overall benefit of humanity. He also wrote a piece in which he pondered, if the story of Noah's Ark were true, where did all the animals shit? For pieces like this he spent six months locked up in the Bastille.

But the works of one writer above all became revered as the ideological justification for the course of the revolution: Jean-Jacques Rousseau.

ROUSSEAU

Every leader of the revolution read and reread Rousseau, in the way leaders of the Russian Revolution referred to Marx. Robespierre apparently carried copies of Rousseau's books with him at all times.

Rousseau was the son of a clock maker in Geneva. We know a fair bit about his upbringing because he wrote one of the world's first autobiographies, called *The Confessions*. Amongst the items he confessed was the effect of being beaten as a boy by his nursemaid, Mlle Lambercier: 'I found in the pain inflicted an element of sensuality which left me with more desire than fear at the prospect of experiencing it again from the same hand.' Which seems to confirm that one of the reasons philosophy has never gained mass appeal in Britain is that British philosophy is shamefully short on spanking.

One night, the teenage Rousseau returned to find the city gates locked, so in outrage he left Geneva to go touring around Europe. At one destitute point he went to a Catholic school in Turin, where his fellow-pupils were mostly bandits. One day, one of the bandits took a liking to him: 'At last he tried by degrees to move to the vilest

**Rousseau demonstrating that commoners
could wear magnificent hats.**

intimacies and, by directing my hand, to force me to do the same. I
recoiled, flinging myself impetuously from him with a cry which communicated so vehemently my shock and disgust that he let me go: but
as his convulsive movements began to subside, I saw something spurt
towards the fireplace and fall on the floor, something sticky and white.'
We can almost hear a publisher howling, 'Magnificent, Jean-Jacques,
now what's the chance of livening up the section on the relationship
between the individual and the state with another spunk story?'

Like many radicals of the time, he became obsessed with science
and carrying out experiments as a way of discovering truth for himself. Following a recipe he learned from a monk, he tried to make
invisible ink. But, he said, 'It began almost immediately to effer-
vesce. I rushed to uncork the bottle but it was too late and it
exploded in my face, and I was blinded for six weeks.' This is an incident you can imagine would have been much worse for him if it had
taken place in an English working-class environment. He'd have
been surrounded by workmates cackling, 'There's nothing wrong

with your eyes – but the stuff's gone all over the place and made *everything* invisible. Haaa haaa.'

Rousseau learned to write out music, and was offered a wage and pension by the King, which he turned down because 'Once I accepted the pension, I would either have to flatter him or remain silent.'

On his travels he was taken in by Mme de Warens, whom he fell in love with, though he had to share her with her husband, who didn't seem to mind the arrangement. There might have been a touch of rivalry between them, however, as when the husband died Rousseau's comment was 'So can I have his clothes?' Then in 1755 he entered an essay competition with 'A Discourse in Inequality'. In this he not only railed against inequality but suggested that it was against nature. The essay ends by stating that inequality is as absurd as 'that a child should govern an old man, that an imbecile should lead a wise man, that a handful of people should gorge themselves with super-fluities while the hungry multitude goes in want of necessities'.

This sort of thing made him unpopular in certain circles and for a while he was forced to flee to Britain, where he was looked after by the statesman Edmund Burke. But his major work, *The Social Contract*, was still to come. This began with the statement, 'Man is born free but everywhere is in chains,' an opening sentence that may explain the book's popularity with the Marquis de Sade. His contention was that each of us is born with a natural desire to play a useful part in the community, but the systems of rule we'd built prevent that spirit from emerging. So he wrote, 'You are lost if you forget that the fruits of the Earth belong to no one and the Earth itself belongs to everyone.'[2]

His attack on the state was connected to his views on religion. Orthodox religion, he wrote, existed only to protect the unfairness of inequality, as 'Christianity preaches only servitude and submission.'[3] Inequality, he wrote, was a curse on all sides of the divide, whether that inequality revolved around social rank or wealth. So man needed a state in which everyone could participate, in which each individual could flourish while submitting to the overall will of that state, which implied a democracy that everyone would have to accept.

The Social Contract made Rousseau famous, and despised by the royal court. But by then he'd moved in with a large maid called Thérèse who could barely read and didn't know the months of the year. This must have produced some of the finest marital discussions in history – Rousseau asking, 'How can we ensure a judiciary protects the state while enshrining the rights of the individual?' while she answered, 'No idea. Now I've got a question for *you* – have we had Christmas yet?' Yet they remained devoted to each other, in an unlikely but perfect romance, except for the fact that they had five children, all of whom they dumped in an orphanage and never saw again.

The theory that men were 'born good' was taken by the Royal court as an attack on the concept of original sin. And *Emile*, Rousseau's novel which suggests a person's intelligence depends on his education, was burned in the streets, to which Rousseau replied with a concise 'Burning is not the answer.' The city of Geneva refused to allow him to re-enter. But so deep were the beliefs Rousseau was challenging that he said of the time he met the King, 'Nothing was more certain than that in his presence I would be unable to recall a single word of what I had prepared.'[4] So the person who set out to undermine reverence towards kings, met the King and thought, 'Oh my God, it's really him, I can't remember what I'm supposed to do, it's the King!'

During the revolution he was revered above any figure from history, and his body moved to the exalted Panthéon. So there was a happy ending, as long as you ignore the fact that when the monarch was restored in 1814 Rousseau's corpse was dug up and his remains scattered in disgust.

THE FRENCH AND THEIR FILTH

Despite the attractions of Rousseau and his colleagues, the most popular radical books, published and sold by the same people who published the rest of Enlightenment writing, were from the genre of philosophical pornography.

These works were admired by the most serious critics of the regime, such as Rousseau, who recommended such books should be read 'with one hand'. One of the chief writers of these books was Count Mirabeau, who became a leading figure in the revolution. In the preface to *My Conversion, or the Libertine of Quality* he wrote, 'May the reading of this book make the whole universe beat off' – an ambitious wish for the most hard-core eroticism, let alone a work of philosophy, though maybe it's a mix that's been sadly neglected in recent times. Perhaps there would be a vast market for a film of *Ideas, Concepts and Their Relationship to the Material World* starring King Dong and Chesty Morgan.

The most influential of these books was *Thérèse Philosophe*, written by the Count of Argens and published in 1748. It follows the sexual and philosophical life of Thérèse, in particular when the two combine. For example, as a teenager she sees Father Dirrag persuading a woman called Eradice that a spanking will lift her soul to an ecstatic state approaching sainthood. Eventually he introduces his 'cord', until Eradice screams, 'I'm feeling celestial happiness. I sense that my mind is completely detached from matter. Further, further, further. Root out all that is impure within me. I see the angels. Push forward. Ah, St Francis.' Which you certainly don't get in *Nurse Vixens Go Bedpan-Banging*.

Much of the book is a guide to masturbation, which in itself was subversive in a country dominated by the Catholic Church. One description of the book says, 'they philosophise and masturbate deliciously together, for page after page'.[5] I suppose that, just as jazz musicians in segregated America felt their improvised style created a space in which they could express themselves freely, some who felt culturally repressed under the French monarchy used masturbation for a similar purpose. But since Thérèse has to read a library of erotic fiction before she can participate fully in sex, it's also a plea for knowledge. And amidst the explicit sexual detail are plenty of passages such as the one in which the *abbé* explains to Thérèse why their actions don't amount to sinning: 'Everyone agrees that God knows what will occur throughout eternity. He has seen that we will commit these acts. Thus God, in creating us, knew in advance we would be infallibly damned. Can these ideas be reconciled with the infinite goodness of God?' What a fantastic chat-up line. You'd feel extremely hard done by if you came out with all that and she said, 'Yes, but I'd rather just see you as a friend.' *Thérèse Philosophe*, packed with graphic illustrations, despite being banned, was a best-seller consistently through the 1770s.

There must have been a complex set of reasons why intellectual rebellion took this form. Certainly, sexual freedom, criticism of the

The original front cover of *Thérèse Philosophe*. You could see this for free, but after page 7 you had to pay or it went fuzzy.

values of the day and the search for knowledge were all anathema to the regime. But then came someone who made anything before him seem so utterly tame that people must have laughed at how they'd ever been shocked before, the way that people now wonder how we ever thought there was something compellingly dirty about Pan's People on *Top of the Pops*.

THE MARQUIS DE SADE

Often the most captivating rebels are those so damaged that their very existence is an act of rebellion. Their unpredictability sets all authority on edge, the way some drunks can when you're not sure whether their next move is to hug you or whack an ashtray in your face. Like Kurt Cobain or Billie Holiday, Alex Higgins or Lenny Bruce, they have a multitude of ways of exploding, which produce either works of genius or appalling acts of self-destruction. Revolutionary France had the Marquis de Sade.

Given his early environment, perhaps it shouldn't be surprising that he dedicated his life to depravity. When he was a toddler his father was arrested after being entrapped, George Michael-style, while cruising in the Tuileries gardens. The young boy was sent to Provence, an area dominated by the Pope, who lived on land granted by the French King. To raise money the papacy had introduced a system whereby sinners could absolve their sins by paying cash to the Pope. There was a strict price list: 'sins of fornication by a layman – 27 livres. 4 livres extra for incest. Adulterous women can receive absolution, be shielded from prosecution and receive dispensation to continue illicit relations – 87 livres, 5 sous. A nun who has given herself to several men but wishes to achieve the rank of abbess – 131 livres, 15 sous.'[6]

The Pope was lucky he didn't face competition from a rival church that could have undercut his prices and advertised themselves – 'Why not switch to Easypray, where prices are going crazy

crazy crazy – masturbation just 8 *livres*, serial adultery just 20 *livres* and anal sex only 20 *livres* and NO EXTRA FOR SUNDAYS. Plus join now and covet your neighbour's ox ABSOLUTELY FREE!'

The brother of de Sade's father's mistress was Count Charolais, who boasted of killing several peasants on his land for sport, and caused outrage by setting fire to a heap of explosives under the Marquise de St-Sulpice's skirt.

As a teenager de Sade was sent to the army, and at twenty-two he was dispatched to marry a woman he'd never met, Renée de Montreuil, daughter of a wealthy judge. It was a classic case of a noble family trying to redress its financial worries by marrying into a bourgeois family, who were equally delighted to acquire noble status to go with their money. The marquis however didn't appear to resign himself to settling down, as he paid a prostitute to watch him masturbating into a holy chalice while shouting, 'Motherfucker, the Holy Virgin is a bugger.'[7] Maybe this sort of behaviour could have been sorted out if only there were problem pages in French news-papers at the time. He could have written to Dear Virginia and been told, 'I'm sending you a pamphlet called "How to Stop Masturbating Into Holy Chalices and Seek a Loving Relationship".' But for the marquis this was just the beginning. He took to paying prostitutes to eat aniseed sweets so he could enjoy their farting in a variety of ways. One Easter Sunday he locked a prostitute in a room and forced her to whip him, and be whipped, with a bundle of canes.

The marquis was no gallant hero of liberty, but he was an explo-sive combination of cruel aristocratic arrogance, and rage against the hypocrisy of his own class. He knew he could indulge in what-ever depravity he fancied as long as he played the game of sycophantic attendance at court and due deference to the Church, but refused to participate in either. Periodically, anger against authority produces a protest that has no other purpose than the joy of shocking the enemy. There was no finer way to outrage the guardians of morality in the sixties than with the *Oz* magazine car-toon of a sexually rampant Rupert Bear. And when punk began, in its quest to shock the generation whose catchphrase was 'We fought a war for you', it knew it was guaranteed instant success by encouraging the wearing of swastikas. The Marquis de Sade seems to have felt a similar need to shock – and was clearly screwed in the head as well.

In Marseille he arranged an orgy, in which his proudest moment involved keeping a tally of the number of times he could be beaten with a broom (he finally gave up at 758). Eventually, after he'd made the mistake of involving the sons and daughters of other nobles in his adventures, at the request of their families the King ordered one of his notorious *lettres de cachet*, and de Sade was arrested and thrown into the prison at Vincennes.

He escaped from prison in Hollywood fashion and spent several nights sleeping in wheatfields, but was recaptured a few months later. He turned to writing the books and plays that would award him a place in history beyond his affections for brooms and chalices. Amongst these were *120 Days of Sodom* in which a duke, a bishop, a magistrate and a banker carry out every act of depravity that can be found in the most twisted corner of the Internet. Following this he was moved to the notorious Bastille prison. Something extraordinary would have to happen if he was ever going to get out of there.

FRANKLIN AND HIS KITE

Meanwhile, the rumblings of discontent had crossed the Atlantic. Of all the battles between the new and old worlds, the one that had the greatest direct impact, politically, ideologically and financially, on the French Revolution was that which took place in America.

The matter of American independence was first brought to my attention during the early years of my primary education by a fierce teacher, who began a lesson by placing a globe on his table, spinning it slowly, jabbing his finger at various points, and repeating, 'This was ours, this was ours, this was ours, this was ours,' until he said the magnificent phrase, 'And that's America; we gave that bit back.' Then we all groaned, as if to say, 'Dur, what idiot did that then?'

The War of Independence directly influenced events in France in several ways, and the actions of one man in particular, Benjamin Franklin. Franklin was an American scientist whose work and philosophy had led him towards opposition to divine rule, like the European scientists. He helped draft the American Constitution, and became a diplomat for the colonies, touring Britain and France to win support for their wars of independence. The French government sent troops and money to back the colonies, mostly in order to boost their own position by causing grief to the English.

In Britain in 1774, Franklin met the radical unemployed corset maker Tom Paine, and persuaded him to try his luck seeking work in Philadelphia, the effects of which we'll return to later. His other contribution to the radical cause in France was to write an essay about lightning.

Diderot's *Encyclopaedia* contained a section on lightning, which claimed a thunderbolt could be broken up by the ringing of several large church bells nearby, as this disturbed the air in such a way as to calm the storm. Such is the journey of science that sometimes it goes backwards in order to go forwards. He was searching for a scientific explanation of what, for thousands of years, had been considered God's most visible and obvious weapon. But in doing so he'd come up with a theory that the best thing to do in lightning is to go up to the highest roof in the neighbourhood and wave around an enormous chunk of metal. As a result, in one region in lower Brittany, where this was tried, twenty-four churches were burned down.

But in 1777 a supplement to the *Encyclopaedia* was published that took account of the work carried out by Benjamin Franklin. Through experiments with electric kites, Franklin had deduced that lightning was an 'electric fire', and that strategically placed rods of metal could act as conductors, guiding it to safety and protecting ships and buildings.

Franklin – and his kite.

So in 1780 a resident of St-Omer installed a lightning conductor on his roof. His neighbours, thinking this would have the same effect as the useless bell-ringing method, went to court to get it taken down. The magistrates agreed with the locals and ordered the rod to be removed, and the resident appealed. The young lawyer who got the job of representing him in court was Maximilien Robespierre. The locals sought their own scientific evidence, and as their chief witness they called an amateur scientist who had written a paper on electricity, Jean Paul Marat. The case became a point of discussion across France, and when Robespierre won the case he became one of the most celebrated lawyers in the region. He sent his closing speech to

Franklin, along with a note to say, 'The human race owes you its thanks,' and Franklin's prestige amongst radicals was greater than ever.

So a coalition of science, radicalism and organization across the continents had won the right to tame a force previously felt to be impossible to control and directed from the heavens. The impossible was becoming possible, even more so as the British were forced to give America back.

4

The Crisis

When they kick at your front door
How you gonna come?
With your hands on your head
Or on the trigger of your gun?

EARLY RIOTS

France had been overtaken by the British in almost every field as the Industrial Revolution gathered pace, and the debt incurred from sending an army to back the Americans was equivalent to the total tax they would raise in four years. Then the Chancellor, Calonne, added further debts of 653 million *livres* over three years, including a handout of 14 million *livres* to the King's brother and 16 million to the Count of Artois. The King behaved like the sort of person who responds to a crippling Visa statement by going straight out to buy a camcorder or a Persian rug. He bought two more palaces, one at Rambouillet for 10 million and one at St-Cloud, for Marie Antoinette, for 6 million. Chancellor Calonne had a similar mastery of personal finance, employing a team of full-time chefs and an army of servants, including three whose job was to look after roast meat.

There followed a rumour that Calonne had delivered to his wife a box of pastilles, each wrapped in its own 300-*livre* note. You have to applaud the genius behind putting someone like that in charge of the nation's finances. He probably spent all day having thoughts such as, 'There's still a couple of million left in the economy. Fuck it, let's blow the lot on a curry.'

The humour may have been lost on some of the French, especially in 1785 when there was a drought, and the worst harvest for decades. The King, aware he had to increase tax, imposed measures such as building a wall around Paris as a customs post; and in 1787 he called a meeting of 144 leading nobles and tried to persuade them, in return for increased local powers, to start paying tax. The nobles refused, and the local authority in Paris, called the Parlement, supported them. The King, his authority challenged from outside the court for the first time, panicked and withdrew most of the planned taxes. The Parlement called for a public celebration, which turned into the first demonstrations of the revolution. Thousands swarmed through the streets, denouncing Calonne and throwing fireworks. When a sergeant ordered his troops to 'Get some lead into the bastards' backsides,' they fired instead into the air, and the riots continued for a week. Discontent was becoming dissent.

So the first 'outside agitators' whose actions led to the mob being stirred were the aristocracy – a bit like a revolution in Britain beginning with a demonstration called by Norman St John-Stevas. What were the nobles thinking of, stirring up the mob like this?

They could have had no idea that the peaceful show of strength they wished for would turn into a riot. They probably agreed with Mercier who, two years before the storming of the Bastille, wrote, 'Dangerous rioting has become a moral impossibility in Paris . . . Any attempt at sedition here would be nipped in the bud.'[1] Typical bloody columnist. And if the French media were like the modern British types, the fact that he was proved hopelessly wrong wouldn't have stopped him being introduced on hundreds of news programmes as 'an expert on Paris affairs'.

In any case, the police were hardly trained for dealing with mass unrest. The bulk of their time was spent dealing with fires, and matters such as peddlers' licences. They were also in charge of certain taxes, and street-cleaning, and they had a special bureau in charge of wet-nurses. From a modern perspective this can create an appalling image: 'All right, sonny, now SUCK. Or are we going to have to do it the hard way?'

The masses had always seemed subservient, so who would consider the possibility of this changing? But also, the nobles could see no way that a demonstration could move beyond support for their own cause. To the aristocracy, the bulk of the population weren't players in deciding which direction was taken by society. They knew no important people, could influence no courtiers, and had no financial clout.

No mass movement starts out revolutionary. Protests may take the form of an appeal to the highest authority, as if the rulers' emotions can be tapped the way the orphan girl wins round the President of America in *Annie*. This is the same optimistic attitude that leads some people on modern demonstrations to carry handwritten placards with slogans such as PLEASE THINK AGAIN, WORLD BANK, AND ABOLISH INTEREST PAYMENTS EVERYWHERE. To the rioters of Paris, the King was someone who now appeared as if he would listen to their grievances.

To move from discontent to riot requires someone respectable signalling the protest as legitimate. When an apparently credible figure makes an appeal for a show of support, it can give protest the official stamp it needs to take off. Just as, strange though it is to recall, the man who made protest seem legitimate in the Soviet Union prior to its collapse in 1991 was Boris Yeltsin.

The organizers of the parades in Paris in 1787 must have assumed the crowds would pour out their affection for the nobility, then return home satisfied. But as the participants arrived and assembled with slogans supporting the nobles, the resentment of sixteen-hour days, of rent men nabbing commodes, of dog dung in the pepper and rumours of diamond necklaces, must have cascaded from every marcher. Like anyone who's been on the wrong end of an abusive relationship, when they finally found a voice to shout back, years of frustration flowed out in a rambling, incoherent torrent. As fireworks and stones soared over the wall of the Palais de Justice, each individual that made up the mob propelling them was probably thinking, 'And another thing . . .'

The protests continued for a week. They burned effigies of Calonne, and attacked the police and troops. In all probability they ran amok for no other reason than that, surprised by their own numbers and audacity, they realized they could get away with it. Over the following months the King sought to restore his authority, but demonstrations took place wherever he did so, given added impetus by a bread shortage. By now the protests were supported by the bourgeoisie, who saw a chance to push for the influence they'd been craving. Along with the nobles, they demanded the convening of an 'Estates-General', a parliamentary body in which they'd be represented.

The royal government began to disintegrate. In April 1787 Calonne resigned in disgrace, fleeing to Britain. Other ministers followed, and the job of chancellor was given to Jacques Necker, a Swiss man popular with the people, though not so much with the King's younger brother, who called him a 'fornicating foreign bastard'. With his options rapidly evaporating, the King agreed to call the Estates-General, to begin meeting in May 1789.

THE RIGHT TO COMPLAIN

For the elections to the Estates-General, France was divided into its three orders. The nobility and clergy each elected their own representatives, and the third estate held an elaborate series of elections in which all property owners over the age of twenty-five were allowed to take part. They elected a smaller group of electors, who in turn chose their delegates. The third estate was also requested to provide a list of grievances from each area called a *'cahier de doléances'*, to which anyone could contribute. The aim was similar to those initiatives taken by office managers who've been on a modern business-course. It was as if the King sat all his subjects in front of him, and walked up and down in front of a flip chart, tossing a pen from one hand to the other and said, 'Now, this country can only operate efficiently if you're happy. And if you're happy, well, then the country's happy and, most important for me, the Queen stays happy, heh heh. But seriously, please write down anything that makes you unhappy and we'll read it out and discuss it together.'

The central problem of this strategy was exhibited when I was at school, and the one liberal teacher sat the class in a circle and asked us to share with him our problems regarding the lesson. He selected the grubbiest, most deprived kid to start the discussion, asking, 'Johnny, what do you think?', to which the answer was, 'I think you're a cunt, sir.'

This was the problem for the King. Thousands of the *cahiers* demanded a constitution, along the recent American model. Most proposed a reversal of the tax burden. Many advocated freedom of the press, reorganization of the Church and an end to royal 'waste'. And the procedure provided an outlet for countless other complaints, few of which could be dealt with without challenging the basis of absolute monarchy altogether. As with the teacher, the question 'What grieves you?' couldn't be resolved without removing the person asking the question.

Between 25,000 and 60,000 documents were filed, each one representing a group within a town, or an entire village. It's easy to imagine the arguing through the night that must have been behind many of these documents, especially for anyone who's been part of a group effort to write a leaflet.

'We've got to mention the frog-swishing.'

'Don't forget the hunting laws.'

'Or fishing rights.'

'Hang on, we haven't mentioned Nicaragua.'

These *cahiers* contained a characteristic common to all revolutions but which contradicts the popular image of revolution. Not one document has been found that advocates the abolition of the monarchy.

Far from being led by bloodthirsty militants, the population pleaded for moderate reform. The grievances may have been impossible to remedy without revolution, but no one at the start of 1789 was aware of that. So the pleas can appear almost pathetic.

From the Town Hall in Paris, for example, came a document called 'Petition of Women of the Third Estate', addressed directly to the King. It complains, 'Having fulfilled the first duties of religion, we are taught to work, having reached the age of fifteen or sixteen, to make five or six *sous* a day. If nature has refused us beauty, we get married without dowry to unfortunate artisans, lead aimless, difficult lives stuck away in the provinces, and give birth to children we are incapable of raising.' A reasonably strident document, it would appear. But it ends:

> We ask to be able to give our children a reasonable education so as to make them subjects worthy of serving you. We will trans-mit to them the love we have for your majesty. We defy Frenchmen to love you better than we. When we, Sire, see you at Versailles, with pounding hearts, and are able to gaze for an instant upon your august person, tears flow from our eyes. We see in you only a tender father, for whom we would sacrifice our lives a thousand times.

It must be almost certain that from among the women who com-posed that paragraph came some of the crowd that four years later cheered the King's execution.

THE CAST

Robespierre

The deputies elected to represent the third estate were almost entirely bourgeois, partly due to the property qualification, but also because of the way the elections were held. In villages and towns, the elections took place after a discussion on the *cahiers*, so public speakers, particularly lawyers, had an advantage. It was at this point that many of the celebrity names of the revolution first appeared. Maximilien Robespierre, from the town of Arras, was a lawyer who stood for election in the region of Artois. By the end of the revolution he was one of history's pantomime baddies, architect of the Terror. And as with Marat, anyone should have been able to tell this from his appearance. The ex-Chancellor Necker's daughter, Mme de Staël, said after meeting him for the first time, 'his features were repulsive, his veins a shade of green ... something suggested an unspoken terror'. The historian Nodier wrote, 'his gaze was an indescribable shaft of light from a wild eye between retractile eyelids'. Other

The repulsive, green-veined, ugly Robespierre.

accounts, such as the one that describes him as 'having the face of a tiger', make you wonder whether you're reading *Harry Potter and the French Revolution*.[2]

Arras is a beautiful town dominated by a stunning cathedral in a huge square surrounded by pavement cafés and those shops full of cheese and olive oil. Unfortunately, to some it seems contaminated with Robespierre's green-veined evil. By way of explaining how such a monster as Robespierre could have been created, the biography *The Incorruptible* by Freidrich Sieburg describes Arras as 'an uninspiring country town' where 'everyone is behind securely locked doors. The noisy cheerfulness of markets, talk across streets, the chattering gaiety of normal French towns are lacking in this place. The footsteps of the inhabitants seem to be always hurrying.' You expect it to continue, 'The shops only open after sunset, there are no mirrors and visitors are always puzzled as to why this is the only French town with no garlic.'

You can visit the house in Arras in which Robespierre was brought up, but your entrance will surprise the woman who works there, as it must attract fewer tourists than most branches of Kwik-Fit. I asked her if there was a statue of him in the town, and she looked aghast before admitting there had been one at one time but it had been pulled down. 'He's not very much appreciated round here,' she said, and I felt as if I'd walked into the town hall at Gloucester and asked where I could find a statue of Fred West.

When Robespierre was five his mother died in childbirth, and shortly afterwards his father ran away, leaving the children with their grandparents. As a star pupil at school, he was selected to read the Latin address when the town received a visit from the newly anointed King Louis XVI. So as Louis listened to this cherubic lad, he may well have looked at the diligent Robespierre and thought, 'What a nice young man. As long as there are plenty like him, I'll have no worries being King.'

Robespierre became a law student, a poet and a devoted admirer of Rousseau. As a lawyer he worked fourteen hours each day, and was then visited by a barber who shaved him and powdered his face. Throughout his adult life he always wore a cravat (carrying a spare in case the first one became creased), lace cuffs and a waistcoat, and carried a hat he never wore in case it disturbed his hair, which was curled into two side-rolls and powdered, while at the back was a pigtail tied in a black satin ribbon. He never drank alcohol, and there's no record of him having a 'girlfriend' or 'boyfriend'. His every action was meticulous and measured, which has led to an image as the archetypal humourless leftie. He didn't really help to combat this image when he wrote to a friend from a relative's house: 'Every moment since our arrival has been devoted to pleasure. Ever since Saturday I have eaten tart. What a temptation to spend the night eating even more!'[3] Even this sordid behaviour was rejected because 'I then reflected upon the beauty of mastering one's passions.' It was an outlook that earned him the nickname 'the Incorruptible'.

From every contemporary account it seems that Robespierre was utterly single-minded, driven and committed to whatever task was before him. He was probably the sort of activist who would ring you at one in the morning and say, 'I want to speak to you because I feel you're not convinced about the political importance of changing the meeting night from Tuesday to Wednesday,' the type who would be invited to a wedding and say, 'Ah that will be handy as Terry will be there and I need to convince him to take over as treasurer,' and then look utterly bemused when Terry says, 'Not now, Robespierre, I'm getting married in ten minutes.'

He was so successful as a lawyer, including his victory in the lightning case, that he was made a judge, and in 1786 he was elected as President of the Arras Academy. The first hint of radicalism came when he befriended some of the peasants in his area and produced three pamphlets recording his horror at their conditions.

As a speaker he was clear and thorough, but with little panache or emotion. His approach seems to have been similar to those modern political activists who judge everything by whether it offers the 'correct' analysis, with no room for emotion to rear its ugly head. For example, when *Schindler's List* first came out, I asked a long-standing professional activist what he thought and he said, 'I was quite pleased as it was ninety per cent historically accurate.'

Robespierre evidently *was* emotional, or the plight of the peasantry wouldn't have driven him to jeopardize a successful career by championing their cause. But Robespierre seemed to view emotions as an impediment to clarity. And he believed the clarity he sought could be found in the works of Rousseau. Throughout the eight turbulent years of his political life he carried a copy of *The Social Contract* in his pocket. When the Estates-General election was announced, he stood for deputy for his region, being elected following an election address that went, 'Our countryside offers the spectacle of an unhappy people, who spray with tears of despair the soil their sweat has fertilised in vain.' Which has to have the edge over 'I am married with three children and wish to serve the people of Croydon North by reducing crime.'

Danton

Equally famous was Georges Jacques Danton, whose image suggests he drank, caroused and debauched his way through the whole event. He became known for having the loudest voice in France, and once insisted on wearing his hat through a performance at the theatre, leading to such an argument with the manager that the play was cancelled for the night.

Danton was brought up in the village of Arcis, and like Robespierre suffered a turbulent childhood. As a baby he was crawling around his family's farm when he was attacked by a bull and left severely scarred for life. Then he got smallpox and was left with scars on top of his scars, and his father, a middle-ranking lawyer, died when Georges Jacques was two. He often played truant to go

The ugly Danton.

swimming, and when he was fifteen he walked seventy miles to Rheims to see Louis XVI's coronation without telling anyone. From a modern perspective this may seem a distinctly swotty thing to do, but the coronation was a vast carnival, and it must have been the equivalent of a teenager from a tiny town in Dorset walking seventy miles to the Reading rock festival.

Most contemporary accounts suggest he surrounded himself with the most extravagant food in the vicinity, and drank with an Oliver Reed-style exuberance. Danton would be the one who, when every-one else was collapsing, would shout, 'Time for some tequilas!' He collected thousands of books, learned English, Italian, Latin and Greek, read Shakespeare, became a lawyer and was besotted with

Gabrielle Charpentier, who helped to run her Italian parents' restaurant. Charming Gabrielle's mother with his fluent Italian, he persuaded them to let him marry their daughter.

Where Robespierre was driven by intellect and inquiry, Danton was motivated by passion. Where Robespierre spoke with a calculating tone, Danton delivered spontaneous drama. History presents him as so diametrically opposed to Robespierre that you wonder whether their relationship has been devised by a Hollywood screenplay writer. The result would be Bruce Willis as Robespierre, Danton played by Jim Carrey, and a trailer that began 'Max liked the Social Contract – Georges liked social drinking. One was incorruptible – the other was irredeemable. But they were stuck with each other in *Georges and Max's Wild Weekend in Paris.*' Then we'd see them yelling at each other, then Robespierre saying, 'I feel so ashamed at what I did with that tart,' and Danton replying, 'I have that feeling every night – you'll get used to it.'

Danton's speeches were like his life: joy could only be unrestrained euphoria, and sadness meant intense, chilling tragedy. If he made a speech reminding a crowd of their role in events, he wanted them charging away at the end eager to grab their pikes. Yet prior to the revolution he never considered becoming a republican, and he told one of the King's friends, 'I am more monarchist than you.' However, he despised subservience, walking away from his job in the law courts, saying of the atmosphere, 'I cannot put up with all these servilities of civilisation, I am unable to indulge in such sycophancy. My lungs need a purer air to breathe.' It almost makes you want to go and work for a sycophantic law firm so you can resign with that speech.

At this point Danton was a cynic, the type who, while they may be appalled by the behaviour of powerful institutions, would never even sign a petition since they believe that unfairness is inevitable. It appears that he felt the only reasonable response to such a world was to pursue a grand life as an individual. Which may not seem radical, but, as he'd discovered at his law firm, under the *ancien régime* individuality and self-education landed you in trouble.

Then, as revolt began to rumble around him, his attitude towards the possibility of reforming society changed. In 1787 he was offered a senior job called Secretary of the Seals, but turned it down because he believed in radical change, saying, 'We are at the dawn of revolution.' He stayed as committed to personal pleasure as ever, but one friend said of him, 'He was bourgeois from head to toe, but his heart was with the people.'

None of this meant he would be an automatic friend of Robespierre, whom Danton described as 'having a face of a cat that's tasted vinegar'.[4] But just as behind Robespierre's apparent coldness there must have been a deep sense of rage against injustice, while Danton gloried in his bountiful personality he would have been a ranting nutcase without his intellect. And his reputation with women reached down the centuries; a French minister at the revolution's 200th-anniversary celebrations in 1989 was asked his opinion of Danton and replied, 'I like a man who screws.' Ah, the French. If New Labour reigned for a thousand years a millennium of Jack Straws and Alistair Darlings would never *say* anything as interesting, let alone *be* as interesting as Danton himself.

Desmoulins

Camille Desmoulins was also a barrister in Paris, and son of a lieutenant-general. And he provides the connection between the French Revolution and *Pop Idol* because he had a stutter that rendered him unintelligible unless he was performing to a crowd – the Gareth Gates of the French Revolution. It's been claimed that this peculiarity first became evident when Desmoulins was about eleven: one of his father's military friends visited the house and made a comment about the laziness of the poor, at which the enraged Desmoulins blurted out an eloquent tirade without a single stumble.

The ugly Desmoulins: 'Because I'm worth it.'

A biography written in 1871 declares, 'He was ugly with an energetic ugliness.'[5] Yet the drawings and busts of Desmoulins suggest a boyish appearance, with 1970s-style longish wavy hair and an air of David Ginola. The description of his ugliness could result from jealousy, but it's more likely that historians through the ages have had such contempt for the leaders of the revolution they've found it impossible to be objective, even about the leaders' appearance. If a revolution in America was led by Brad Pitt and Gwyneth Paltrow, in a hundred years' time historians would write, 'Pitt's frame jerked in ungainly fashion, his bulbous pot belly wobbling hypnotically with each malevolent cry of "Power to the People," while Paltrow's straggly unkempt hair hung menacingly across her piggy nose and obtrusive, unaligned eyes.'

Desmoulins was sent to a religious boarding school, where he met and became friends with the young Maximilien Robespierre. But unlike his friend, when Desmoulins later stood for election to the Estates-General he failed to win in the final round, so went to Paris to continue his career as a lawyer while pursuing his ambition to become a writer.

He was considerably more flowery in his writing than Robespierre, which is how he came to write that monarchy 'bastardises us by surrounding our youth with places of seduction and debauchery and besieging us with prostitutes'. Of all the arguments against monarchy, the charge that it leads to too much seduction and debauchery is probably not the strongest. Desmoulins also attempted satire, though, unluckily for him, one of the only surviving passages is the line, 'In order to pay taxes I must sell saucepans.'

Where Robespierre and Danton appear never to have been troubled by self-doubt, one because of his intellect and the other through the power of his personality, there appears to have been a certain uneasiness about Desmoulins, perhaps embodied in that stutter. Before each action, such as a speech made from on top of a table, he had to tell himself this was the right thing to do, then overcome his trepidation and jump into it, like someone jumping off a diving board for the first time.

Desmoulins became a close friend of Danton, though like all close friends of people like Danton he spent much of his time saying, 'No, don't do that, it's going too far,' and 'I think the best thing might be to go home.' He was certainly too wild for Robespierre, who once declined Desmoulins' invitation to a party by saying, 'Your light champagne brews are poison to freedom.' Anyone else would have said, 'I'm a bit skint 'til Friday' if they didn't want to go. But you can't help but love him for that, and it will be almost tempting, the next time I get one of those invitations with RSVP on the bottom, to ring up and say, 'I'm not coming – because your champagne brews are poison to freedom.'

Where Danton was a natural, Desmoulins had to work for his achievements, the grafting batsman to the flamboyance of an Ian Botham. By these efforts he taught himself Sanskrit, and began to produce his own newspaper. And five years before the revolution he befriended the Duplessis family, who lived in Paris and had a twelve-year-old girl called Lucile. Later on the relationship between Camille and Lucile would be one of the revolution's great love stories, though, if the rumours are true, he overcame his natural anxieties on one other occasion and managed to have an affair with her mother.

Mirabeau

For the money the aristocracy had cost the French nation, the least they could do was behave in an interestingly debauched way, and Count Mirabeau did his best to oblige. To start with, like anyone worth knowing, it seems, he was renowned for his ugliness. Madame de Staël, in an account of the Estates-General, wrote, 'Mirabeau is swart, prodigious, patched with foul moles and eye-offending remarks.'

Mirabeau had a typical noble upbringing: sent to military school, provided with an annual allowance of ten times the average income, married off to the heiress of the largest estate in Provence – that sort of thing. At first it seemed he would fail in his quest to marry Marie de Marignane, as she was already engaged, but fortunately his sister sent him a letter saying 'don't grieve', and went on to explain the good news that his rival could be persuaded to pull out of the marriage as 'Marie is hideous and very short.'

A deal was struck, and once married the couple lived rent-free on the family estate, but Mirabeau's habit of employing servants for every occasion, including a valet whose job was to shine the buttons on his clothes, meant that within fifteen months he was 200,000 *livres* in debt, at which point he secretly pawned his wife's jewels and began discreetly selling off the timber from the estate – the aristo-cratic version of flogging your records.

When he discovered that a baron in his sister's village had posted placards on every door in the area suggesting his sister was a 'lady without morals', Mirabeau attacked the baron, snatch-ing the baron's umbrella and snapping it on his back. The baron sued him for attempted murder, and at this point Mirabeau's father decided his son had become such an embarrassment that he appealed to the King to publish a *lettre de cachet* against him. Mirabeau was locked up, coincidentally in the Chateau d'If, the infamous island prison on which Dantes is held in *The Count of Monte Cristo*.

During his sentence Mirabeau met Sophie de Monnier on an early form of day-release, and as soon as his sentence had ended he ran off with her to Amsterdam. So his father arranged through the French Embassy in The Hague for them both to be arrested for the second time. Mirabeau was locked up at his father's request for three and a half years, this time in the castle at Vincennes, and Sophie was sent to a convent prison. While inside he took to writing philosophical pornography, such as *Erotika Biblion* and *The Education of Laure*.

Sophie was released first and waited for Mirabeau, but after his release it was clear his passion had evaporated during his sentence. So Sophie stayed in the convent until she became engaged to a man who died on the day before their wedding, at which point she com-mitted suicide. This family shouldn't have been in the aristocracy, they should have been in *Brookside*.

Understandably, Mirabeau felt like getting away, and went to Switzerland, where he met a group of liberals who convinced him of the need for a French constitution. He began writing pamphlets arguing this case, such as his *Essay on Despotism*, and despite being a count was elected to the Estates-General as a member of the third estate.

THE ESTATES-GENERAL

When the Estates-General convened in May 1789, of almost three hundred third-estate deputies about half were lawyers, around one hundred were bankers, some were ex-clergymen and one, Bailly, was France's only celebrity astronomer. But none was a republican. Even Robespierre proposed that the campaign for rights should be led by the King, through 'moral virtue'. Like Rousseau and the writers of the Enlightenment that inspired them, the radicals of the third estate believed the reshaping of society would come about through mutual agreement with the old order. At the same time, every area of France was deluged with further protests.

The rising price of bread, combined with the growing belief that the authorities could be forced to retreat, led to demonstrations in almost every town. In the Alps, the peasants of three villages ransacked the chateau of Lord d'Espraux to take back the grain they'd handed over as part of their feudal dues. And the people of Provence stoned the local bishop for protecting hoarders of grain.

Posters went up around Marseilles proclaiming, IF YOU HAVE COURAGE, SHOW IT NOW, from which was organized a citizens' militia. In Aix, the First Consul was besieged in the town hall by protesters demanding a reduction in the price of bread, until he escaped out of a window. In every area mills, monasteries and castles were invaded for food, and tax-collection offices were broken into, the records taken and burned. In the town of Limoux the records were thrown into the River Aude, creating the magnificent image of tax officials on the riverbank, stretching out fishing nets and tearfully squeaking that the whole of D to F had just sailed under the bridge and into the weir. Perhaps the peasants should have held their own public-information campaign, informing each village, 'Avoid having to make any unnecessary tax payments this year by making sure you burn down your tax office by 31 March.'

By the late 1780s the initial rush of protest had settled into a series of deliberately planned actions, and over 2,500 pamphlets were published throughout France. The early alliance between the nobility and third estate broke down, as their separate class interests ran into conflict. The nobles may have called a march, but they were always likely to draw the line at burning down tax offices. Also, the exact nature of the forthcoming Estates-General was a source of some dispute. The King's proposal was that he would maintain his absolute rule, merely advised by this new body. He also proposed that votes should be counted as three blocks, so the clergy, nobility and third estate would have one vote each. Since the nobility and clergy were bound to side with each other on most issues, this would have made it pointless for the third estate to turn up. This reminds me of the socialist group that held a conference in the late 1990s; and when it came to the first vote it was announced that one delegate, who was a union official, had a block vote that counted for more than all the other votes put together. Given the strange nature of the British left, for some reason the conference carried on.

The third estate were less tolerant, demanding that each individual vote should be counted and that, as they represented most of the population, they should have as many deputies as the other two orders combined. The royal court, aware that the body was meaningless if the third estate refused to take part, backed down and accepted these demands.

This was the atmosphere in which the Estates-General met on 4 May 1789, in Versailles. The tension between the orders rumbled immediately. To start with, the nobility and clergy were presented to the King individually, in his private office, while the third-estate delegates had to walk past in a group to a spare bedchamber. For all the concessions forced on the King, he couldn't contemplate the unnoble deputies in his private office, as if the place would reek for ever of their commonness. This was a level of snobbery that even in England I have only encountered once, when a landowning woman from Berkshire told me she'd asked around the village for someone to do her ironing, but 'I only sent it round there once as the woman was too common and my clothes all came back smelling of chip fat.'

Perhaps the third-estate deputies should have tried some twentieth-century techniques, such as marching confidently to the office door and saying, 'I'm on the guest list.' Even then they would have failed the dress code for the opening ceremony. The clergy were ordered to wear glittering robes; the nobility had silk coats and plumed hats; and the third estate were ordered to wear plain black coats. The following day the opening session began, in an open coach-house. This didn't trouble the nobility or clergy, who sat either side of the King, but the third estate were seated on wooden benches at the back of the room, from where they couldn't hear a thing.

As the King entered, protocol obliged the nobility and clergy to remove their hats, sit down after him and replace their hats on their heads. But the third estate were expected to remain standing and without hats for some time after everyone else had sat down. At this point they must have felt like schoolkids in morning assembly, squashed together and expecting the King at any moment to clap his hands and say, 'NO talking during the Estates-General. And that applies to YOU as well, Robespierre.' So the first act of rebellion was when the third estate sat down at the same time as the other orders.

The royal advisers decided to let this pass, saying in effect, 'Leave it, Your Majesty, they're not worth it.' Then came the King's opening speech, followed by possibly the greatest ever failure of a human being to rise to the occasion. For the opening session of this momentous event, the new chancellor, Necker, was to propose his remedy for the country's bankruptcy. But he went on so long that he made himself exhausted, and handed his speech to a court official to finish for him. Most of us have heard dreadful speeches, but this is the only occasion I know of where a speaker has bored *himself* to sleep. The only explanation I can think of is that Necker had only ever spoken before within the royal court, and was petrified at having to stand before the deputies of the third estate. I saw something like this when an Oxbridge newspaper editor had to make a speech to trade unionists, and mumbled so nervously and incoherently that almost the entire audience left before he was halfway through; throughout his speech he looked as if what he really wanted to say was, 'Look, take my credit cards but please don't break my glasses.'

Worse still for Necker, the official had a particularly monotonous voice which, combined with the poor acoustics, meant no one up the back could understand what he was saying. The deputies only found out the Chancellor's proposals by reading the next day's newspaper. And Necker's friends must have had quite a task consoling him: 'You were fine, honestly, it was just a really quiet audience, and don't worry about the bit where you gave up and got the bloke from Accounts to take over, I don't think anyone noticed.'

It may seem puzzling that the royal court apparently went out of their way to antagonize the third estate, but they must have been trying their absolute hardest not to. The difficulty was in combining a system of values based on superiority through birth with a system based on merit and democracy. Before royalty was challenged as irrational, it didn't have to justify its individuals as worthy rulers. They were rulers because they were born that way, divinely ordained. It's only since royalty has conceded its divine authority, that it's tried to justify its position through merit, which is how we ended up with stories of the Queen Mother's dancing prowess. Even then, their real feelings are exposed occasionally such as when the butler accused of stealing Diana's nick-nacks revealed the story of his meeting with the Queen. He'd stood throughout the entire three-hour session because 'One does not sit in the presence of Her Majesty at a private audience.' Maybe this is a royal game and they see how long someone can keep going without keeling over. Perhaps Charles and Andrew were looking through the keyhole, sniggering, 'Keep it up, Mum, ten more minutes and he'll wet himself.'

In Versailles in May 1789, the court couldn't begin to grapple with the conundrum of what purpose they might serve if they abandoned their absolute rule. They could condescend to invite democratically elected individuals to the same building they were in, but not to the office, and only if they wore plain black coats.

THE PAMPHLET, THE TENNIS COURT
AND A REBELLION

The Palais-Royal, owned by the King's brother, the Duc d'Orléans, was the unlikely venue for the meetings of radicals that took place in parallel with the Estates-General. The palace was already used as a trading area, packed with clothes shops, cafés and clubs, but the *duc*, who disliked his brother intensely, allowed it to be used by the growing opposition. The police weren't allowed to enter the palace compound, which meant the square soon became a centre for radicals to debate and produce pamphlets, making it the heart of radical thought. During the volatile years of the Estates-General, these debates attracted thousands. The English traveller Arthur Young visited, and wrote:

> The business going forward at present in the pamphlet shops of Paris is incredible. At the Palais-Royal, every hour produces something new. Thirteen pamphlets came out today, sixteen yesterday, and ninety-two last week. But the coffee-houses in the Palais-Royal present yet more singular and astonishing spectacles; they are not only crowded within, but other expectant crowds are at the doors and windows, listening to certain orators. The eagerness with which they are heard, and the thunder of applause they receive for every sentiment of more than common hardiness or violence against the present government, can not easily be imagined.[6]

France was transforming not because of outside agitators, but because thousands on the inside were *becoming* agitators. Many of those people distributing pamphlets or climbing aboard tables would never have believed, a year or two before, they would ever do such a thing. Peasants and artisans who had never imagined their views or actions could have an impact on society were sensing that they mattered.

The third estate were consistently winning votes in the Estates-General, by attracting the poorer sections of the clergy to their side. The King, in an attempt to reassert control, announced on 14 June the postponement of the Estates-General until after a special royal session. Somehow, though, the message didn't get through to the third-estate deputies, and on Saturday 20 June they arrived as normal at their meeting hall, to find their room locked.

They could hear banging from inside, and found carpenters preparing a platform for the King. The stages that must have followed will be recognizable to anyone who's tried to organize a meeting and discovered the room to be unexpectedly unavailable. Stage one – indignation: 'There must be a mistake, we meet here all the time.' Stage two – making it worse by annoying the blokes who work there: 'Look, for Christ's sake, you must be able to do something.' Stage three – pathetic backtracking: 'All right, mate, sorry, I know it's not your fault.' Then panic, then confusion. And then a series of unworkable suggestions – 'I know a bar with a room at the back, as long as we don't mind sharing with the Irish dancing club,' or 'My brother-in-law's a security guard at the aquarium, I'm sure he can let us in to meet there.'

At this point Dr Guillotin, who'd been elected as a third-estate deputy, had his second most historic moment. He announced that he knew the manager of the nearby indoor tennis court, and the elected representatives of the French nation walked off in a crowd behind him as it started to pour with rain. Guillotin had over five hundred deputies behind him, and his heart must have been fluttering a bit, wondering whether, having led the entire French parliament to his mate's tennis court, he'd have to say, 'Er, apparently it's fully booked until four o' clock this afternoon.' Luckily for Dr Guillotin, the manager was as amenable as he predicted, and the doctor must have assumed that as a result of this incident future generations would remember his name for ever as the bloke who found a place for the third estate to meet. Perhaps he also thought, 'That's a shame, because I've always fancied myself as an inventor, but I don't suppose anyone will ever remember me for that.'

Bailly the astronomer chaired the session and Mirabeau proposed an oath 'never to break up, and to reassemble wherever circumstances may demand it, until such time as the Constitution was passed and established on firm foundations'. The oath was passed unanimously except for one person, M. Martin d'Auch of Castelnaudary, which must have spoiled the effect a little. Here was this great dramatic moment and there was one man with no sense of occasion.

The deputies had, in effect, declared themselves to be the government of France, a national assembly pending a constitution, which would be organized by Mirabeau. The King responded by saying directly to the rebellious third estate, 'I command you to disperse immediately and return to your rooms,' as if they were naughty kids on a school trip. But the third estate were feeling defiant. The following week, when they were allowed back in their chambers, the

The Tennis Court Oath

King sent a messenger, the Marquis de Breze, with an instruction to finish their session for that day. Mirabeau rose to tell the messenger, 'Sir, you are a stranger in this assembly, you have no right to speak here. Return to those who have sent you and tell them we shall not stir save at the point of the bayonet.'

As word spread of the oath, the King's reaction and the growing conflict, protests intensified. Bakeries and mills were looted in every area. Sections of the army pledged never to fire against supporters of the third estate, and in some areas the Gardes Françaises began helping the looters. Perhaps the most spectacular looting was at the St-Lazare monastery, where fifty-two cartloads of hoarded grain were taken. Then every part of the monastery was pilfered, and one boy took a skeleton, which he dragged up five flights of stairs to his room. Obviously a student.

5

On to the Bastille

Kick over the wall, cause governments to fall
How can you refuse it?

THE SEARCH FOR WEAPONS

In the last week of June, the royal government ordered around 20,000 troops to march to Paris, to threaten the third-estate deputies and deal with any further protests. Then on 12 July the King dismissed Necker and replaced him with a hard-line militarist, Baron de Breteuil. This was the equivalent of the moment in a pub argument when a look, an under-the-breath comment, a sudden movement or a facial twitch, leads to everyone shuffling out of the way, knowing a line has been crossed and a bundle is now inevitable.

Thousands flooded into the courtyard at Versailles to demand the reinstatement of Necker, surely the biggest display of support in history for someone unable to stay awake during their own speech.

Mirabeau stood before the deputies and made a rousing speech, reminding them of their oath and urging them to stick together. This was the moment for Camille Desmoulins to impose his name on the forthcoming revolution. Desmoulins had ridden to Versailles to report on events for his newspaper, and as soon as he heard the news of Necker's replacement he galloped back to Paris, where he was the first to reveal the news to the crowds at the Palais-Royal. Pamphlets were circulated through every garrison. Local troops refused to fire on the demonstrations demanding the reinstatement of Necker. Forty of the fifty-four customs posts that made up the wall around Paris were destroyed. Marat made his first appearance, publishing a paper that warned, 'Their aim is to dissolve our National Assembly, and the only means at their disposal is civil war.' To a vast crowd outside a café, Desmoulins made a speech from the top of a table that ended, 'Citizens, Necker has been driven out. After such an act they will dare anything, and may be preparing a massacre of patriots this very night. To arms. To arms. The famous police are here; well, let them look at me. I call on my brothers to take liberty.' Then he waved his pistol in the air, shouting, 'I am ready to die a glorious death.' Within days he wrote, 'The great are only great because we are on our knees. Let us rise.'

Crowds from the Palais-Royal marched to the Abbaye prison, where they forced open the doors to release eleven guardsmen who'd been jailed for not firing on demonstrators. Throughout the city, troops were offered drinks by the crowd if they shouted, '*Vive le tiers-état.*' Other crowds marched to the theatres, where afternoon

Woman spanked for spitting on Necker's portrait.

performances were about to begin, and demanded the shows be cancelled out of respect for the uprising. When the theatre managers refused to refund the ticket prices a crowd of 3,000 invaded the Opéra to demand everyone be given their money back. A waxworks was broken into, and dummies of Necker and the Duc d'Orléans were stolen, to parade as heroes in the demonstrations.

The deputies and other prominent members of the third estate met at the Town Hall to formulate their strategy. They knew the defence of the third estate depended on the mass movement growing around them; on the other hand, they were afraid the crowd would get out of control. So they set up a people's militia, which recruited 13,000 volunteers immediately, although they insisted that 'all unemployed and vagrants were excluded'. This is another recurring feature of revolutions in general, to start out with a bizarre sense of decorum. The deputies were saying, in effect, 'No beggars, this is a *respectable* violent uprising.' Some districts even demanded employers' references before admitting recruits into this militia. Volunteers must have been hoping for references that read, 'Alain is punctual, co-operates with colleagues, and shows the initiative to make him well suited for attacking a landlord with a pike.'

By the evening of 12 July, as an English observer, Dr Rigby, wrote: 'The regularly armed citizens almost exclusively occupied the streets.'[1] Each district of Paris was to provide at least eight hundred armed citizens, who would direct the procuring of more arms to repel the King's troops. Historians usually record this as a smooth act, no more problematic than if a modern government wished to recruit extra police or firemen. Simon Schama, for example, says, 'Units of eight hundred in each district were to be mobilised, making up in total a citizens' army of 48,000 . . . it was an imposing force.' So we visualize it as if portrayed by Hollywood, when someone would stand up, shrug their shoulders and say, 'Well, looks like the King's made up his mind. There ain't nothin' us poor simple folks are gonna do to change it.' Then a man with bushy sideburns would say, 'Now just you listen to me. I'm sick and tired of this fancy King with his high-falutin crown puttin' up the price of bread and shuttin' the good folk of this town out of their hall. I say we all sign up until there's eight hundred of us willing to stand up and fight for what we believe in. Well, what are we waitin' for?' Then the first man would stand again and shout, 'He's right. Let's throw our hats in the air.'

But anyone who has witnessed a meeting of union members, or angry people debating the strategy for a campaign, whether opposition to the poll tax or an unwanted by-pass, will know these meetings must have been chaos. Someone will have been saying, 'I'm sure if we talk to the King politely, it will turn out he meant to hand over the keys all along.' Someone will have been over-enthusiastic, yelling, 'I know some builders, maybe I can get them to knock us up a castle.' A hippy will have announced he was no good at fighting, but he and his mates could stand at the back juggling. An anarchist will have explained how he could make bombs out of flour and vinegar. A group from an estate will have been shouting, 'Never mind the third estate, when's someone going to fix my drains?', and an old man will have wandered through the middle asking if this was the right place to get a dog licence.

One problem that doesn't appear to have been anticipated was that numbers willing to sign up varied enormously according to the district. In the poorer areas the figure of eight hundred was reached easily, with 1,200 enrolling at Le Petit-St-Antoine. But in the district of Les Minimes they only managed to get four. You have to feel for the poor sods in charge of recruitment there. They'll have taken the names of their recruits to a central office, and it must have been someone's job to lean across a table and have the conversation that went: 'Did you get eight hundred, citizen?'

'Not eight hundred, no. There's four. But they're ever so keen.'

While the newly formed militia dedicated themselves to finding weapons, the royalist authorities were equally desperate to hide them. Besenval, who was responsible for public order, was in charge of this task. Fifty-two thousand muskets had been stored in the hospital, and the hospital governor, M. de Sombreuil, promised to ensure they were dismantled, asking the pensioners based in the hospital to remove the triggers and ramrods. The next day he took Besenval into the basement, after which Besenval wrote, 'in six hours, twenty pensioners whom he had detailed for this job had only put twenty muskets out of action. He said that a spirit of sedition was rife in the hospital. A legless cripple, whom no one suspected, had introduced into the establishment bundles of licentious and subversive songs.'[2]

STORMING

On 14 July the search for weapons became so desperate that the museum in the Place Louis XV was raided. The insurgents procured pieces such as a crossbow and a sword once owned by Henri IV. So somewhere in the revolution must have been this museum battalion, easily recognizable by their tendency to threaten royalist troops with an axe discovered in the remains of a Roman villa, perhaps informing their victim, 'By the eleventh century, improvements in metallurgy techniques made possible strengthened swords such as the one I'm attacking you with here.'

More productively, a crowd of 8,000 invaded the Hôtel des Invalides, taking around 30,000 muskets. By now the Paris electorate, still at the Town Hall, had decided that a crowd should march to the Bastille.

The fortress was a symbol of royalist France, partly because political prisoners were held in its notorious dungeons, but also because the simple existence of such an enormous and apparently impregnable building must have been a constant reminder of the power of the old regime, especially situated in the heart of one of the poorest areas, by St-Antoine. There was also a more practical reason for a raid: over the previous two days, Swiss Guards had moved 30,000 lb of gunpowder in hundreds of barrels to the area behind the draw-bridge, precisely because it was deemed to be impenetrable to the rebels.

A crowd of around one thousand, mostly made up of small tradesmen, including dozens of locksmiths, arrived at the gates at ten in the morning and demanded the handing-over of the gun-powder. The prison Governor, de Launay, invited a delegation inside for breakfast, but the breakfast went on for three and a half hours, while outside, rumours circulated that royalist troops were mas-sacring local citizens throughout Paris. Anyone who's been on a large anti-fascist demonstration or a mass picket will be able to imag-ine the nature of these rumours. A group of three blokes dressed all in black will have arrived in the crowd, yelling, 'Don't just stand there, our comrades are being hammered round the other side!' So a huge contingent will have set off and bumped into another crowd coming the other way, who will have said, 'No, we heard they're massacring people round *that* side.' So the first crowd would reply, 'We've just come from there.' Someone would yell, 'What the bloody hell are they doing in there?' A few will have had to go home to pick up their kids, someone will have had to leave for a dentist's appoint-ment, and someone will have grumbled, 'This is the last time I come on one of these things, I *told* you nothing would happen,' and stomped off home. And throughout, a revolutionary group with a national membership of nine will have handed out leaflets entitled *Why We Aren't Supporting This Demonstration.*

The deadlock was broken by someone who must have been the mad kid at school. The kid who, on the trip to the War Museum, goes missing and is found dangling upside-down from the top of the statue of Wellington. Who never learns to read but is astounding at climbing. One man, studying the angles of the drawbridge, decided he could get to the chains that held it in place by climbing on to them from the roof of a nearby perfume shop. He succeeded and, using a variety of tools, cut through the chains. The one flaw in his genius was that as the drawbridge collapsed it fell on a fellow protester and killed him. None the less the rest could now get into the outer courtyard. De Launay broke off his negotiations, but despite his promise not to fire, late in the afternoon cannon shots were aimed at the crowd. Hulin, personal laundryman to the Queen, persuaded two companies of French Guards to march to the Bastille and defend the rebels, as de Launay's cannon were now killing demonstrators. In response the crowd set fire to the Governor's house. A Swiss Guard handed the keys to the second drawbridge through a slit in the wall, the drawbridge was opened and the crowd surged through. But now the crowd faced another moat, which they had no idea how to cross, so a clerk from a pawn office ran to a carpenter's shop

**Maillard walks the plank over
the moat of the Bastille.**

to fetch some planks. He got eleven, one of which was long enough to be a bridge. Surely it would be worth the while of some historian to investigate whether the carpenter charged for these planks. And if he stood there lovingly planing the ends and stroking his wood the way carpenters do, while the anxious clerk screamed, 'Never mind that, just chuck the things over here, we're trying to storm the fucking Bastille.'

Once inside the inner courtyard of the Bastille, Hulin the laundryman tried to protect de Launay, but an unemployed cook ran past him and sliced off the Governor's head. Altogether, six defenders of the Bastille were killed, and ninety-four protestors. The crowd then swept down to release the prisoners, but the keys to the dungeons were part of the same set that included the key to the drawbridge, and the bloke who had them had gone home. So they had to batter down the doors anyway. It was then that they realized the dungeons of the most famous jail in France only contained seven prisoners. There would have been an eighth, but the Marquis de Sade had been moved earlier in the month because he'd been upsetting passers-by by shouting at them through the pipe he was given to piss through. Worse, as they released the seven, it became clear that one of them was convinced he was Julius Caesar – which must have created possibly the greatest anticlimax in all history, to go through all that, finally open the door and find a decrepit old boy saying, 'Thank you very much. Did you know I came, I saw and I conquered?'

Governor Morris, at the Royal Gardens at Versailles, wrote, 'A person came in and announced the taking of the Bastille, the governor of which is beheaded, and a crowd carries his head in triumph through the city. Yesterday it was the fashion at Versailles not to believe that there were any disturbances in Paris. I presume that this day's transactions will induce a conviction that all is not perfectly quiet.'[3]

The King, in his diary for 13 July, and again on the 14th, wrote one word – 'Rien'.

NOW WHAT DO WE DO?

As news of the storming of the Bastille spread through Paris, most of the city was strangely euphoric. The King's will had been over-turned by the locksmith and the laundryman. Parisians were experiencing a sensation that would become familiar in modern revolutions, the notion following the opening battle that it was much easier than expected, and that virtually the whole population supports the outcome. Not only was everyone from the starving people of St-Antoine to the ugly Count of Mirabeau united in cele-bration, but much of the nobility proclaimed their support as well. As with the uprisings in Eastern Europe in 1989, so many people heralded the revolution that you wondered who had ever backed the old regime. It was as if a united population had defeated a typhoon or a pride of escaped lions. Like the bureaucrats of Eastern Europe, prominent figures from the overturned government appeared, waving at crowds, shouting in effect, 'Congratulations for overthrowing me.' And this process reached its logical conclusion when the storming of the Bastille received support from the King himself.

To start with, Louis XVI agreed to recall Necker to his job as Chancellor. Then he agreed to recognize the National Assembly, made up of the third-estate deputies along with the poorer clergy and a portion of nobles that came over to the third estate's side. The Paris electors at the Town Hall appointed Lafayette as head of the police and army, which would now be known as the National Guard, and Bailly the astronomer became Mayor of Paris. But the most radical body to be formed was the Paris Commune, in charge of the city. This divided Paris into forty-eight sections, and anyone could vote or stand for election, which led to it becoming the heart of all action by the *sans-culottes*. So France was to be governed by a mix-ture of royalty and elected representatives, and the tussle between the two over which held ultimate power shaped the next three years of the revolution. Louis XVI agreed to come to Paris, where he would accept a gift of the cockade that had become a symbol of the revolution. One witness wrote, 'The King took it in very good humour and fastened it onto his hat. When the Maréchal de Beauvau tried to keep the crowd away, he said "Leave them alone, they love me well." There was a burst of applause and cries of *"Vive le Roi"* were heard everywhere.'

The King's attitude is relatively easy to explain: his hope for survival depended on conveying an attitude of humility, as if summoning 20,000 troops to destroy the Assembly was all a silly misunderstanding. But why did so many people agree? Partly it must have been that most people would rather resolve a conflict by mutual agreement than by having to extinguish their opponent. It was easier to believe the King was the victim of bad advice. But also, to believe the King was honest in his sentiments was to believe the battle was won. Everything would be all right now; he'd seen the error of his ways and the democratic assembly would work hand-in-hand with the monarchy. The people of France had accomplished an extraordinary feat, they'd compelled a centuries-old dynasty to submit to their will. To suggest that such an achievement amounted only to a beginning would have been like telling someone crossing the line at the end of a marathon that they couldn't have their medal unless they ran all the way back again.

There were *some* from the aristocracy who expressed their horror at events, and many of these reacted by running off altogether. The Duchesse de Gontaut, in her account of her journey out of Paris, wrote, 'We set off in a two-horse carriage with a groom in livery in front. A curious way of travelling incognito!'[4] Proving she hadn't quite got it, as shown by her jovial use of the exclamation mark, reminiscent of a modern holiday postcard. You could expect her to continue, 'The people here are very lively, though their novel use of pikes leaves a lot to be desired!' She goes on, 'When we arrived at Saint-Roch the crowd surrounded us, stopped the carriage and forced us to get down, while they ransacked the carriage hoping to find treasures. I had a painful surprise on seeing among the crowd my wet-nurse. Her ingratitude was such that she added an obscene gesture, which I will not describe.'

More tragic was the tale of the Duke of Dorset, British Ambassador in Paris. In June 1789 he asked the English Foreign Secretary, the Duke of Leeds, for a gesture of good will towards the French government. So Leeds, who was a cricket lover, agreed to send a team to play a French team that would be picked by Dorset. Unfortunately the English set off on the day after the storming of the Bastille, and so they got to Dover to find the Duke of Dorset fleeing in the opposite direction.[5] Personally I'd have found this cancellation most distressing; what better way to spend a couple of days off than storming the Bastille followed by a leisurely day at the cricket?

6

Taking Sides

Let fury have the hour
Anger can be power
D'you know that you can use it?

THE GREAT FEAR

The notion of a 'bourgeois revolution' can seem a peculiar concept. From a twenty-first-century perspective it raises images of the board of Microsoft linking arms round a mahogany table to shout, 'The partners united will never be defeated,' at a line of police down a videophone.

But one incident displayed how these two words with apparently opposite meanings could combine. A wealthy architect called Palloy made several speeches declaring his patriotism and commitment to the revolution. The day after the storming of the Bastille, Palloy applied to the Paris Commune for the contract to demolish the building. Once that was attained, he established a thriving business in selling pieces from the ex-prison as souvenirs to revolutionary societies throughout the country.

A more immediate task was to spread the word around France that the Bastille had been captured at all. Most major towns heard the news between three and five days after the event, but in some regions they didn't know for two weeks. Even then their information must have been unreliable, dependent on travellers arriving on horseback, and no doubt breathlessly gasping something like 'This is breaking news' before repeating the one piece of information they had forty times.

As the word spread, the peasantry greeted the revolution with hope that feudal dues would be abolished, but soon became embroiled in a whirlwind of panic over the expected aristocratic revenge. This became known as the Great Fear. Rumours of a vengeful King's army were everywhere, and there are almost identical accounts from hundreds of villages, of a traveller arriving to inform the locals that an aristocratic army was on the way, destroying all peasant life in its path. In a number of villages, panic was sparked when someone mistook the sunset for a burning village in the distance.

Many villagers defended themselves against imaginary threats by forming peasant militias. Bridges and roads into the villages were manned by armed peasants. Which is why, though the panic became known as 'the Great Fear', Marat referred to the events as 'fires of sedition'.

From the peasant point of view, the change that had swept society must have been staggering and terrifying. Anyone who ever shoplifted anything as a kid knows the fear and excitement that runs through you as you imagine everyone you pass is looking at you, about to shout, 'Thief!' Through their protests, alongside those that had taken place in Paris, the French peasantry had overturned the divinely ordained ideology ingrained in them from the moment of their birth. Now they were fearful of the consequences.

Or there's another explanation, that the paranoia represented, as Simon Schama put it, a 'concentrated form of general anxieties about vagrants'. Which is to say, it had little to do with the revolution, it's just a coincidence that at that time hardened rural French folk, who had just spent months burning tax offices and fighting local militias, went all weedy and became frightened of the local beggars. In every village. By coincidence. Because when you're a peasant in a revolution, it's not the nobility that worries you, it's the prospect of a couple of old boys spilling Special Brew on your crops.

DECLARATION OF THE RIGHTS OF MAN

The rural uprising was the crucial question for the National Assembly in Paris, which responded on 4 August by passing a motion to 'destroy the feudal regime entirely'. There was a catch, though, which was that to release himself from dues to a landlord a peasant had to pay twenty times the annual rent in a lump sum. You can tell this was a revolution run by lawyers. The slogan appeared to be 'You're now all free. The fee for that piece of information is five thousand quid.' This is a forerunner to the 1989 revolutions in Eastern Europe, following which all citizens, no matter how poor, were now free to buy Rolex watches and Gucci handbags.

However, the Assembly's decision was followed up by a Declaration of the Rights of Man and of the Citizen, while the royal court was still too shell-shocked to offer much opposition. This was an immense moment, for a law had been passed annulling the right of nobles to demand taxes, tithes and labour from peasants working on their family land. Compare that to the speed of modern legislation. One of New Labour's most unequivocal promises was to ban fox-hunting. Five years later they were still pondering how to do this, when any rational government would have passed a bill on day one that went, 'So – you arrive in red tunics to drink sherry and send dogs across fields, then blow bugles to celebrate the ripping out of a fox's intestines. You are clearly ill. We will provide medical care but from now on you really must stop.'

The declaration was inspired by the documents of the American Revolution, and was partly written by one of the heroes of that event, the Marquis de Lafayette. Lafayette was an orphan whose parents had been wealthy landowners. At sixteen he married a fourteen-year-old; she had a child and was expecting another when, at the age of nineteen, he decided on a more adventurous career than farming. So he bought a boat, raised a miniature army and sailed off to America to fight alongside the colonies against Britain. It must have surprised the Americans to find an unsolicited noble teenager from France showing up in their army with a boat, but he became so influential that he ended up helping to draft the American Constitution, which made him ideal to help write the French version. The declaration abolished noble privilege, internal tolls and trading monopolies. All men were deemed equal before the law. The right of Frenchmen to rebel was enshrined in the constitution, and the guillotine replaced the water wheel as an instrument of death. One deputy voted to abolish the death penalty altogether, which was Robespierre.

THE KING'S VETO

As the dust settled from the demolition of the Bastille, euphoria was superseded by debate, but the discussions that swept France were different from the political arguments that rumble in pubs and offices in normal times. Instead of arguing about what 'they', meaning the government, the council, the BBC or the FA, should do, debates revolved around what action 'we' should take. In revolutionary times, even an argument about bread can take on political connotations. The direction of the revolution would determine whether there was bread or not, so no discussion on the supply of bread could go far without leading to the most pressing political issue: what to do about the King's veto.

At this time, we must remember, no one could imagine a royalty that didn't rule. The French monarchists wouldn't have understood the arguments I heard put by the editor of *Royalty Today*, justifying Queen Elizabeth II's role in the state opening of Parliament by saying no constitutional harm is done, as she has no part in writing the speech. In other words, it's all right to spend billions of pounds on her because she does nothing. Maybe the miners should have tried this when they were told they were no longer needed. They could have proposed that, as they no longer had the power to actually dig anything, but were a great British tradition, for a million quid a month they'd do nothing except stage a symbolic 'changing of the shifts' once a day by the winding wheel.

If Louis XVI continued to have a veto over every issue, from military matters to who became the chancellor, then what was the point of the Assembly at all? A thousand permutations were discussed, and two camps emerged. Mirabeau was one of the leading figures trying to bring public protest to an end. He appealed for calm, suggesting that further protests would cause the royals to pull out of the discussions on the new constitution. Alongside Mirabeau was Lafayette, who walked around Paris carrying a sword, a proper huge sword in an Errol Flynn scabbard which you can still see in a Paris museum. And he was a moderate, exhibiting the sort of moderation I could live with. How refreshing if Shirley Williams or Chris Patten appeared on *Newsnight* saying, 'I'm proud to be a moderate but I won't stand for that,' and unsheathed a sword. Instead, modern politicians are so dull that you can't even disagree with them because you never hear what they're saying. I had to interview Alistair Darling once on the radio, and off he went in that monotone drawl about sustainable economic growth and I found myself thinking, 'Shall I have a curry tonight?' Stupidly, when he finished, I tried to debate the point he'd made, when I *should* have said, 'You what? Oh sorry mate, do you know I completely drifted off.'

At the other extreme from Mirabeau and Lafayette was the doctor and scientist, not even a member of the Assembly, with his unaligned eyes, Jean Paul Marat.

THE TOAD-LIKE MARAT, MARKED BY BULGING EYES AND A FLABBY MOUTH

Marat, possibly the most fervent French patriot of the whole revolution, wasn't French. He was born and brought up in Neuchâtel in Switzerland. As well as his failed attempt to scupper the lightning rod, he wrote a paper on aeronautics following a ballooning disaster and studied in England, where he got his degree, before becoming a physician to the Count of Artois. Several historians claim that none of Marat's work was of any value, but Marat had been a prominent member of the French Academy of Science, and at one point was in the running to be its governor. It's suggested that it was his bitterness at being rejected for this post that swung him towards revolution. This reminds me of the theory espoused by the historian Robert Service, who said the Russian Revolution happened in 1917 because 'Lenin was ill, and he wanted it to happen before he died.' I suppose he also thought, 'But we'll leave it until October as I'm hoping to go to the Lake District in the summer.'

Marat's motivation was more complex than personal bitterness. He was appalled by inequality, and wrote that if people are denied the necessities of life they will consider themselves outside the social system and therefore not subject to that system's laws. So he proposed free education, paid for by taxation on the rich, and public workshops to eliminate unemployment, and that anyone not wishing to work should be banished from the state. And he stood on street corners reading out sections from Rousseau's *Social Contract*. Yet he felt the best system for bringing this state about would be rule by a 'good monarch'.[1] Or maybe he thought, 'I know what will be a laugh – I'll start a revolution, overthrow a dynasty and cause a European-wide war that lasts for twenty years. *That* will teach them to turn me down for that science job.'

In his role as physician to the aristocracy he was in daily contact with the excesses he despised, but he didn't mix with the circle of radical lawyers who had a voice in the Estates-General. He wrote a barrage of letters to the Assembly, but when he received no reply he decided to create his own newspaper, *L'Ami du peuple*, the 'Friend of the People', with the aim of giving his views a platform. He summed up those views as 'recalling to the sovereign people that since they had nothing more to expect from their representatives, it behoved them to mete out justice for themselves'.

Marat's style was a little confrontational. At one point he demanded that the new constitution should contain the phrase, 'Man has the right to deal with their oppressors by devouring their palpitating hearts.' Did he discuss this with anyone, I wonder? Did he stand in the room with everyone squeaking, 'I'm not sure about the palpitating hearts,' while he yelled, 'What's wrong with it? It should be our constitutional right. Look, if you're going soft you can all fuck off and join the Liberal Democrats'? Marat's doctor read his newspaper, and when he felt it had gone a little over-exuberant he would call Marat in and cleanse his blood with leeches.

The other fascinating aspect to Marat's paper is its title, as there is a paper currently produced called *The People's Friend*, which is written specially for old people. I don't know if that was going back in Marat's day, but you wouldn't have wanted some poor pensioner to get the wrong one delivered by mistake. That could cause dreadful confusion as they turned over expecting a recipe for rhubarb crumble and saw, 'It's time to slice off the heads of aristocratic parasites and devour their palpitating hearts.'

Marat's main subject was the King's veto. He argued for universal suffrage and for the King to retain only an advisory role. He and other radicals thought the King should be made to move from Versailles back to Paris, where he would be less capable of organizing another attempt to summon his army.

Typical of the language of the day was an article written by a colleague of Marat that declared, 'People of Paris, open your eyes at last and shake yourselves out of your lethargy. The aristocrats are surrounding you on all sides, they want to condemn you to chains and you sleep on. Destroy them, or be reduced to servitude, misery and desolation. So wake up! I repeat, wake up!' It would be difficult, after receiving a leaflet like that, to say, 'I agree with what you say, but I can't do anything this week, I'm decorating.'

THE CAKE

Marat also wrote in defence of the seizure of grain. Speculators and hoarders of grain, hoping to keep the price up by controlling the supply, were being raided in every city. By September the new Assembly had placed guards in almost every bakery, to prevent riots that were forcing the bakers to lower their prices. Which is an unfathomable concept today, when bakers are the symbol of genteel village life, and it's difficult to imagine one saying, 'Usual sliced granary, Mrs Armitage? Here you are, love, now put it slowly in your bag with no funny business or these muskets will be pumping lead in your arse. Now GO.'

Wig makers were suffering from the collapse in their industry following the emigration of so many aristocrats, and began demonstrating for unemployment benefit as compensation. Which must stand as the most audacious claim for dole money in history, when you consider that the answer to 'Why did you leave your last job?' was 'I was made redundant when the governor fled because I chased him through the streets with a pike.'

Meanwhile, in Paris, a priest at St-Jacques-de-la-Boucherie refused to bury a carpenter without the normal payment, although the carpenter's family was skint. So a mob stormed the church and forced the priest to back down. Hundreds came to the free funeral, but afterwards a choir leader from another church announced to the crowd that he'd just been sacked for singing in the dead carpenter's service. Then the second church was stormed as well, and this riot was only ended when the choir leader was reinstated.

The spirit that had injected such passions extended to a man called Jean Jacob, whose birth certificate declared him to be the oldest person in France, at 120. He was invited to the National Assembly, where he gave thanks that after all this time he was finally a free man. And I bet there were still some cynics who said, 'Oh, he's full of the revolution now, but wait until he's 125, he'll grow out of it.'

On 1 October the King's bodyguard threw a party at Versailles, at which the King and Queen, in a drunken stupor, took the cap of liberty they'd been presented with and ceremonially trampled it underfoot. Which raises the idea of the King, the following morning, seeing the crumpled cap through a hangover and thinking, 'Oh no, I never, did I?'

Later they denied the rumours, though even the King's nephew said this was 'at least probable'. Word of the royal behaviour spread around Paris, and those, like Marat and Danton, who had been campaigning to bring back the King from Versailles suddenly had more support. In particular the women who campaigned on a daily basis for bread gathered for a march to the palace. The tocsin in the Town Hall steeple was rung, a sound that was becoming known as a call to arms. One contingent of women raided the Town Hall for weapons, and by the time they set off from Paris on the fifteen-mile walk they'd become a crowd of around 10,000. They were joined later by the National Guard, partly wishing to keep the demonstration under control.

When they arrived at Versailles, guards shot at the crowd, who responded immediately by chopping off two of the guards' heads. The National Guard won an agreement that a small delegation of women should be allowed in to meet the Queen, but one of them

**Some angry-looking women
on the way to Versailles.**

was apparently so overwhelmed by the beauty of the palace that she
fainted. If anything conveys the contradictory nature of the human
mind during revolution, this was it: 'We should burn this place
down. Ooh, but isn't it lovely?'

The crowd, once again, were kept waiting, until at around six in
the morning a militant section including a group of fishwives
broke in, killing two more bodyguards before finding their way
into the Queen's bedroom. According to the Marquis de Ferrières,
'The conspirators approached the Queen's apartments crying, "We
are going to cut off her head, tear out her heart, fry her liver and
that won't be the end of it."'[2] This may have been believable if he
hadn't spoiled it by adding the last bit: surely even the most
bloodthirsty crowd would be satisfied with frying their victim's
liver. At the very least there'd be a split, with the moderates
screaming at the militants, 'No, fair's fair. Once we've fried her
liver, let's leave it at that,' and the militants shouting back, 'Bloody
compromisers.'

This was the incident, apparently, during which Marie Antoinette
is reputed to have replied to the statement 'Ma'am, your people

have no bread' with 'Well let them eat cake.'[3] Which seems just a little too convenient to be true.

A member of the National Guard, Stanislas Maillard, wrote later that the women were armed with 'broomsticks, lances, pitchforks, swords, pistols and muskets'.[4] He also says the women were insistent they would be more forceful than the men. The royal camp was short on bargaining power at this point, so a deal was agreed in which the court would move immediately to Paris if their safety could be assured.

So *this* was why the royal family ceased to occupy the palace after 1789, following one of the most dramatic incidents in history, which is somehow omitted entirely from the tourist attraction the palace has become. It would be like organizing tourist expeditions to Pompeii on which visitors were told, 'Then for some reason nobody lived here any more.'

Not only was the King forced to march back to the capital, protected by the National Guard and surrounded by the poorest women of Paris, but he was made to carry out the whole journey wearing a fresh cap of liberty. Which must have been like making Peter Mandelson walk from Hartlepool to London selling copies of *Socialist Worker*.

THIS IS CLASS

After the Versailles demonstration, the Assembly became more confident, while the King was aware he was in no position to veto everything it said. So almost every week the Assembly passed a new law abolishing a tradition that, up till a few months earlier, most people had believed would last for ever. Just after the march to Versailles, the Assembly abolished the ceremonial costumes that classified the deputies according to their orders. Coats of arms were declared incompatible with citizenship, as was the practice of certain pews in church being reserved for the nobility. The tradition of weathercocks bearing insignia denoting nobility was dispensed with, which must have had nobles blustering, 'This is political correctness gone mad.'

Historians who argue that the revolution was not propelled by class divisions but was merely a vengeful scrap between individuals have difficulty in explaining these measures. Schama argues that the aristocracy weren't opposed to these acts, since aristocrats were on the committees that proposed them, and even some of the third-estate deputies were of noble stock. But if the aristocracy genuinely supported the introduction of these laws, why did they never suggest them before? They could have relinquished these privileges at any time during the previous centuries if they'd wished. Instead they declared their support for them at exactly the same time as a major victory of the revolution. It reminds you of the bloke who never washes up but as soon as he sees someone else has done it, says, 'Oh, I was going to do that.'

The aristocracy had no choice but to back down if they were to have any chance of surviving as a class at all. The rulers of apartheid South Africa eventually realized they had to let go of their system if they were to avoid annihilation, but that hardly means the divisions between black and white were imaginary. The fact that individual nobles backed the third estate, or that individual businessmen backed the nobles, doesn't affect this either. To say a conflict is driven by class divisions isn't to suggest that each side lines up as if preparing for a pitched battle between football hooligans, one side in silk shirts with a NOBLES logo, the other handing their victims a card saying, 'You Have Been Visited By the Third Estate Firm.'

Every strike has its workers who side with the management, and every ruling class produces rebels who back the battles of the poor. The ideals fought for by the leaders of the French Revolution favoured the specific interests of a particular faction in society, the bourgeois class, and the *sans-culottes* who were crucial to the revolution. It suited them that people were no longer seen as inferior just because they didn't have a noble coat of arms on their weathercock. It didn't suit the aristocracy quite so much.

CLUBS

As the momentum of change gathered pace following the march on Versailles, pamphlets and newspapers were published by, as Carlyle said, 'thousand wagon-loads'. So much reading material was circulating that Desmoulins could say, 'Some citizens employ the liberty of the press for a private purpose, when a patriot finds himself short of his handkerchief.'

Western politicians ponder why so few people bother to vote, citing 'apathy', as if it's a result of laziness. For many people not voting is a conscious decision, involving no more apathy than if I heard Chris de Burgh was singing 'Lady in Red' at the local polling station and didn't go to that. The main reason why someone doesn't vote must be that they can't see it making an apparent difference to anyone's life. If someone feels their participation in an activity will have an impact, they will take part. Even the most idle person visits the toilet, because not doing so creates a discernible difference in their living conditions. If they felt voting changed anything, they wouldn't say, 'I want to see a society along the lines of what one party is trying to build, a society of co-operation, caring and encouraging the talents of the community, but I'm not going all the way to the primary school, it's nearly a quarter of a mile.'

There was no such problem of 'apathy' in revolutionary France, which was divided into eighty-three sections, with elections in each area, so that 60 per cent of men had the vote, compared to 0 per cent a few weeks before. In every village, local councillors were elected at meetings called by parish priests. In Paris, hundreds of posts were open to elections, which would take place after debates in church halls; and the National Assembly was open to the public, with debates often affected by the cries from the galleries. These bore little similarity to the image created in modern Britain by the phrase 'election following a debate in the church hall', at which one person speaks for an hour and a half then elects himself and his wife to every post, and remains oblivious to the fact there are only seven in the room, one of whom thinks he's Julius Caesar.

At certain points in history, the type of society people lived under really did depend on the outcome of debate. Such arguments during the French Revolution led to the formation of political societies, known as clubs. These clubs weren't political parties, and there was no expectation that every member of a club would hold the same views, but each club was bound to attract supporters of similar ideals. Robespierre joined the Jacobins Club, which became a thriving centre of debate amongst supporters of the third estate. But the subscription rates excluded the poor, who went instead to the much cheaper Cordeliers Club, of which the most prominent members were Danton, Marat and Desmoulins.

Danton was the most popular speaker, and crowds would leave local bars to squeeze in the door and hear him, in scenes that must have been similar to when everyone used to stop what they were doing to watch Ian Botham batting. It was in one of those sessions that Danton proclaimed the aims of the revolution as *'Liberté, Egalité et Fraternité'*.

Camille Desmoulins described a typical night at their headquarters: 'A patriot proposes his motion; if it finds any supporters, they make him mount on a chair, and speak. If he is applauded, he prospers. If he is hissed, he goes on his way.' Which must have made political speaking seem like doing the late show at the Comedy Store. I can imagine them backstage, peering out mournfully at the courtyard and mumbling, 'Rough crowd tonight,' before one of them looks at the running order and says, 'Oh no, I'm following Danton.'

The Assembly Splits

However, it's never as easy to categorize everyone as historians would like, as most people could fit into several different boxes at the same time. I recall an evening in the Crystal Palace end at Tottenham's ground, when a black Palace player received some calls of 'You're fucking useless' from his own fans after making a series of mistakes. When another Palace player scuffed the ball off for a Tottenham goal-kick, one woman stood in the middle of the crowd and yelled, 'You don't have a go at him, do you?, 'cos he's white. You only have a go at Bruce 'cos he's black. You should be ashamed of yourselves, you racists.' I didn't happen to agree that the fans were racist but none the less I admired this gutsy show of liberalism. Meanwhile the Tottenham goalkeeper began his run-up to take the goal-kick, at which point the same woman, who hadn't yet sat down, led an ear-splitting chant of 'Tottenham keeper, Tottenham keeper takes it up the arse.'

During the first year of the revolution, factions were gradually developing, each groping towards a set of ideas and principles. In general, the small traders were the most adamant about preventing a restoration of absolute royalty, and, because they were amongst the poorest, supported the most radical measures to narrow the gap between rich and poor. In general, the wealthy bourgeoisie, such as shipowners and slave traders, were delighted that the revolution gave them a greater political voice, but uneasy at the way it had unleashed a mass movement of peasants and *sans-culottes*. The attitude of another group, centred around Mirabeau, was illustrated by one incident on the Versailles march. Having won the King's acceptance that he would return to Paris, the crowd called for Mirabeau to make a speech. But, as his closest friend put it, 'Mirabeau was not the man to waste his energy on occasions like this.' The surest way to antagonize a crowd is to refuse to make a speech when called for, as anyone who's been to an office leaving party knows. So the fishwives of Paris were left to mumble, 'Too good for us, are you?' The problem for Mirabeau and his faction was that, to keep the *sans-culottes* on their side, they had to show support for the uprisings, but they wished they would come to an end. So their attitude to the mob was like that of a teacher whose class has erupted into laughter because the headmaster farted as he was leaving the room. They were saying, 'All right, I like a bit of fun as much as anyone, but now can we please calm down and get back to normal.' When the King demanded, amongst other things, the sole right to declare war, Mirabeau supported him. And proposals were made to introduce further restrictions on who could vote in elections.

At the other extreme, Marat continued to publish his paper demanding 'eternal vigilance' against the King and aristocracy who, he said, were plotting to restore their rule. But the momentum seemed to be with Mirabeau. The police declared Marat's paper illegal and he was forced into hiding. He emerged after a month and in his next issue condemned the proposed voting laws, finishing, 'The people have already thrown off the yoke of the nobility, they will in like manner throw off that of the rich.' He was threatened again with arrest, which was carried out by three hundred officers. This would be remarkable enough, but Marat got carried away when he described the event, claiming there were 4,000. The next time he told the story, he said there were 12,000 armed with cannon. Why did he do that – wasn't 4,000 ridiculous enough? Even in my home town of Swanley, surely Europe's bullshit capital, I never heard a pub regular claim, 'So the Ol' Bill have come for me, I've turned round, there's only 12,000 of 'em, ain't there? I've gone, "Come on then, who wants some?"' None the less, as he was awaiting trial he was helped to escape by Danton and fled to England. Marat's discomfort was Danton's gain as news spread of his role in organizing the escape, and he became a hero.

While Mirabeau and Marat represented the two extremes of opinion, the majority were somewhere in the middle. More accurately, they were in the middle on some issues, while tending to one side or another on other issues, just like the Crystal Palace supporter.

Factions were forming in the Assembly, though they didn't represent clear-cut ideologies. But they were aligned to layers in society that had specific interests, even if they weren't yet sure what they were. We know from our own times that the lonely old man in a damp terraced house can be the world's staunchest royalist. But however much he identifies with the Queen, he'll still dread his gas bill in a way she never will.

THE BATTLE OF NANCY

And while the civilians were deciding their priorities and allegiances, the army was doing much the same thing.

I happened to be in Paris on 1 May 2002, just after Jean-Marie Le Pen had got into the final ballot for the post of President of France, as leader of the National Front. On that day there were two marches planned for the city, one by supporters of Le Pen and one by his opponents. The grotesque nature of the Le Pen march derived not just from its hateful demands but from its obsessive orderliness. Almost everyone carried a French flag, and not just any French flag, but one that was compact, pristine and perfectly ironed. Everyone stood in perfectly symmetrical rows, under giant screens conveying their leader's speech. One contingent carried banners with shiny gold tassels bearing the words GOD, FAMILY AND COUNTRY. They clapped and cheered at the designated points, but with no spontaneity or joy, just a sense of duty. In a nearby café a man from Mauritius told me he was 'having a look' before attending the anti-Le Pen march, and launched into a sophisticated critique of the rise of French fascism and the abuse he'd received from Le Pen's supporters that morning. Then he grabbed me dramatically, looked directly into my eyes and said, 'You are English, so tell me' – I prepared myself for one of those life-defining moments – 'are Arsenal going to win the Premier League?'

The anti-Le Pen march was such a relief, not just because of the political differences but because by contrast it was so joyfully *dis*orderly. The central squares were enveloped in the seductive aroma of dozens of kebab stalls. Vast sound systems competed with each other so that at certain points you could hear a new musical form, a cocktail of African drumming, a Kurdish kazoo and the first Specials album. Loudest of all was the Arabic folk music booming from the stall of the Turkish Communist Party, oozing inspiration from every syllable, though for all I knew they were singing, 'Hoorah, for corn production has risen thirty per cent since we tipped that Trotskyist down a mineshaft.'

Everyone seemed to be travelling in every direction, jumping, dancing and climbing on each other. Teenagers in baggy jumpers would run across the street and greet a friend with a shriek and a monumental hug as if she were a long-lost sister, when she was actually a mate who'd nipped off twenty minutes ago to get some tobacco. There *were* French flags, but they were creased, smudged and lived in, so that any young girls carrying them looked like the child in the *Les Misérables* poster. For a march whose rallying cry was defending the family, Le Pen's procession had virtually no kids at all, whereas the anti-Le Pen march included thousands of kids, proper kids with scratched knees, ice cream in their hair and unidentifiable sticky things on their trousers. And instead of perfect banners were self-made placards, such as the one lamenting that the choice for voters was between the fascist Le Pen and the Conservative Jacques Chirac: NO TO THE DANGEROUS RACIST XENOPHOBIC NAZI – VOTE FOR THE DEMAGOGUE SICK WITH POWER AND PRAY, MY BROTHERS, THAT GOD WILL CALL HIM TO JUSTICE VERY VERY QUICKLY. So much effort, and yet only the slimmest chance he'll ever be able to use it again.

Paris has seen this contrast between demonstrations of disorderly joy and orderly joylessness before. On the first anniversary of the storming of the Bastille, an enormous ceremony was held in Paris, at which Lafayette, chief of the National Guard, and the King pledged themselves to 'law, the nation and the King'. Whereas the original event had been an emotional, unpredictable explosion of disciplined chaos, the celebration one year later was a dutiful expression of how that revolution had been moulded into a new, tidy order. Instead of the shambolic *sans-culottes*, the heroic watch makers and laundry-men with improvised weapons, museum axes and pilfered wax dummies, were immaculate uniforms, shiny symbolic pikes and marching with precision. Flags and banners, ranks of militia and prepared speeches from dignitaries were all in their designated place. Within this triumph of order, the King had to make his pledge. It might not seem much, that he made a pledge to himself, but at least it's honest, as if an actress accepted an Oscar by saying, 'But mostly I'd like to thank me, without whose tireless efforts none of this would have been possible.' But the pledge was important: it represented a compromise struck between the King and the Assembly. Never before had a French king pledged allegiance to anything other than himself. Now he had to honour himself *and* the nation, *and* a law that stated that all men were equal.

The trouble was that, as each Frenchman recited the pledge, their emphasis was on a different word depending on his viewpoint.

The revolutionary moustache. These three had clearly taken part in a *sans culotte* makeover show.

Many soldiers asked how their officers could pledge their allegiance to the nation when they were almost exclusively noble. A campaign began to bring the spirit of the Declaration of the Rights of Man into the army. Aristocratic officers were locked in their mess rooms for abusive behaviour, and according to the royalist officer Bouille almost the whole army joined political reading clubs.

Military class division also displayed itself in the peculiar form of facial hair. Officers were expected to shave their upper lip as part of their loyal uniform, so every soldier who supported the revolution went out of his way to grow as bushy a moustache as possible. Even more worrying for the officers, several regiments went on strike because they hadn't been paid for several weeks.

The most turbulent of these incidents involved the Château-Vieux regiment near the eastern town of Nancy. Again they hadn't been paid, but their fury was compounded when they heard of an Austrian regiment marching just across the border, which the troops feared was part of a plot to disarm the mutinous regiments. Thomas Carlyle refutes this possibility, explaining the presence of these troops by suggesting they were marching to Belgium and had come across a 'short cut'.[5] Maybe other armies in history should have tried this excuse. Who knows what Hitler would have got away with if he'd said he was just out for a ramble, cut through the back way to Austria, and had no idea his tanks had gone slap into the middle of Poland?

The Château-Vieux regiment mutinied, eventually Bouille brought his specially selected troops, and the mutinous regiment sought to strengthen its hand by distributing weapons amongst the people of nearby Nancy. Bouille came through the city gates in the middle of the night and began firing. The estimates of numbers killed range from 300 to Carlyle's claim of 3,000. The next day Bouille hanged forty of the surviving leaders.

Forty thousand people in the district of St-Antoine, Paris, demonstrated against this massacre. Marat dedicated the next two issues of L'Ami du peuple to tirades of rage against Bouille. And throughout France people wore badges of tiny cannonballs as a gesture of soli-

**A wonderfully surreal page from Desmoulins'
journal captioned, 'General Alton chased
by patriotic street lamps'.**

darity with those slain by the somewhat larger cannonballs fired by
Bouille's troops.

MIRABEAU'S FINAL TRAGEDY

Having supported the revolution, Mirabeau despaired of the agi-
tation it had unleashed, and moved ever closer to royalty, declaring
himself a 'zealous monarchist'.[6] Then in the spring of 1790, with
the same admirably reckless spontaneity he'd displayed throughout, he became more fervent than ever about the need to protect the

King's wishes – at the same time as, despite being broke, he moved out of the moderate apartment he rented from an actress and into a huge house, where he employed one of the best chefs in Paris; and a valet, who was able once again to shine his buttons; and a secretary; and he acquired a country house with a park. When he was asked how he could afford this with all his debts, he proudly informed people his debts had been cleared. You didn't have to be a conspiracy theorist to imagine a deal had been struck, and in time it emerged that the King had put him on his payroll, his brief being 'to save the monarchy'. His method was to push the line at all times that the King supported the revolution, no matter how untenable this became.

At this point he had the complete trust of the King, and he was President of the Assembly, with all the kudos that came from having led the third estate in its tennis-court oath. But in 1791 he became increasingly ill, eventually coughing up blood after spending the night with two ballet dancers. He insisted on playing a major part in a debate in the Assembly that lasted the next three days, then went home to announce, 'I will have a shave, because today I am going to die.' He prepared and delivered his deathbed speech as if it were a piece of performance art, declaring that at the point of death 'All one can do is be perfumed, crowned with flowers, enveloped with music and wait comfortably for the sleep from which one will never awake.' His thunder was stolen however by his secretary, who performed a more dramatic artistic statement by knifing himself in sympathy.

At the time of Mirabeau's funeral, despite his payments from the King, he hadn't finished paying for his wedding suit. The response to Mirabeau's death was one we would recognize from our own times, as his royalist friends and third-estate opponents alike agreed this was a 'tragic loss', and that he was a 'colourful character', even if they'd called him a fat pompous oaf the week before. Of his family, not one even turned up for the funeral except the sister whose neighbour Mirabeau had attacked with his

The ugly Mirabeau.

own umbrella. Marat wasn't swept along by the outpouring of grief, and called on the French people to rejoice at Mirabeau's death.

The King and Queen, still forced to live in Paris rather than their preferred Versailles, referred to themselves as prisoners, though even they would have had to admit there was one difference between their position and that of most prisoners, which was they were allowed to be King and Queen. Their major restrictions were that they weren't allowed to travel more than twenty miles out of Paris without an escort from the Assembly, weren't allowed their original bodyguard, and weren't allowed to hunt. I believe they have similar rules at Pentonville. But consider this from the King's point of view.

From the day he was born he was groomed to believe he was the natural ruler and father of his people, and that his authority came from God himself. The loss of privileges wouldn't just be an inconvenience, they would seem a travesty, a blasphemous affront. His status had to be restored, not just so he could hunt again but in order to re-establish the natural order. After Mirabeau's death it seemed this could no longer be achieved without a counter-revolution.

THE REVOLUTION HEADS WEST

It had taken two months for news of the storming of the Bastille to reach the slave island of San Domingo. The Assembly in Paris authorized the setting up of an assembly in San Domingo, using the French version as a model, except that any election would be solely for the whites. As in France, the merchants jumped at the idea but the noble bureaucrats in charge of the island, placed in position by the French court, were horrified, and refused to relinquish control. As there was only a handful of them, and the Governor, de Peynier, was old and frail, the royalists sought an alliance with the mulattos.

The mulattos were the mixed-race section of the population, the product of decades of illicit relationships between masters and slaves. There were around 15,000 of them, divided by how dark-skinned they were. One that was three-quarters black was deemed slightly inferior to one half black, and so on, with the intermediate shades creating 128 degrees of blackness. Mulattos were forbidden to carry a sword or to wear European clothes. They were forbidden to play European games, and if a white man entered their house they were forbidden to sit at the table with him. Seventy per cent of mulatto women were prostitutes. But after years of this abuse, the Governor, suddenly in need of friends, instructed his officers to 'treat them as friends and whites'.[7]

Mulatto leaders accepted the offer of an elevated status in return for fighting alongside the royalists against the Assembly. But

Assembly members in Paris began to debate granting full political rights for mulattos, including the right to vote. Then a mulatto leader, Oge, inspired by the French radicals, pleaded with the colonial rulers for equal rights as a price for supporting the royalists. He was turned away with such contempt that he tried to organize an uprising. He was captured and tortured, each limb broken on a scaffold, then he was bound on wheels, and finally decapitated. Which pretty much brought the alliance to an end.

In Paris an anti-slavery group called Friends of the Negro, which included a few deputies in the Assembly, referred to slavery as 'aristocracy of the skin'. The Assembly voted against granting the slaves equal status, but the royalists in San Domingo were outraged that the issue should even have been discussed. In and around the city of Le Cap, the slaves began discussing their own rebellion, at the one place they could gather legitimately, their regular voodoo meetings. What a wonderful place to organize a rebellion. Anyone who's shivered in the cellar of a Labour club, waiting for someone to say, 'Well we might as well start then,' as it's obvious no one else is coming, would give anything to be part of a campaign that met during voodoo. Boukman, a high priest amongst the slaves, became their commander. He signalled the official launch of the rebellion by marching his slave troops to the middle of a forest, where he recited voodoo incantations and sucked the blood of a stuck pig. Which, if you're going to go to war, must be the way to do it, rather than with a news flash on BBC2 and a speech from the American president. How much more peaceful would the world be if the weedy-looking Western leaders who make grandiose speeches about 'resolve' and 'courage' had to suck on a stuck pig before launching air strikes on an impoverished town in the desert?

Fires at designated points signalled the slaves' involvement, and throughout the region plantations were burned to the ground and the masters murdered. C. L. R. James, in his account *The Black Jacobins*, describes the events: 'The slaves destroyed tirelessly . . . seeking salvation in the most obvious way, the destruction of what

they knew was the cause of their suffering . . . Now that they held
power they did as they had been taught. In the frenzy of the first
encounters they killed all . . . "Vengeance! Vengeance!" was their
war-cry, and one of them carried a white child on a pike as a stan-
dard.' And he follows this with the magnificent statement, 'And yet
they were surprisingly moderate.'[8]

7

The King Reacts

Should I stay or should I go?
If I go there will be trouble
If I stay there will be double

ECHOES IN ENGLAND

In recent times we've enjoyed the excitement of the fall of apartheid and the Berlin Wall, but the French Revolution must have created an exhilaration almost beyond our comprehension. This wasn't just the demise of an oppressive government, but the replacement of an entire social and political system run through one man, anointed by God, with an order in which everyone shared a stake. So the euphoria wasn't confined to France; it made liberals and radicals everywhere feel that what had once been utopian was now possible.

For example, in 1789 the poet Robbie Burns was working in the Scottish Excise Office when he captured a consignment of smuggled guns. He sent them straight to the Assembly in Paris for use against the royalists. Maybe he wrote a poem to go with his action – 'Away tae France heads ma wee bairn Kalashnikov'. But we do know for certain that almost every poet agreed with Burns, and with Wordsworth's pronouncement that 'Bliss was it in that dawn to be alive'.

Even parts of the establishment supported the revolution (though sometimes only from the joy of seeing France in turmoil). Revolution was respectable. You can imagine the artistic world saying, 'We've discovered a lovely new bar in Islington called Pikes, where the bottles of lager have miniature cannonballs in the top and there's a collection of severed heads hanging from the ceiling.'

In Britain, part of the attraction was that, although the country was ruled by a parliament, it was a parliament riddled with corruption and with little democracy. Cornwall, because of its royal connections, had forty-four MPs, whereas the cities of Birmingham and Manchester didn't have one between them. The hamlet of Old Sarum, which consisted of one farmhouse, elected two MPs. And I bet, if the Tories got in, the farmer said, 'I never voted for them.'

The rumblings against the system of government spread from academics and poets to the poor. Amongst this number were radicals such as Thomas Hardy, the cobbler who founded the London Corresponding Society, aiming at parliamentary reform and support for the revolution in France.

Not so keen on the revolution was the Whig MP for Wendover, the Irishman Edmund Burke. He wrote a book, *Reflections on the Revolution in France*, which declared that those who stormed the Bastille were a 'swinish multitude'. He complained that the French Chancellor had declared 'all occupations were honourable'. And he gave his reply: 'The occupation of a hair-dresser, or a working tallow-chandler can not be a matter of honour to any person, to say nothing of more servile employments.' And to confirm his point he quoted the book of Ecclesiastes: 'The wisdom of a learned man cometh by opportunity of leisure: and he that hath little business shall become wise. How can he get wisdom that holdeth the plough, that driveth oxen, and whose talk is only of bullocks?'

TOM PAINE

When Burke's book was published in 1790, a corset maker called Tom Paine was staying near the Angel at Islington.

After leaving penniless for America on Benjamin Franklin's advice, Paine had arrived penniless in Boston, aged thirty-seven, and got a job in a bookshop. Soon after that, troops in nearby Lexington shot at a crowd, and Paine was moved to write a pamphlet, which he called *Common Sense*, backing the protests against British rule. It contained phrases such as 'Nature disapproves the hereditary right of Kings, otherwise she would not so frequently ridicule it by giving mankind an ass for a lion.' Perhaps worried that he hadn't made himself clear, he added that George III was king only through being descended from a 'French bastard landing with an armed banditti and declaring himself King of England against the consent of the natives'. Something for everyone there. Even a royalist cabbie could say, 'Mind you, he's got a point about the French.'

Common Sense became the best-selling pamphlet ever up to that time, motivating thousands of Americans to join the fight against the English troops. Its success was not just a result of its content, but because it was written in a style comprehensible to the common person. Paine was also the first to argue for complete independence from England. George Washington was so impressed that after the war he gave Paine the job of being America's first foreign secretary. Enormously flattered, Paine invited Washington to 'spend a part of an evening at my apartment, and eat a crust of bread and cheese'.[1] Which is a cool way to react to being given a job by George Washington. Most people would be fawning and slobbering and panicking with a recipe book, but he prepares a crust and cheese for the first US president. If Washington had asked for anything more, you can imagine Paine would have said, 'What are you complaining about? I've got the King of Spain coming tomorrow – he's getting a bowl of Sugar Puffs.' How refreshing, given the current official attitude to the American President which results in Bush and the British

Tom Paine

ministers sounding like these pairs of old women you get on buses. Bush says, 'Saddam is a monster, prepared to use his weapons of mass destruction,' and Jack Straw says, 'Mass destruction, hmmm, destruction, yes.' Bush says, 'He's a threat to the civilized world,' and Blair says, 'Oh, yes, a threat to the civilized world – and you've got to be careful these days, that's right dear.'

Paine eventually fell out with Washington over the direction of the new country; Paine felt that independence and democracy should be a step towards eradicating inequality, writing, 'For rich and poor to live in the same society is like dead and living bodies being chained together.' Washington disagreed and sacked him, so Paine returned to England, again penniless, where he became obsessed with the idea of building a bridge. But the finance he received wasn't sufficient to build it over anything, so he had to make it in a field in Paddington.

Paine was so preoccupied with the bridge that he barely seemed to notice the outbreak of revolution in France. But across from his room at the Angel was a bookshop, and seeing the prominent display of Burke's *Reflections*, he bought a copy. Instantly he began composing a reply. Continuing his theme of the simple illogicality of the monarchy, he wrote, 'A hereditary ruler is as absurd an idea as a hereditary mathematician.' And while he's probably right, you *can* imagine that idea being supported by the aristocracy. So students would walk into a maths lecture, and the teacher would say, 'Look at those delightful squiggles on the blackboard. I've absolutely no idea what they mean but they were left to me by my grandfather.'

He reiterated the point he'd made in *Common Sense*, that 'the state of a king shuts him off from the world, yet the business of a king requires him to know it thoroughly'. Which certainly applies to modern royals. For the Queen is head of state, but the only person in that state who's never had to run for a bus, never had to walk across town looking for a cashpoint machine that isn't broken, never had a car mechanic saying, 'Wooo haaa, that will need a new gearbox, Your Majesty,' and never had to sit in a public toilet with the lock busted, whistling the National Anthem so no one bursts in.

Paine condemned 'men in all countries who get their living by war, and by keeping up the quarrels of nations'. Even more controversially, he added, 'Aristocracy has a tendency to degenerate the human species by intermarrying constantly with each other.' And there he may have a point. I've always wondered whether the reason the Countryside Alliance found it so easy to get 400,000 in London on the same day was that this was just a family outing. The book ends with an explanation of why people such as Burke disliked the French Revolution: 'That which is a blessing to nations, is bitterness to them. They tremble at the approach of principles, and dread the precedent that threatens their overthrow.'

Paine called the book *The Rights of Man*, and within weeks of its publication it had sold thousands of copies, leading to panic in the English government. A supporter of the government, Hannah More, wrote, 'The pernicious pamphlet is in every cottage, highway, mine and coal-pit.'[2] Newspapers reported that in Staffordshire a copy was 'in every hand', and that in Sheffield 'every cutler owns a copy'.[3] Within six months 300,000 copies had been sold – to a population of 10 million, of whom 40 per cent couldn't read. In Ireland, peasants debated the book in pubs and markets, and the Protestant revolutionary Wolfe Tone declared it 'the Koran of Belfast', thereby rendering himself liable to assassination by just about everyone in the world.

Again the book's success wasn't just due to content but to style. Before Paine's book, political writing was *supposed* to be incomprehensible to the majority, like the Shipping Forecast. Paine's books were as much of a shock as hearing 'Bloody hell, I'd keep clear of Rockall and Finistaire if I was you.' Which is why, whereas Burke's book was full of passages in Greek or Latin, Paine received reviews such as 'His language is coarse and debased by vulgar phraseology.'[4]

Paine responded to his critics by writing Part Two, detailing the ways in which a republic could organize Britain's finances. He wrote, 'The Duke of Richmond alone takes away as much for himself as would maintain two thousand poor and aged persons,' proposed a land tax, and argued that the abolition of the monarchy would pay for a welfare state. He proposed free education, pensions for anyone over fifty and a death allowance to cover funeral expenses for the poor. Even now you could see that causing uproar at the *Daily Mail*: 'We uncover the cheats with nothing wrong with them, deliberately dying to get their free coffin.'

The second part of *The Rights of Man* was too much for the government, and Prime Minister Pitt brought in a law aimed at 'seditious and wicked writings'. It became illegal to publish or even to own a copy, and Paine had to flee for his life. He went to France, where he wouldn't need to stir up revolution, as he had in his last two countries, because there was already one going on. Almost as soon as he arrived he was elected as deputy to the Assembly for the region of Pas-de-Calais. You get the impression that if you went to see a band at Wembley with Tom Paine, somehow by the end of the evening he'd be on stage playing lead guitar with Bruce Springsteen.

THE FLIGHT TO VARENNES

By the spring of 1791, almost two years after the storming of the Bastille, there were 133 political journals in Paris alone.

Parish priests had been dismissed, replaced by priests elected by the village, and the clergy had to swear an oath to the constitution. Robespierre advanced plans for the emancipation of Protestants and Jews, equal treatment for all ranks in the navy, and to abolish the property qualification for membership of the National Guard. On the economy he suggested, 'Legislators, you will have done nothing for freedom unless your laws tend ... to diminish the extreme inequality of fortunes.'[5] And he remained as incorruptible as ever, refusing to be a guest of the Duc d'Orléans in case it affected the clarity of this thinking. But Robespierre let himself down a little when he wrote a speech advocating his plans for freedom of the press, but lost the manuscript on his way home from the Jacobins Club. The next day he placed an advert in a newspaper: 'Lost manuscript. M. Robespierre left in a cab he had taken at 9.30 p.m. Thursday night on the quai des Augustins. He beseeches all good citizens to help him find it.'[6]

In this atmosphere, the King and Queen embarked on one of the most extraordinary escapades in history. Soon after the Versailles march they had begun to consider how to organize a foreign force to restore their power, and sent a secret agent to discuss the possibility with the King of Spain. And in December 1790 Louis XVI wrote to the King of Prussia requesting what he called a 'European congress backed by an army', though he and the Queen couldn't decide whether they would be in a better position to aid this army from Paris or abroad. In the spring of 1791 the momentum of events persuaded them they had to go. Several radicals warned that this was likely – a journalist for the *Annales patriotiques* reported that the King's stables were preparing horses for the journey, and Marat claimed to know of their plan to fool the guards by putting a replacement boy in the bed where their son slept.

The King then enlisted the support of Bouille, whom he had congratulated for putting down the mutiny at Nancy. Their other chief ally was Count Hans Axel von Fersen, a Swedish officer devoted to Marie Antoinette. Most of Paris believed they were having an affair, but as the Paris paparazzi were yet to perfect their craft we can't know for certain. But he did visit her almost every night, and he did deliver to her hundreds of boxes of calfskin gloves. Fersen offered to procure a coach for the journey to Montmédy, near the border, where Bouille was fortifying a camp to receive his friends.

But the issue of the coach didn't bode well for the plans. When Fersen described the coach he had found them, Marie Antoinette was aghast. She had to have a *berline*, with inlaid ivory and rose-wood, and it had to have room for two chambermaids as she couldn't possibly travel without them. It was as if the British Queen needed to escape discreetly and said, 'I know, the royal yacht *Britannia* should do nicely.' Eventually Fersen found a suitable model, though it could only travel at around seven miles per hour; but then the Queen delayed plans further by insisting on new clothes and boxes of perfumes for the journey.

Passports were arranged. The Queen was to assume the identity of a Russian, Baroness de Korff; the King would leave the palace disguised as a servant, through the gate that the National Guard discreetly left open every night to allow Count Fersen to leave if he wished. Which means the Queen must have had to tell him, (a) the good news is there *is* a gate we can escape through; and (b) it's to provide an escape route for this Swedish count I've been knocking off.

The Queen was supposed to meet her husband, the count and fellow-refugees at a bridge across from the palace. But she'd never had to walk anywhere in the town before, so she got hopelessly lost. For an hour she strolled through the centre of Paris, presumably in a state of panic, fretting each time she passed a fellow-pedestrian that they would shout, 'Bloody hell, isn't that the Queen?' Eventually she found her king and her count and they set off for Montmédy at seven miles per hour.

At six in the morning Lafayette was woken by a servant at the palace and informed that the Royal Family was missing. He rushed to the palace and found the King's letter to the Assembly, detailing his complaints at the indignity he'd suffered and condemning the constitutional measures he'd claimed to support over the previous two years. As word got round a crowd of thousands swarmed to the Tuileries palace, with the customary pikes, and invaded the royal apartments. A fruit-woman climbed on to the Queen's bed and took the opportunity to offer plums and cherries for sale to the other invaders.

As this sale took place, the royal posse, consisting of the King, the Queen, the Queen's sister, the royal children, their governess and the two essential chambermaids, driven by Count Fersen, successfully passed the Paris gates. They changed drivers and headed towards Pont-de-Sommevel, where a royal regiment had been placed by Bouille to protect them for the rest of the journey. But the cumbersome carriage broke down, and there is some dispute about whether the King insisted on stopping for dinner. The children's governess insisted this was a slur, saying, 'The King got out of the carriage only once the whole way and went into an empty stable, spoke to nobody and got back into the carriage in a very short time.' Presumably she's trying to tell us he went to relieve himself, but protocol forbids the admission that the King participates in such activities, especially not in a stable. Similarly, with a senior royal visit today, a toilet is reserved that no one else must use for some time before or after. Which can only be to preserve the myth of them as other than human, which would be spoiled if someone came charging out of a toilet yelling, 'Bloody hell, the Queen ain't 'alf dropped one!'

Either way, the royal party arrived so late that the troops had assumed the plans were cancelled and galloped back to their base. Concerned, the royals rode on to Ste-Ménéhould, where they had to stop at a staging-post on the way out of town. The town had already been full of mumbling that day, about the presence of a regiment of dragoons that had been placed there by Bouille. Then the royal carriages arrived, and Drouet, son of the postmaster, checked the occupants' papers. It was the King's misfortune that Drouet was a staunch supporter of the revolution, and had been to Paris to attend the celebration of the fall of the Bastille. In his later statement he said that as he looked at the 'servant' in the corner, 'I was struck by the resemblance of his face to the likeness of the King printed on a banknote I had with me at the time.'[7]

Drouet allowed the party to leave, but rushed round to the town hall to discuss the incident with a friend. To answer why he didn't act immediately, consider his position. Imagine if this *wasn't* the King, and he chased after this traveller through the night. For the rest of his life, wherever he went he'd be known as the idiot who'd thought he was chasing the King. Any bar he was in, people would mutter just loudly enough for him to hear comments such as 'Oy, I've just seen the King rollerskating towards Prussia, let's get him.'

Eventually he and his colleague, Guillaume, mounted their horses and chased the carriages. The royals were resting at the start of the village of Varennes, about thirty miles from their destination. Drouet and his friend galloped past them across the river and stopped at a bar where they could see a light. They said something to the landlord to the effect of 'You'll never guess who we've just passed at the top of the hill.' It may have been just as well for Drouet that his audience was at the fag-end of a late drinking session, because that's the only time anyone would hear a stranger announce that the King was over the road trying to escape and believe him.

The occupants of the bar found a discarded cart full of furniture, which they used to barricade the bridge. Others knocked on doors to alert the neighbours, and Drouet rode through nearby villages sounding the church bells to spread the news. When the royal coach moved on, it was blocked at the bridge, and the mayor of the village, a grocer named Sausse, asked to see their papers. Still uncertain, Sausse asked the royals and their entourage to come into his house while the papers were checked. As they were there, 5,000 peasants from the surrounding villages gathered around Sausse's house. At which point Drouet must have been thinking, 'I bloody well hope this turns out to be the right bloke.' To verify the travellers' identities, a local judge who had known the King at Versailles was sent for. He came into Sausse's house, marched into the bedroom and immediately went down on one knee, pining, 'Indeed, sire, you are my king.'[8] At which the King must have thought, 'Well thank you *very* fucking much.'

Meanwhile, Bouille's troops decided to march to Varennes in search of their missing guests, but were delayed when one fell into a hole in the forest and it took forty-five minutes to get him out. The first hussars to arrive were captured by the town's National Guard. Drouet pushed his pistol into the chest of a royalist officer and threatened to fire unless they surrendered, which they did. In his

Louis XVI dining while being arrested at Varennes, 21 June 1791.

statement he said, 'They made a great mistake in giving in so easily, as the guns were not loaded.'[9]

When the King and his family were returned to Paris, posters informed the enormous crowd that came to witness his return: WHO-EVER APPLAUDS THE KING WILL BE FLOGGED; WHOEVER INSULTS HIM WILL BE HANGED.[10] The result was the greatest insult, a silent crowd, and as a deliberate mark of contempt they all wore hats. This was the beginning of a new phase of the revolution. The King had been caught red-handed in opposition to the constitution, and large numbers of people became capable of imagining a country not just without Louis but without a king at all.

For two insurgents, the journey from Varennes to Paris was especially memorable for other reasons. The Mayor of Paris, Pétion, who rode back in the same carriage as the royals, insisted afterwards that the Queen's sister had spent the whole trip coming on to him, as she'd laid her head on his shoulder throughout. What a terrible indictment of the male psyche, that at this pivotal moment in human history the thought occupying the mind of a leading figure in the revolution is 'Bloody hell, I reckon I'm in here.' It probably even crossed his mind to ask whether, if the royals were all to be executed, would there be any chance of leaving it a few weeks first?

On the other hand, Drouet was an instant hero, riding at the front of the procession, a symbol of this new world in which the plight of a king could be determined by the actions of a postman. He was even elected as a delegate to the Assembly. However, every time he spoke he went on at some length about his heroics of that night, until hardly anyone would spend any time with him.

Varennes is still a tiny village, with a selection of plaques marking the key points of the night's events. The bar, the *Bras d'Or*, which was so crucially serving late drinks when Drouet and Guillaume arrived, is still there, run-down and bearing no sign of its place in history. There are two bars by the bridge on which the barricade was built, one called the Bar Grand-Monarque and the other the Bar Louis XVI. The village seems almost embarrassed by its place in history, whereas you can imagine if a minor pop star or regional weatherman had been brought up there, they'd probably knock up a statue to them in the square opposite the church.

The Ste-Ménéhould staging-post is now a *gendarmerie*, but the road it's in is named rue Drouet. And the bar opposite proudly displays on its wall a sign saying that this is where National Guards approached the dragoons on suspicion of being there for the King. The people I spoke to in Ste-Ménéhould reckoned that around 15 per cent of the local population were aware of the events in their town that turned history. Amongst that number is not, I suspect, the manager of the creaky railway station, who told me around midday that 'the next train leaves at half-past five'. At six o' clock, as the unoiled sign squeaked above the grass growing through the tracks, there was clearly no train imminent. Out came the manager, looking magnificently French with his stubble, beret-shaped railway hat, vast stomach and pungent cigarette that would stink anywhere else but seemed pleasantly rustic in the French countryside. I asked if he was sure about this train and he said with a gruffness worthy of a million Gitanes, '*Oui – cinq heures et demi – demain matin.*' And I could still hear him laughing as I passed the *gendarmerie*, unwilling to wait until 5.30 the following morning, to hitch-hike back to Paris along the road the King's carriage came down in 1791.

THE CHAMP DE MARS

Most of the third-estate delegates had desperately tried to hold together the compromise of a constitutional monarchy. But when your head of state flees in disguise to try and help a foreign army invade the country he's supposed to be head of, you have to accept your system hasn't quite worked. Alternatively, you can behave like a woman who won't admit her partner's having an affair, which is what many deputies did. They insisted the King had been kidnapped, and dispatched National Guards to find his abductors.

When General Bouille wrote a statement accepting responsibility for the King's attempted escape, the compromisers replied that Bouille must be lying. Even if the King had said, 'Listen, I was trying to set up an invasion so I could kill you all,' the delegates would have said, 'Oh I know you didn't mean it. It was a one-off wasn't it? This Bouille means nothing to you. I forgive you.'

The only sanctions taken against the King for his attempted escape stripped him of his veto over matters of law and finance. But the episode had the opposite effect on the *sans-culottes* and the more radical supporters of the revolution. Danton and the Cordeliers Club openly proposed a republic, as did Robespierre and most of the Paris Commune. Danton and the Cordeliers called for a demonstration and mass petition to demand that the Assembly should consult the people before deciding what to do with the King. The demonstration took place on the second anniversary of the fall of the Bastille, at a field called the Champ de Mars. After about 6,000 demonstrators had signed the petition, Lafayette ordered the National Guard to open fire, killing about fifty demonstrators, and the section of the Assembly that had urged compromise with the monarchy adopted the slogan 'The revolution is over.'

Where the storming of the Bastille represented the moment in which everyone felt they'd won an easy victory, the shooting at the Champ de Mars signalled the realization that the battle hadn't been won so easily after all. Lafayette and his colleagues still wanted an end to the weird values of the feudal regime, but they resented the mass of the population having any say in the outcome.

If, at this point, the competing factions seem to make the story a little complicated, Marat did his best to provide a simple solution in the issue of *L'ami du peuple* that followed the shooting. He wrote, 'If I could have found 2,000 men filled with the anger that tore my heart, I would have placed myself at their head, stabbed Lafayette to death, burned the despot in his palace and impaled our odious representatives on their benches.' And he added, in apparent surprise, that when he'd proposed this to Robespierre, he 'listened to me in horror, paled and for a while remained silent.' Whatever else you say, it's refreshing for a politician to come so directly to the point.

THE WOMEN'S MOVEMENT

If the women's movement in 1789 had adopted similar attitudes to some women's groups in Britain in the 1980s, you could be forgiven for assuming that their role in the French Revolution was to debate whether the cannon was phallic; or to stand round a guillotine holding hands in the belief the peaceful energy would blunt the blade; or to claim that Marie Antoinette was a feminist icon, for challenging gender stereotypes by advising people to eat cake without suggesting a recipe.

Simone de Beauvoir, who *was* a feminist icon, wrote in *The Second Sex*, 'It might well have been expected that the French Revolution would change the lot of woman. It did nothing of the sort.' She describes the law of 1790, that for the first time property was no longer inherited solely down the male line, as an 'insignificant victory'. The real significance of the legal and economic changes, and they became grander as the revolution went on, lies not just in the letter of the law but in the way men and women thought about the status of each sex. Just as the changing status of the sexes between 1970 and 2000 can be measured better by counting the number of men pushing buggies along high streets than by studying the subclauses of the Sex Discrimination Act.

Before the revolution, women's education was, according to a document sent to the Estates-General from Paris, 'neglected or very defective. They go until they are able to read the service of the Mass in French and Vespers in Latin.'[11] In the strict hierarchy of the *ancien régime*, women were seen as unfit to hold office, to be granted a divorce, or to inherit property. So the first effect the revolution had on many women must have been a transformation in their self-esteem. You can almost imagine a shrink suggesting to a woman

who feels worthless, 'Perhaps you should get some friends to march
with you to a palace and remove a royal family – you'll feel so much
more valued.'

The role of women in the French Revolution wasn't confined to
the march to Versailles. The bread riots were mostly led by women;
one incident was reported in January 1792 at a sugar warehouse
when 'residents of Saint-Marceau forced open a warehouse, and the
sugar hoarded there was sold at twenty-one sous per livre. All those
who took it paid for it faithfully.'[12] That must have been the politest
looting in the world. Maybe they even introduced a special offer –
pay for two bags, steal one free.

The dramatic changes led many women to reassess their position
in society. The first woman to articulate this was Olympe de Gouges,
a butcher's daughter, who wrote a document, 'The Rights of
Women', in 1791. She began by stating, with a nod to Rousseau,
'Women are born free,' and claiming to 'sound the *tocsin* for reason'.
She argued for women's education and suggested the women's vote.
She also advocated the abolition of the current form of marriage,
which she called a 'tomb of trust and love', suggesting it should be
replaced with a 'Social Contract between Man and Woman'. She
designed a form that would need to be completed by both partners,
which began, 'We, moved by our own will, unite ourselves for the
duration of our lives.' All talk of honouring and obeying was missing from this scheme. Which is why she added, 'I see rising up
against me the hypocrites, the prudes, the clergy.'

Surely it was only possible to conceive of such ideas because of
the turmoil enveloping French society, which had taken every belief,
no matter how entrenched, and held it up to the closest scrutiny. Or,
if we believe the theory that the revolution had little impact on
women, maybe the fact that it was written in 1791 was yet another
coincidence, and she'd hardly noticed the revolution at all.

Other groups were set up by *sans-culotte* women, such as the
splendidly titled Fraternal Society of Patriots of the Other Sex. But
the most influential was the Society of Revolutionary Women,

founded by Claire Lacombe, who had been an actress in a travelling company when the revolution began. When she heard the news of the Bastille she rushed to Paris and met Pauline Léon, a chocolate seller. Léon spoke at the National Assembly demanding that women should be allowed into the army, though she was outdone slightly by Théroigne de Méricourt, who proposed an entire women's battalion. The society was one of the main groups organizing the protests in shops and was a major influence on the Commune.

So, clearly the revolution changed the lot of women. At the very least they wouldn't have the old man complaining there wasn't any sugar in the house.

MADAME ROLAND AND THE GIRONDINS

While one section of Paris was declaring, 'The revolution is over,' the other was becoming more audacious than ever. After the shooting at the Champ de Mars, the 'revolution is over' section appeared to be winning. Elections were held for a new National Assembly, with the vote withdrawn from the poorer sections of France. The radical groups found themselves continuously threatened, and this time it was Danton who was pursued by police and forced to flee to England, while Desmoulins hid in Versailles. Only Marat, now a prominent Jacobin, remained in France, to write that 'the monarchy is as much use as the fifth wheel on a cart'.

Eventually, the divisions in the revolution became formal. Lafayette and his colleagues were openly trying to undermine the revolution they'd helped to begin. Opposing them was a republican group in the Assembly, including deputies connected to the ship-owners and traders of an area called the Gironde, who adopted the unimaginative name of Girondins. Amongst the Girondins' most prominent supporters were Monsieur and Madame Roland, who stuck together like a sort of revolutionary Neil and Christine Hamilton.

Jean Marie Roland

Condorcet, the secretary of the Assembly, said, 'When I wish to see Monsieur Roland I can never see a glimpse of anything but the petticoats of his wife.'[13] She was known as viciously rude, saying of Danton, 'He has a repulsive face . . . I cannot associate an honest man with such a countenance.' Mme Roland also incurred the wrath of Pamela Oldbury, the original owner of my second-hand copy of a biography about her. Throughout the book, next to quotes from Roland are notes made in pencil such as 'This is the sort of envy and class spite we have to put up with now!' At one point Roland gives an account of the King's coronation: 'It made me indignant that its object was to exalt a few individuals already too powerful.' Next to this, in deeply gorged pencil, is the note 'Who was she to lay down the law about her betters?' But who was Pamela Oldbury? To have continued reading a book that made her so angry, suggests she had to read it for work, so it's likely she was a history teacher. Wouldn't it be marvellous if she was the same one who was so adamant that the Vikings came in hordes.

The daughter of an engraver, Mme Roland became a public figure initially because of her husband, though she'd always been the more impressive character of the two. He was hardly romantic; while he was begging her to marry him he wrote her a letter to say he'd found a house they could live in, but it was full of lines such as 'I have knives and forks for eight persons and two stew ladles.' How often, when we're trying to seduce someone but don't seem to be getting anywhere, we think, 'I bet I'd be in here if only I had an extra stew ladle'?

Something must have clicked, because they were married. They moved to the town of Amiens, where M. Roland pursued his career as a clerk working on the details of the manufacturers' statute, and in his spare time he corrected the vast notes he'd made while travelling in Italy, with his new wife copying out each new version for him. And that, it seemed, was her life. You can imagine him saying, 'Tomorrow night, dear, for a treat, we'll do the page where I took a wrong turning in Naples.' But she must have felt uneasy with the traditional role allotted to all bourgeois women, as bored servant to a husband. Especially as her own notes were far more interesting than her husband's. Following a trip into the countryside she wrote of the peasantry, 'There is nothing but poverty! I have just seen the death of a woman of sixty, who could have been saved but these people suffer for months without stopping their work. They never think of calling a doctor, and fearing the expense of one they call a priest and in agony depart this life thanking God for having delivered them.'

So she spent her time learning the harpsichord and studying botany, and then came the storming of the Bastille. Such was the magnitude of this event that even M. Roland was stirred by it, and Mme Roland persuaded him they should move to Paris. Now her talents and personality were unlocked. She wrote articles and leaflets that so impressed Robespierre and the others that they agreed to come to discussions at the Rolands' flat, all of them staggered that the writer was a woman. She wrote an amazingly detailed plan for the military defence of Paris against a future attack from royalist troops, which, she felt, was inevitable. She wrote that 'The revolution, imperfect as it may be, has given France a character. Fatherland is no longer a mere word. It is a being we love as much for the sacrifices it costs us as for the hopes it inspires.'

None of this was sufficient to win the respect of Marat, who described her as 'the woman Roland, who leads her kitchen scullion husband by the ear.'

The revolution had transformed the couple. M. Roland was eventually invited to be a minister, as a government inspector for manufacturing, employing his talent for detail. Mme Roland became a person in her own right (then, just to make it perfect she started having a lesbian affair with a radical called Sophie Grandchamp).

Though Mme Roland was the most influential Girondin, the leader of the faction was a man called Brissot. Brissot came from a wealthy family but had run up debt through failed business projects, and had done time in the Bastille for writing a pamphlet attacking Marie Antoinette. Despite being known as one of the most business-friendly revolutionaries, he was so broke he owned only three shirts, which his wife had to wash in a constant rotation system.

Another leading Girondin was Louvet, possibly the French Revolution's only transvestite. But it's unclear what sort of women's clothes he wore; presumably in a republican club he couldn't very well pursue the normal tranny preference for glamour and come as a duchess. By the time the *sans-culottes* were at the height of their influence he must have been wandering round in a ragged dress and finding himself dragged along to riots to break into warehouses full of sugar.

THE RISE OF THE JACOBINS

The most coherent opposition to the Girondins came from the more radical Cordeliers and Jacobin Clubs. This can appear confusing, firstly because they were very different from modern political clubs.

I don't suppose many people joined the Jacobin Club thinking, 'I don't take any notice of Robespierre, I just come for the cheap beer and a game of snooker.' People became a member of a club purely to take part in political debates. But there was *one* way in which the Jacobins behaved like a modern left-wing party: just before the elections to the new assembly, they split. Over half their deputies left after Robespierre's speech supporting a republic. The remaining Jacobins responded by reducing the club's subscription rates, and five hundred new branches were set up across France. In Lyons alone they reached 3,000 members. And you can bet the ones who had been members right from the start were slightly peeved, like supporters of a lowly football team that gets into the Premier league who grumble, 'I preferred it when we were shite.' In Marseille, around 10 per cent of the population took part in Jacobin activities. In Paris there were mass meetings to listen to readings of Marat's paper.

The Jacobin Club – 'Where's the bar?'

Marat was now calling for 'vigilance', not just against the King and aristocracy but against a foreign invasion, which he felt certain would happen soon. He was especially vigilant about his own safety, and fled to London. Before he left, he promised his lover, Simonne Evrard, that they would get married as soon as he returned. Which they sort of did, in a ceremony involving no priest, in which they pledged their commitment 'before the Supreme Being . . . in the vast temple of nature'. While this would sound reasonably whacky if it took place in a field in Wales in 2003, in France in 1792 it must have been remarkably awkward to explain to the neighbours. Marat was not much of a catch at this time, as he was broke, vilified and fled to London with alarming frequency. His paper would never have been published again if Simonne hadn't come to its rescue, both financially and with help in printing, hiding the copies and distributing them.

Saint-Just

A new radical who would help shape the revolution was entering the scene, Louis Saint-Just. By the time he was twenty-five he was one of the most influential characters in France. Even before that, he'd got about a bit. At seventeen he went out with an older woman, whose parents considered the St-Justs too lowly and arranged for their daughter to marry a lawyer. In response, full of teenage angst, he ran around Paris accruing huge debts from his debauchery, and to pay off his creditors he burgled his own parents. Then, when his mother realized he'd run off with a ring, the family silver and his father's pistols, she wrote to a magistrate begging him to put her own son in jail. He was sentenced with a note that he was 'imprisoned on the demand of his mother'.[14] He was actually the son of a small landowner, though from this description you would imagine he'd escaped from *EastEnders*. When he came out of prison he went to Rheims to study law, and made contact with the local peasants, where their indignities and their enthusiasm had an enormous impact on him, and St-Just pledged to become a deputy in the Assembly.

St-Just stood for election, but his opponents questioned whether he was old enough. Anyone who's experienced the humiliation of being sixteen and facing a pub landlord leaning across a bar and saying sharply, 'Are you SURE you're eighteen?' can imagine how he felt. Maybe he should have found a mate with stubble and a deep voice and got him to stand instead. He was kicked out of the election, and spent the next year studying Rousseau, supporting every protest in his area and following every speech of Robespierre, Danton and Marat, still at an age where he might be expected to have their pictures on his wall.

The growing popularity of the radical figures was a sign that the attempt to curtail the revolution after the shooting at Champ de Mars was failing. The leaders who had fled to England or gone into hiding returned, to greater acclaim than ever. Danton was elected Public Prosecutor, and celebrated by restocking the wine cellar at the Cordeliers Club.

THE MADMEN

After the start of the revolution, two productive harvests had eased the problem of urban hunger, but in 1792 there was another bread shortage, which some of the rich responded to by indulging their hobby of hoarding. But the *sans-culottes* were becoming adept at forcing hidden goods on to the market. Now many of them demanded a 'law of the maximum', a prices policy that would make it illegal to sell any item above an amount fixed by government. This may seem an odd demand from a modern perspective. You can imagine the chaos if, instead of wage claims, there were price claims, and union officials screamed, 'We want spaghetti hoops on special offer or we're out of the door.' But whereas modern workforces are united by working for the same employer, in the France of 1792 most *sans-culottes* worked either for themselves or for tiny employers, so the demand that could unite them was not wages, but prices.

The most active contingent formed a group with possibly the best name in the history of agitational politics: the 'Enragés', meaning 'the Madmen'. Their long-term aim was to push the republican faction in the Assembly to be as egalitarian as possible. They must have been aware that once you've called yourself 'the Madmen', you've set your stall out. If you're giving out leaflets in the shopping centre you can't very well say, 'Maybe we should pack up and go home 'cos it looks like it's going to rain in a minute,' not if you're called 'the Madmen'.

WAR BREWING

It was obvious that France was becoming as polarized as ever. On the one hand there was an opposition movement called the Madmen, and on the other hundreds of nobles fled to Koblenz to join a potential invading force from Austria and Prussia. The Duke of Brunswick, who would lead this force against the revolution, said, 'I perceive with regret we shall have no obstacles to get over. I would have preferred that the allies should encounter some resistance, for the French need a lesson they will never forget.'[15]

Around 25,000 *émigrés* gathered for battle, and the Marquis de Falaiseau described a day in his life: 'We passed into the dining-room. The custom here is to take what is brought to you. It is true that you are offered something fresh every minute or two. There is a footman to look after every two guests.'[16] Presumably, not all the *émigrés* were like the Marquis de Falaiseau, who you can imagine wandering through the battlefield looking for a waiter carrying a tray of canapés. The *émigrés* brought with them stories of the atrocities of the French Assembly, and anyone who watched the build-up to the wars America has fought in recent times will be familiar with the techniques of making conflict seem inevitable. The Austrians cried that, in effect, 'If we don't stop them now they will continue to make pikes of mass destruction.' The Duke of Brunswick declared, 'We will be marching on Paris soon.'

In France, most republicans supported the idea of declaring war before the *émigrés* declared war on them, claiming this would be the best way to unite the country. But they debated the matter for some time, not on grounds of pacifism but because they didn't have an army. Of the 10,000 officers they'd had in 1789, 6,000 had run off to join the *émigrés*. The army was in such chaos that on New Year's Day 1792 some grenadiers in Picardy went to wish volunteer soldiers a Happy New Year, but a fight broke out over something someone said, and ended with four grenadiers dead. Which suggests a fraught atmosphere, as even in a small town in Kent you don't often get a crowd of lads in a pub saying, 'These geezers came in and wished us Happy New Year. We sorted them right out; they won't do that again.'

One faction surprisingly keen on going to war with the royalist armies was the French Royal Family. They supported war in the hope that they would lose; as the counter-revolutionary force would restore them to their original position. Marie Antoinette wrote to Count Fersen about the supporters of war in the Assembly saying, 'The fools! They do not see that it is in our interest!'[17] Fersen pressed the Swedish government to back war against France, following a request from Marie Antoinette, which put her in the unusual position of pleading with a lover to declare war on her, a fetish it would be hard to get catered for in the seediest club in Amsterdam.

The Girondins, especially Brissot, were confident the army could resist the invading forces. But as things stood, they were being very optimistic. The leaders of the army had all been nobles, and had almost all run off. On 20 April 1792 the King, who was still head of state, declared war against the Austro-Hungarian Empire, who wished to restore his power. Within days the French were being torn apart along the border, but as each defeat was reported to the King, he must have replied, 'Oh dear, how – er – terrible.'

HERE WE GO

In modern Britain we're meant to feel proud of where we were born, because of our supposed greatness in the past. You can still witness teenagers chanting, 'Two world wars and one world cup, do-da, do-da,' which makes as much sense as kids from Luxembourg singing, 'Two Eurovision Song Contests and one radio station, do-da do-da-day.' At the time of the French Revolution, citizens were asked to take pride in France not just because they'd been born there but because they were helping to create the nation France would be. There was no assumption that citizens were nationalistic, for nationalism was in its infancy, and duty to the nation had only been a concept with any meaning since the revolution had begun. By the summer of 1792, the flurry of appeals to defend the nation weren't glib calls to 'buy French fruit' or boasts that 'We're the paper that supports our boys,' but pleas for the defence of the revolution. The nation meant the revolution, as when the Assembly declared, 'All those who hate liberty are taking up force against our constitution. Citizens, the fatherland is in danger.' Loosely following Rousseau's model, republicans saw the nation as the body of people who had chosen to be part of the new society, and should be prepared to defend it. As distinct from the modern definition of nations as places that you should support in the Olympics because you were born there. To the French, Tom Paine was a patriot, despite being English. The French King, on the other hand, was no patriot at all.

With foreign armies, not entirely made up of foreigners, advancing on the nation, the position of the King became increasingly surreal. The Assembly ordered the dispersal of the King's bodyguard, a force of 6,000 that was sure to act as a fifth column if the invading forces got to Paris. But they had to get the King to ratify this. Not surprisingly, he said something like 'No fucking way,' and blocked the measure with his veto. The Assembly then called for 20,000 patriots to come from across France to defend Paris. Again, the King blocked this with his veto. From the French side, the war began to resemble a game of cricket in which one captain has been paid to throw the match. It's surprising that, amongst the historians who argue there were no class interests at work in the French Revolution, there hasn't been one to claim the King's behaviour can be explained by his links to a Far East betting syndicate.

The immediate result of the King's actions was an audacious demonstration, called by the Girondins, for the French people to plant a tree of liberty by the King's palace. But it seems once again a door was left open at the side of the palace, and the demonstrators poured in. Chanting, 'Down with the veto,' they broke into the royal apartments, where they forced the King to wear a red cap of liberty and sit on a chair listening to their insults. For several hours the demonstrators marched past him, offering slogans such as 'Fat Louis' and 'Tyrants must tremble'.

After this demonstration, the notion of compromise evaporated almost completely. On one side, Lafayette tried to plan a coup that would restore the monarchy to its old power, using the National Guard. On the other, armed citizens marched to Paris to defend the Assembly against any such threat. In particular, six hundred marched from Marseille, becoming celebrities amongst republicans along the route. Not everyone found them so endearing. One deputy, M. Blanc-Grilli, described them as 'a scum of criminals vomited out of the prisons of Genoa and Sicily'.[18] Our Book Society Choice friend *Paris in the Terror* described them as 'neither French nor from Marseilles but a collection of foreign vagabonds, the dregs of all nations, Genoese, Corsicans, Greeks . . . and a Pole named Lazowski'. And what does any idle vagabond do for an undeserved free handout? Walk eight hundred miles for no money whatsoever, of course. A journalist, Thiebault, added, 'They are the criminal scum of the city. One cannot imagine anything more horrifying than these fanatics, three-quarters of them drunk, marching bare-armed and dishevelled.' He goes on, 'we left them moving towards the Champs-Elysees, where they indulged in satanic dances before taking part in an orgy'. Maybe someone should have dropped a journalistic tip to Thiebault, that sometimes less is more.

There's a more lasting legacy of this particular march. Just before it took place, a Marseille engineer wrote a song for the revolution, as the most popular up until then was 'Ça Ira', which translates loosely as 'Here We Go'. And as anyone can testify who recalls the striking miners of Britain in 1984–5, while this is fine as it goes, it's not as rounded in content as it could be. So Rouget de Lisle wrote a song called 'The Marseillaise', full of calls to arms to defend the fatherland, of bloody banners and tainted tyrants, perfect for playing in Casablanca bars to drown out the Nazis at the nod of Humphrey Bogart. That scene certainly wouldn't have been as moving if the French had tried to trump the German band by singing, 'Here we go, here we go, here we go.' At the time, the Chronicle of Paris reported, 'In all our houses of entertainment the public always call for the song. They sing it with the greatest fervour and the passage where, waving their hats and brandishing their swords, they all sing together "To arms, citizens" is truly thrilling.'

As Robespierre predicted, the French Army was in such disarray that the war began disastrously. They were thoroughly beaten by the Austrians, and one of their generals was captured and lynched. Then on 25 July, as he prepared to exploit the French chaos by marching towards Paris, the Duke of Brunswick, commander of the Prussian forces, issued a manifesto which pledged to return the French Royal Family to its original status, though it also declared 'no intention of meddling with the domestic government of France'. The manifesto went on to explain how it would do this. Anyone in any town who 'may dare to defend themselves against the troops of their Imperial and Royal Majesties' would find 'their houses pulled down and burnt'. Then, 'The town of Paris and all its inhabitants without distinction shall be bound to submit on the spot, and without any delay, to the King.' Otherwise the Prussian and Austrian Armies would 'take an exemplary and never-to-be-forgotten vengeance, by giving up the town of Paris to military execution . . . and the guilty rebels to the death they have deserved'. The Royal Family, it went on, must be restored to the 'respect to which the laws of nature entitle sovereigns'. If not, there would be 'military execution without hope of pardon' for 'all members of the National Assembly as of the districts, the Municipality, the National Guards and Justices of the Peace'. And all this without meddling with the government of France.

THE RISE OF TOUSSAINT

At the opposite end of French society, but just as concerned with military affairs, was a slave of San Domingo, Toussaint L'Ouverture. His job had been to look after his master's cattle, which led to his becoming a competent horseman. He added to this talent by finding the time to read Caesar's commentaries. Already unique as a Caesar-reading slave, following the first slave revolt he had committed himself to the cause of raising a disciplined slave army.

Toussaint was aware that, although the slaves had been effective in the short term, they hardly constituted an army that could defeat their owners. But many slaves believed that on their death they would be reborn in Africa, which gave them a fearless attitude we

Toussaint

recognize in modern suicide bombers. The problem was, fearlessness may be admirable but it's pretty useless. No one wants to be on a plane flown by a fearless pilot – they might say, 'Hey, let's fly into a mountain, to see what it feels like, wahey!' So Toussaint's troops charged into bayonets, happy if a handful got through. And, less successfully, they would run up to a cannon, reach into the barrel and try to pull out the balls. One military leader, with the unlikely name of Hyacinth, believed that his talisman of a bull's tail would chase death away.

But at the very least the slaves had fought their way into the revolution, and they became another matter for debate within the French Assembly. A law was passed that the colonies were at liberty to decide for themselves the status of the blacks. This accepted the possibility of freedom in theory, though the slave owners were hardly likely to give away their slaves just because they were legally allowed to. But the Assembly also announced an inquiry into the revolt, to be reported by the Colonial Commission. The colonists' case was put by Millet, who offered an intriguing insight into the world of slavery. The slaves had a 'pleasant and easy life which they enjoy in the colonies . . . Sheltered by all the necessities of life, surrounded with an ease unknown in Europe, cared for in their illnesses, protected and respected in the infirmities of age.'[19] By the end the delegates must have been wondering why the whole of Africa wasn't begging for an interview for the job of slave. The result was yet more compromise. The mulattos were granted full political rights, but no mention was made of blacks.

Meanwhile, Toussaint was recruiting, training and drilling. Most applicants weren't even sure which end of the gun to fire from, but he taught them how to fire, and to retreat as well as advance, by using his knowledge of Caesar, a warrior whose life was dedicated to extending an empire of slavery. It would be like if, in 2,000 years' time, an Iraqi army conquered America using a strategy devised by General Tommy Franks.

8

The Second Revolution

The reign of the super powers must be over
So many armies can't free the earth

MOVING ONTO LEVEL 2

I n our times, amongst those who defend the British monarchy, most accept the rules that govern them as meaningless nonsense. For example, very few people can make sense of the regulation that the monarch can't marry a Catholic. What are they worried about, that if they drop this rule the Queen will run off with Martin McGuinness?

In France in the summer of 1792 the matter wasn't so frivolous. Twenty thousand Parisians signed a petition supporting the return of rule by the Royal Family. The 20,000 who signed were declaring their support for counter-revolution, including a foreign invasion committed to military execution without pardon. Republicans were divided about how to respond. Mme Roland and her supporters proposed abandoning Paris and setting up an alternative government in the countryside. Danton especially was furious with her for this proposed surrender. Marat, in a special edition of *L'Ami du peuple*, urged volunteers to 'hold as hostages Louis XVI, his wife, his son, his ministers, all unfaithful representatives, all the members of the old departments and the new, and all the venal judges of the peace'.

Robespierre and Danton spoke nearly every evening at the meetings of the Paris Commune, and felt the mood leaning towards support for another insurrection, this time to remove the royals altogether, until forty-seven of the forty-eight districts supported the move. On the night that the group from Marseille arrived, Robespierre and Danton organized a secret meeting to plan the insurrection. Danton and Desmoulins were to tour the districts on the night of 9 August, urging the people to storm the Tuileries palace and remove the royals from power. On that night Danton began at the Cordeliers Club, where he yelled that all members should 'Rise in your might and strike down the usurper. Lose no time, for this very night satellites concealed in the palace are to sally forth upon the people and to slaughter them. Save yourselves. To arms. To arms.' Throughout the night they rang church bells in every district to signal an uprising, though dispensation to cease the ringing was granted in some areas between 1 a.m. and 3 a.m. Nevertheless many people must have been lying in bed screaming, 'I don't care who runs the state as long as they shut the fuck up.'

Whereas the storming of the Bastille was the result of spontaneous uprisings, this second revolution was meticulously planned by a group committed to the ideals of revolution. Delegates from each section of the Commune met to plan a military strategy. Each area was designated a route to the palace which they would control, and arms were allotted and issued. But none of this meant the outcome was certain. Lucile Desmoulins described the evening before the insurrection: 'Danton was resolute but his mother was weeping, very distressed. So we walked up and down the street and sat by a café. Several sans-culottes passed by shouting, "Vive la nation," but at last, in full sight of everyone, fear took hold of me. Danton's wife made fun of my fear but in doing so became frightened herself, and when we arrived back I saw that Danton [too] was nervous.' When she returned she became more frightened than ever when Desmoulins came into the room carrying a gun.

MARCH ON THE PALACE

Anyone who's witnessed a demonstration that has ended in confrontation can imagine the tension as the march to the palace set off. August 10, 1792, wasn't going to end with a rally and a call to hand in your placards. They weren't protesting that there shouldn't be a king, they were setting out to *remove* the King.

One of the tensest situations I've known was in Prague, where I was writing an article on an anti-globalization protest, outside a World Bank conference. Just across from the conference was a bridge, every inch of which was covered by military hardware, protected by 11,000 police. From a van at the front of the march came an announcement in Italian, which sounded dramatic and exciting, although for all I knew it could have been explaining the car-parking restrictions, and then in English: 'The police are beginning to er, er . . .'

'Er what?' thought the linguistically hopeless English. Er fire on us, er give us all an ice cream? What a time to forget your verbs.

'. . . er, use tear gas,' she said.

A spate of rumours swept the English contingents about how to stop the effects of tear gas. Lemon, vinegar, water – definitely not water, that makes it worse – Vaseline and a special type of salt were all suggested in the space of ten minutes. Next was a recorded announcement from the police, played over and over again in several languages, which in English was 'We warn you to disperse. If not you are violating the laws of the Czech Republic and you will be dispersed,' repeated with all the dramatic flair of the man who says, 'Mind the gap.'

As puffs of gas circulated, the riot police stood still and nervous; the water cannon remained smugly poised; and men with lots of padding shuffled from foot to foot and jangled their guns. Some demonstrators continued to sing and whistle and climb up poles, one was pedalling a cardboard tank and another was running amongst the crowd stark naked with his knob through a one-dollar note. And it crossed my mind, was this combination of tension, drama and surrealism the atmosphere that must have prevailed just before the troops fired at Amritsar or Derry or Lexington? For demonstrators in an explosive situation, there is no command compelling them to stay. No one can have you court-martialled for desertion. For most people in Prague, the tension fizzled out and they went home. But everyone there tasted something scary, the sense that at any moment there could be a major battle. But on 10 August 1792, the crowd went through all this, not suspecting there could be a major battle, but knowing there *would* be a major battle. So as the hum of imminent violence fizzes, everyone has to reassure themselves and each other that there is a reason to stay. Rumours circulate of a crowd being battered nearby, someone jokes that they're scrawling out their will, and everyone tries to sing to hide the fact that everyone's cacking themselves.

To avoid complete chaos, military formations were planned in advance, under a series of professional commanders, one of whom was a young Napoléon Bonaparte. The defence was offered by 6,000 Swiss Guards and royalist troops, probably experiencing an equal sensation of trepidation, yet one for which they'd been trained. But the mere appearance of the insurrectionists won them an early advantage in the crucial battles of the mind, as Minister of Justice Dejoly, upon seeing the armed demonstration, said, 'I was convinced there was no dike powerful enough to stop this torrent.'[1] Twenty-eight of the forty-eight Commune districts had been won over to active support for the insurrection, and it can't have helped the morale of the King when a large contingent of the National Guard announced they were leaving because they wanted breakfast. Palace officials desperately searched for an improvised breakfast to stop them leaving, but I think in reality there was more to the guards' announcement than a yearning for a croissant.

This is reminiscent of the day in Prague, firstly because that's the only demonstration I've attended that began at seven in the morning, but also because, at that time of the morning on this anti-Gap, -Nokia and -McDonald's protest in the freezing cold, the English section of the march was preoccupied with one issue alone: where to get a cup of tea. Eventually a union rep nipped off and returned with a dozen cups. As the last cup was finished, we asked him where he'd found them, and he said, 'McDonald's. I had to go through a line of armed riot police but it was the only place open.'

Every account from the Swiss Guard suggests chaos. One commander, Desbouillons, wrote, 'There was no formal plan, no overall commander.'[2] This was more than a failure of military strategy. At one point the commanders discussed introducing martial law to stop the insurrection, seemingly unaware that their problem was a result of the population no longer recognizing royalist laws. When you're storming up the left bank of the Seine with a musket to overthrow the King, you're not going to be put off by someone saying, 'I hope you realize that's against the law.' Many of the National Guards sent to defend the King had marched with the women to Versailles, so many must have had divided loyalties. Which may be why only 200 out of the 1,500 remained at their posts.

The Swiss Guards were more resolute, their Sergeant Blazer declaring when asked to surrender, 'We are Swiss, and the Swiss only abandon their arms with their lives.'[3] The *Swiss*? Is this historically accurate? Is the phrase 'Quick, run, it's the Swiss' more common than any of us imagined?

Despite the Swiss, the King was advised by Général Roederer to take refuge with his family in the National Assembly, where he was likely to be safer. As he accompanied the King there, the monarch's only comment was, 'Ah, have you noticed how the leaves are falling early this year?'[4]

Outside the Tuileries palace, the first royalist troops were arrested. Their fate was in the balance when Théroigne de Méricourt, dressed as an Amazon warrior with a sabre and bandolier, leaped on to a cannon and urged that the arrested troops be put to death. Shortly after Théroigne's intervention the troops were thrown from the upstairs window, followed by the grisly business of heads on pikes. All but the most loyal sections of the royal defence changed sides, after which a ferocious battle took place. The royalists retreated across the Place Louis XV and clambered on to the monument in the square, whereupon a debate took place amongst their attackers about the ethics of damaging the statue. It was decided to try and charge their enemy with bayonets rather than risk unnecessary damage with a cannon. After this, republicans forced their way into the palace, leaving 600 royalists dead, along with 390 republicans. Lucile Desmoulins wrote that the sound of the firing was sufficient to cause Danton's wife to faint.

This had been an orchestrated battle with definable leaders, but this doesn't mean the second revolution wasn't part of a popular movement, or was solely the work of a handful of activists. Yet this is the claim of many modern historians. For example Simon Schama claims, 'The whole sans-culotte "movement", at its height in Paris was made up of no more than two to three thousand committed revolutionary zealots.'[5] So all the meetings, the clubs, the storming of the Bastille, retrieving the royals from Versailles, invading the stores, the insurrections and eventually the Terror were all carried out by 2–3,000 extremely busy people. Not only that but the reversal of every aspect of society and ideology was allowed to take place against the will of the other 25 million, who let the 2–3,000 get on with it.

Every protest, from the flimsiest picket to the most overwhelming uprising, is usually dismissed in a similar way. As the Romans walked through the field of 10,000 slaves to ask, 'Which one is Spartacus?' they probably said to each other, 'Look at this, the usual suspects. Most of this lot are probably middle-class students *pretending* to be slaves.' Revolutionary action does usually involve a committed minority, but that applies to state-led action as well as to opposition. The difference is that then the minority become official heroes. After the Battle of Britain, Winston Churchill didn't say, 'Oh typical, just a handful of activists with big mouths and Spitfires.'

The *sans-culotte* activists who drove the revolution *were* a minority, but a far bigger minority than 2–3,000. Just as important, they would have been helpless unless they had won support at some level from the majority. If 3,000 people in London in 2003 erected a guillotine and started invading royal palaces and cutting off their opponent's heads, they'd be stopped. They might buy themselves a bit of time if they began with Jeffrey Archer and Noel Edmonds, but that's all. A revolution can run on the activity of a minority, but only if they connect with the aspirations of the majority. A handful of activists organized the raids in the stores, but thousands came with them and tens of thousands more liked the idea.

Those who attack the revolution as undemocratic take a strange line, when the avowed aim of the counter-revolution was to restore a state of affairs whereby the number of people with a vote was one. But traditional historians' biggest objection to the validity of revolution is the disbelief that the majority can take an active interest in the direction of society. History, for them, revolves solely around kings and queens, presidents, popes and generals. Or, to put it another way, a handful of activists.

THE NEW REGIME

The republicans immediately called an election, in which all French males could vote, to take place in six weeks. In the mean time the King was suspended from duties; the Assembly would rule, in conjunction with the Commune of Paris, headed by Robespierre, with Danton on the Executive Council. Marat came out of hiding for the first time in three years, and in an 'insurrection special' wrote, 'No one more than I abhors the spilling of blood; but to prevent floods of it from flowing, I urge you to pour out a few drops.'

Camille Desmoulins responded in his own way, by writing to his father. His letter began, 'Despite all your predictions that I would never amount to anything, I have now been promoted to the highest post which a man in our walk of life could hitherto expect.' Somehow you don't associate parental pride with revolutionaries. During the Cuban missile crisis, did Mr and Mrs Guevara say to their neighbours, 'Our Che's doing ever so well, he was in the papers *again* this morning'?

The one position that had almost completely disintegrated by 10 August was that of the compromisers. Compromise might have been desirable, but it had been demonstrated to be simply impossible. The King believed, with every fibre of his being, he'd been sent by God to rule. His family, his court and his followers believed the same. And foreign armies were prepared to inflict carnage to defend his belief and that of the aristocracy that they were a higher species than commoners, just as slave owners believed their property was a sub-species. The peasants and supporters of the third estate had come to believe equally passionately in the rights of man, and had tasted the experience of feeling in control of at least some part of their destiny. For three years almost the entire country had longed for compromise, but it didn't happen. The King has been derided for weakness, but he didn't do badly. He negotiated a veto, fooled almost everyone into believing he supported the new constitution, plotted secretly with foreign armies and planned an escape that might have succeeded but for a sharp-eyed postman. The more forceful Duke of Brunswick only managed to persuade republicans that they had nothing to lose in staging an insurrection. Had the King been the most flexible compromiser in history, even conceding power to the Assembly, he would simply have been replaced by a less compliant royal by the army of counts, dukes and nobles whose wealth and power depended on his rule. The King wasn't weak; he became weak. Almost everyone involved was ordinary, but became extraordinary. And compromise wasn't undesirable, but it became impossible.

THE SEPTEMBER MASSACRES

To understand the atmosphere of anxiety as the foreign armies approached Paris, we just have to look at fear in our own relatively calm times. People shake their heads and say, 'Have you heard what these criminals are doing now?' Then comes a story about how they're watching you tap in your PIN number at a cashpoint machine using satellites they've stolen from NASA; or are dressing up as sheep on country roads and stealing cameras from people who stop to take a picture. You're warned that if you don't lock everything, with alarms and if possible a moat and a nearby sniper, it's almost certain to be stolen. Yet even if you drop your credit card or wallet, the most likely outcome is that someone will either point it out to you or hand it in to the police. And the majority of people who steal cars are car thieves, who aren't too bothered whether they're locked or not. Even if you don't lock a car at all, it's unlikely someone will come past and think, 'Ah, hang on. I'm not normally a car thief, but seeing as that one's unlocked I'm going to climb in, hot-wire it, respray it and sell it to a bent dealer in Germany.' So, if the Duke of Brunswick was marching towards your town with an army bent on levelling the whole neighbourhood, and local criminals and prisoners could potentially be his allies, you can imagine the gossip this would cause in the average old people's home.

After the battle at the Tuileries there was a collective sense of 'Blimey, now we've done it.' If the revolution was a pub fight, the Duke of Brunswick had said, 'Put my pint back or I'll do you,' and the revolution had thrown it in his face. Surviving Swiss Guards were jailed, along with royalist priests and nobles, and the royals were gaoled in the Temple prison. Within days of the King's overthrow, uprisings against the revolution started in Brittany and the Vendée, and on 2 September the Prussians captured Verdun, the last major town between them and Paris. Panic swept the city, along with stories that the royalist soldiers would be released from prison by the invading army to murder the families of anyone at the front.

The tension broke on the afternoon of the 2nd, as a coach of suspected royalists was being transported towards the prison. A crowd surrounded the coach, a royalist priest struck a bystander and he, along with twelve co-defendants, was slaughtered on the spot. This started a rampage that ended with a killing spree in the prisons. A lawyer called Maton de la Varenne described how he heard from his cell a crowd enter the prison: 'I saw two men, one of whom had one arm and the sleeve of his coat covered with blood as far as the shoulder. He said, "For the last two hours I have been cutting off limbs right and left and I am wearier than a mason who has been slapping plaster for two days."'[6] Whatever else, you have to be slightly impressed that he appeals for sympathy, as if to say, 'I never even got a tea-break.' As Maton sat in his cell, a prisoner who could see the murders called to him, 'My friend, we are as good as dead. They are murdering the prisoners as soon as they come out.'

At the Abbaye prison there were similar scenes, when every prisoner in one wing was killed. One, Masaubre, hid up a chimney.

September Massacres – Heads on pikes.

The assassins knew he was in the prison, so threatened the jailer until they found out where he was hiding. They fired a cannon up the chimney, but Masaubre stayed silent, a feat for which anyone ought to be pardoned, no matter what they've done. But then they started a fire underneath him, and eventually he suffocated.

Meanwhile, Maton was dragged from his cell and placed before an instantly arranged court. He quotes one of his interrogators as saying, 'Ha! You smooth skinned gentleman, I'm going to treat myself to a glass of your blood.' But within moments, following a search through the prison register, the same man said, 'I find there is nothing whatever against him.' And after urging him to join in a chorus of 'Vive la Nation', which he had no hesitation in co-operating with, Maton was freed. So Maton at least was actually *better* off, except that on his way home, protected by a gendarme, a fired-up citizen took him for an escaping criminal and cried, 'Let's do him in here,' and set about him again. This time a pedestrian saved him, after which he can never have complained about having a boring day for the rest of his life.

One of the victims of the night was the Princesse de Lamballe, who was butchered into countless pieces. But the only inquiry into the case was against one man accused of eating her heart. One typical part of the hearing, a series of questions asked of the man's lawyer, went as follows:

INQUIRY: Was it not true that he roasted the heart on the cooking-stove supplied by the wine-shop man?

LAWYER: He had neither seen it or eaten it.

INQUIRY: Had he not carried the sexual organs of the deceased on his sabre?

LAWYER: No – only a part of her comb.

INQUIRY: Isn't it true his wife refuses to live with him because he went round with the Princess's head and ate her heart?

LAWYER: No.

We can only hope the lawyer was telling the truth, or feel sorry for whichever Marriage Guidance counsellor tried to patch up that marriage.[7]

Whatever, someone did take her head, which turned up later on a pub table. Between 1,100 and 1,400 prisoners were slaughtered that night, and their bodies dumped in a quarry. So how can this outbreak of mass murder be explained? One theory is that offered by an otherwise excellent book on Danton by Charles Warwick, who suggests it was simply the work of uncontrollable brutes. Of the attackers, he says, 'They were of the labouring classes, their woollen caps, hob-nailed shoes, and coarse aprons revealing this fact. They smoked and drank during the proceedings and ignored every feature of judicial demeanour and decorum.'[8] As if it would have been any better if they'd asked each prisoner if they wanted to be dismembered in a smoking or non-smoking area. Other theories suggest the killers were paid by Danton and his colleagues, but even after several months on the dole very few people would agree to chop up random strangers, saying, 'It's a bit grisly but at least we'll have a decent Christmas.'

On the other hand, there's something disconcerting about the glib justification offered by, for example, the nineteenth-century socialist Belfort Bax, who wrote, 'The so-called massacres were strictly a measure of self-defence, and as such were justified by the result.'[9] No conflict is as black and white as some on the left try to make out. You can be almost certain that around the world there were left-wing groups answering questions on these massacres with arguments such as 'How do we know they weren't carried out by the CIA to discredit the revolution?', or 'Can it just be coincidence this story came out at the right time to divert attention away from the unemployment statistics?' No more convincing are statements such as 'These things happen in revolutions,' or 'It was necessary in the circumstances.'

The first point about understanding an episode such as this is that it's pointless and a little superior to judge acts, no matter how ghoulish, from the perspective of twenty-first-century Western comfort. If the people who carried out the September massacres had been living in modern Epsom they probably wouldn't go round decapitating people before sauntering into the local, ordering a pint, placing a head on the table and saying, 'Now don't let me leave without that.'

The September massacres can be explained as something other than madness, but it has to be accepted they were a disgraceful, inhuman and despicable act. You wouldn't fully trust anyone who could sit in a pub with a head on the table, saying, 'Well, you have to see this in its overall context.' None the less, to make any sense of this episode does require an understanding that here was a city in fear of the slaughter they would be subjected to if it was recaptured by royalist forces. Every potential supporter of those forces appeared as a menace. And many of the prisoners were regarded as potential allies of those royalists, which may be why the one prison untouched by the assassins was the debtors' prison. And there *were* trials, however unorthodox, that led to prisoners such as Maton going free. This suggests that there was a military rationale to the massacres and the slaughter wasn't entirely indiscriminate. The revolutionary authorities certainly saw it like that. Although no individual took responsibility, Danton had been named Minister of Justice, and did nothing to prevent the slaughter. Nor did any National Guardsman, and the Paris Commune issued a statement afterwards that 'a number of the dangerous conspirators detained in the prisons have been put to death by the people of Paris. This act was judged indispensable in order to restrain by fear the traitors concealed within the city.'

Either way, judging solely from the standpoint of modern society without acknowledging the extreme circumstances in which the massacres took place is as dishonest as condemning someone for cannibalism without acknowledging they'd been floating in the Pacific for six weeks in an open boat.

VALMY

One of the travesties of the way history is traditionally taught is that battles become reduced to a series of arrows on maps, as if we were watching a football pundit or a choreographer for a West End musical. For the traps, retreats, land-bridges and cutting-off of supplies may be vital elements in battle, but are all subordinate to the fact that the people carrying out these acts are human beings, and if things go wrong they'll be killed.

In casting out the noble officers, the French Army had lost its strategists and its technicians and the enemy was on the road to Paris. Mme Roland again suggested abandoning Paris and moving the Assembly to the south, which would almost have amounted to surrender, to which Danton replied, 'Audacity, more audacity, always audacity will save the Republic.'

The Assembly called for 50,000 volunteers, and recruiting agents were sent to every area of France to insist that, 'after all the efforts that have been made, it would be heartbreaking to be forced to return to our former slavery'. They promised this would be an army unrecognizable from the one that had collapsed. Officers and men would wear similar uniforms and receive the same pay. They would march into battle singing 'The Marseillaise', and 80,000 *livres* were spent on supplying the army with songbooks for this purpose. Two-thirds of officers would be chosen by a ballot of the soldiers. Church bells and silver were melted down to make bullets, and the makeshift army travelled from Paris under Generals Dumouriez and Kellerman to meet the most professional and well-equipped force in Europe.

The Duke of Brunswick swung his army to meet the novice opposition, on the fields that lay behind the tiny village of Valmy. The ease with which they'd strolled through the French up to then led him to believe this battle would be a formality. The French were grouped at the top of a hill, around a windmill, where they placed themselves throughout the night. One of the peculiar aspects of nineteenth-century battle was how huge numbers of people lined up in areas that were usually pictures of tranquillity. At some point the miller of Valmy must have turned a corner, as he did every morning, and seen that instead of his gently turning sails were 150,000 people facing each other with muskets and cannon. And there was probably a moment where he tried to see if he could get through, perhaps calling limply, 'Excuse me, only I've got a lot of orders, you see, because it's a Wednesday.'

The battle was of little interest to the people who draw arrows on maps, involving a day-long exchange of cannon-fire in pouring rain, most of the shots landing in the mud. But the untrained novices didn't flee as expected. For the first time since the war began, the French held their line. The Duke of Brunswick, having expected to march on for Paris, was shocked and exasperated, and to add to his misfortune amongst his troops was Johann Goethe, who later became one of the most famous writers of all time, there to record the whole event. The Duke must have felt like an actor who forgets his lines and then hears that all the critics were in: 'Oh not bloody Goethe, not today of all days. Why couldn't he have been at Verdun? I stormed the place that night.'

Goethe wrote, 'In the morning we had been talking of spitting and eating the French. Now everyone was thinking again. Almost everyone remained silent. Only a few men spoke and their reflections seemed illogical or frivolous.' They had been stopped, not by an adept formation, but by the changes in people's heads. Four years earlier the watchmakers, peasants and laundrymen that made up this army had been resigned to a life in which their highest aspiration was to avoid discomfort. If they could get through a few years with the minimum of cold, hunger and pain, that wouldn't be so bad. But then a new world opened up, which they would play a part in shaping. They would read, write, discuss and argue the issues not just of the day but other days. And when they considered a return to the old ways, not just for them but for future generations, they must all have taken the enormous mental leap required to volunteer for a battle in which they may well have ended up dead in the mud. Somehow, in whatever fashion the human mind converts these thoughts to actions, this led them to continue standing when every instinct for survival was urging them to run. Which may be why the Prussian officer Massenbach said, 'Today is the most important day of the century.' And Goethe, being a writer, put it more poetically: 'From this place and this day forth commences a new era in the world's history and you can all say you were present at its birth.'[10]

As news of the resistance reached the rest of France, the effect on the mentality of the revolution is hard to overstate. The war was only just beginning, but for the first time it must have dawned on people that they really could win. The army was reinvigorated, and one month later, as the retreating Prussians were attacked by local peasants, the French recaptured Verdun. The Prussians must have felt that if they were being analysed by football pundits, it was with the joy of watching a top team being knocked out of the FA Cup by non-league part-timers, with all the cries of 'And here's one of the *sans-culotte* heroes, who last Monday was selling fish at his stall in the market.'

The windmill, however, was demolished halfway through the battle by General Kellerman, because it was a target for Prussian artillery. So at least one person must have ended this historic day shouting, 'It's all very well commencing a new era in history but what am I supposed to bloody do about my weekly orders now?'

The English Respond

The week after Valmy, 5,000 republicans marched through Sheffield in celebration, carrying posters of Edmund Burke riding a pig, and an angel of peace carrying Paine's *Rights of Man*. In London there was a surge of popularity for the London Corresponding Society. A porter wrote that a typical meeting consisted of tradesmen and journeymen, but that 'the most numerous consist of the very lowest order of society. Some are filthy and ragged, that it requires some mastery over that innate pride, which every well-educated man must possess, even to sit down in their company.' And that from a porter!, whose own contributions to the meetings, if we're to go by the modern characters in his occupation, must have consisted of an eloquent defence of the republic followed by, 'Mind you, don't get me wrong, I fucking hate the fucking French 'n' all.'

In Stockport, a member of the 'Friends of Universal Peace and Rights of Man' wrote how he approached the town's firework night on 5 November: 'I proposed making an effigy of Brunswick, and after some persuasion it was adopted, and carried on with considerable spirit . . . and some excellent toasts were drunk.'[11] Sailors in Aberdeen planted a tree of liberty in honour of the French. It was uprooted by the authorities, so the sailors went on strike for the replacement of the tree and won. It was lucky they weren't represented by certain modern union leaders, who would have called the strike off after five minutes, announcing, 'Great news, they've agreed to a tulip.' Groups from London, Manchester, Nottingham and Norwich sent addresses to be read out at the Jacobin Club in Paris.

Prime Minister Pitt was enraged on two fronts: that the disquiet about the English government was reaching a dangerous level, and that the French armies could be a threat to English rule in Europe. The Mayor of London sent agents into Corresponding Society meetings as spies, and the leaders were arrested; pub landlords were threatened if they allowed meetings on their premises; and teachers were sacked for 'traitorous expressions'.

In February 1792, Pitt had declared that Britain would be at peace with France 'for fifteen years'.[12] In August, after the second revolution, he amended this to 'they hold out encouragement to insurrection and rebellion in every country in the world. They order this decree to be printed in all languages. They mean to carry their principles into every nation, subvert and destroy every government.' In other words, they had 'declared war on the civilised world'.

The authorities turned on English radicalism. King George III imposed the custom that after any military setback the people should be subject to a national fast, which protesters took delight in ignoring. That must have been the only demonstration in history that involved *not* going through physical discomfort such as walking three miles with a banner, while it was all the conformists who couldn't wait for it to end. The paranoia of the government was suggested by the arrest of three Corresponding Society members over 'the pop-gun plot', after a disgruntled ex-member claimed the society had invented a special pop-gun that could shoot the King with a poison dart.

Mass meetings took place supporting the French republic. Thousands went to a meeting by the Globe Tavern in Southwark, and it was reported that 'several thousand' attended an open-air meeting on Primrose Hill in north London. Several spies were in the audience, and one reported he saw Thelwall, one of the speakers, blow the head off a pint of beer and say, 'Such should all tyrants be served.'[13]

But it was the founder of the Corresponding Society, Thomas Hardy, that the police became really obsessed with. One night a group of the King's messengers, along with two Bow Street Runners and a locksmith, raided Hardy's shop. Hardy was arrested for high treason along with three of his colleagues, and virtually the entire contents of his house removed. Internment without trial was introduced, and the courts announced that if Hardy was found guilty they would hang him, release him before he was quite dead, then disembowel him, burn his innards before him while he was still alive, and then tie him to four horses who would gallop off in different directions. Hardy's wife Lydia would have to witness all this while she was six months pregnant.

While he was awaiting trial, the country received reports of a victorious naval battle. A crowd of English patriots toured London to check that everyone had lit a lamp in their window to celebrate, as ordered. Feeling especially patriotic that night, they smashed into

the Hardy house and tried to drag Lydia away, who was only rescued by her neighbours. But she was severely beaten and weakened,
and when she went into labour a few weeks later, the child died.
Feeling herself growing weaker, she wrote a letter to her husband
beginning, 'You are never out of my thoughts, sleeping or waking,'
without getting much further before she collapsed and died herself.

Then Hardy stood trial. There were four acts for which you could
be charged with treason: plotting a war against the king, plotting to
kill the king, allying with the king's enemies and having sex with the
queen. Hardy was accused of the first three. The fascination with the
trial reached O. J. Simpson proportions, with crowds outside the
court each day and every newspaper reporting every angle. The trial
became a debate about the rights of man, with each side quoting
Paine and Burke; eventually the jury, having taken three hours to
arrive at a verdict, found the defendant not guilty. What a shame
Hardy didn't say to the prosecution afterwards, 'And if only you'd
known I've been fucking the Queen.'

Hardy was caught in the most turbulent mix of emotions. Instead
of being tortured to death he was free to go, but to a home in which
his wife and child had just died. He left the courtroom wishing to be
alone and come to terms with this grief, but a crowd of his supporters spotted him and carried him through the streets, then into a
carriage that, according to the *Morning Chronicle*, 'took him to the
church-yard of St. Martin where he was shown the grave of his wife.
The multitude kept a distance, respecting his feelings with a sympathy that did them credit.'

9

The Republic

It's kill or be killed
A nation of destiny has got to be fulfilled

THE PACE OF CHANGE

One factor in the establishment of a French republic that has been overlooked is the glory of the French language. I once saw *Jurassic Park* dubbed into French, and even that acquired a certain sexiness, so much so that it was a disappointment to find the dinosaur roars weren't dubbed into French as well: instead of 'Raaaargh', a sort of *'Reaaaeu'*. To sense the difference between French and English, it's worth considering our separate words for the noise of a contented cat. We say it 'purrs', which sort of describes it, but not really. A fed cat doesn't look up from your lap, clear its throat and say, 'Purr.' But the French word is *'ronronner'*. Which, when said with a French 'rrrr', sounds not only like a cat but like a *French* cat. For example, *'Le chat est content, il rrronrrrone'*. (The word in German is probably 'katzensnoren'.)

And so it was in the French government. On the day after the Battle of Valmy, the newly elected French parliament, called the Convention, declared France an 'indivisible republic'. The Convention was made up of three factions, the Girondins, the Montagnards and the Grenouilles de la Marais. Before you even know what they stood for, that has to be an improvement on Labour, Conservative and Liberal Democrat. The Girondins were named after the region of the Gironde, the Montagnards were the more radical faction of Jacobins and Cordeliers, including Danton, Robespierre and Marat, and got their name from their habit of sitting in the highest seats in the Convention, so were dubbed 'the Mountaineers'. Even if British political parties *were* named according to their seating position in Parliament, they'd have called themselves something as unpoetic as 'Near the Fire Escapes'. The Grenouilles were the 'Frogs of the Marsh', because they hopped to and fro between the other factions. Just as interesting, since the Montagnards not only sat upstairs but on the left of the building, this was the origin of the terms 'left' and 'right' to describe political attitudes. And the nature of this building was confirmed when Robespierre won his argument for a public gallery, which was to allow 1,400 citizens to view the daily debates of the Convention.

All factions supported the deposing of the King, but the divisions between them developed quickly. The Montagnards saw the eradication of divisions in status as the first step towards bridging the economic gap between rich and poor. As Robespierre said, 'Royalty has been destroyed, now the reign of equality is beginning.' Attacking the wealthiest businessmen, he said they saw 'those goods which are necessary to keep people alive as nothing more than an ordinary item of trade', a statement not so far from Marx's assertion that businessmen see objects not for their use-value but as commodities.

Marat also sounded like a Marxist: 'Without the workers, society could not exist for a single day. Yet these unfortunates look with disdain upon the scoundrel who grows fat by their sweat.' But, being Marat, he couldn't leave it at that. So he went on, 'These publicans drink the workers' blood in cups of gold.' You can almost hear his colleagues shouting, 'All right, yes, we get the idea.'

The Jacobin ideal, based on Rousseau's model, was a republic of small property owners, in which everyone worked in small units. The government, elected by those property owners, would protect the will of the majority. Beyond that everything else was still up for debate. Until recently they'd had no idea they even supported a republic, let alone that they wanted to make or lead it themselves. Unlike Lenin or Mao or Castro, they hadn't been preparing for power over many years, so they were like a character in a film who's being chased then suddenly finds himself in a speedboat or a helicopter, desperately pulling all the levers and yelling, 'Let's see if this works.'

Rousseau imagined his ideas would be put in place by mutual agreement, not by a regime that existed because it had knocked over a castle, jailed the King and stood firm by a windmill. But he and the other Montagnards *were* clear about their sense of fashion. Whenever in public they wore their red liberty cap, a low-cut shirt exposing the top of their chest, short-cropped hair and wooden shoes. Which must make them the campest revolutionaries in history. Maybe Robespierre said, 'Now the reign of equality is beginning,' then St-Just spread his arms and screamed, 'Ooh hark at her. I said there's one part of the mountain no one's been up for a while.'

The Girondins were becoming convinced the Mountaineers were preparing a dictatorship. The transvestite Louvet accused Robespierre of 'having quite obviously set your sights on a position of supreme power'. Brissot said the Montagnards were 'mad anarchists'.

But the Girondins had lost credibility following their suggested retreat from Paris. This hadn't been just a tactical error, but came about because they lacked the social roots of the Montagnards. Even if they'd desired it, it's doubtful they would have possessed the mechanism for motivating thousands of *sans-culottes* in the way that Danton, Desmoulins and Marat could, through their clubs and publications. Most leading Girondins were allies of the wealthier businessmen, and their support for the republic had struck an impasse – they found the mob distasteful, but only by mobilizing the mob could the revolution be protected. None the less Danton tried to repair relations with Mme Roland, breaking into her box at the opera so as to greet her when she arrived. Unfortunately for Danton, as Mme Roland approached she could see 'Danton's inflated figure, as well as three or four women of questionable appearance'.[1]

For all the complexities of the debate between Montagnards and Girondins, one argument, between Danton and M. Roland, may have encompassed the whole row. Roland referred to the problem of the 'rabble', and Danton replied, 'Are we not of the rabble ourselves? It is this rabble that has raised us to power. If we ever forget that, we are making the most disastrous mistake of our lives.'

M. Roland resigned his post as a government inspector in despair, partly because he no longer felt he could work for a regime that lived by principles so different to his own, though his mental condition may not have been helped by the fact his wife was now having an affair with another Girondin called Buzot.

The arguments within the Convention reflected the company kept by the delegates outside it. After the petition at the Champ de Mars, Robespierre was walking back to his lodgings when he met M. Duplay, a cabinet maker. He was invited back to the Duplays' flat and met the whole family, discovering that they'd been trying to let out their spare room to help the finances. So Robespierre took it himself, and lived there for the rest of the revolution.

It's worth considering this for a moment. At the start of this business, the ruler of France was waited on throughout several palaces, by countless courtesans, with someone employed solely to supervise his wife as she got dressed in the morning. By the height of the revolution, the most important man in France, on his way to dealing with war and famine and establishing a reign of equality, would have to wait for a carpenter to leave the bathroom so he could clean his teeth.

THE *SANS-CULOTTES*

L'homme du Sans Culotte   **La femme du Sans Culotte**

The *sans-culottes* were the Jacobins' trusty but slightly embarrassing best friend – unshakeably loyal, but when your parents come round they're sitting on the settee in their underpants eating a pork pie. They were the crowd that had saved the third estate, overthrown the King and fought the Duke of Brunswick. They were the wheel-wrights, potters, locksmiths and carpenters who would produce for the society the Jacobins wanted to build. But they weren't lawyers or journalists, and whilst they shared the Jacobin aspirations they were all too aware that before these could be realized they needed bread. One writer of the time said, 'If the poor are going to help you bring about the Revolution, it is a matter of the greatest urgency that you provide them with the wherewithal to live.'

Led by the Enragés, the *sans-culottes'* campaign to fix prices became more daring. In one sweep through central Paris, they forced stores to sell sugar at 25 *sous* (unrefined at 12), candles at 12 *sous*, soap at 12 *sous* and coffee at 20 *sous*. These prices were co-ordinated across the city, and it's just a shame there were no TV adverts for anyone involved in this action to say, 'Hurry hurry hurry to Henri's soap store where you simply won't *believe* the prices. You can see why we're called madmen!' But the remarkable side to the price campaign was the continuing politeness in paying the agreed sum. A grocer invaded by the Enragés presented the police with a report that showed that the money they'd left was almost exactly in keeping with what he would receive if his prices were as they demanded.

In the rue Saint-Lazare, washerwomen staged what may well be history's only ever soap riot. A lorryload was taken by the mob, and the laundry workers fixed a price and handed this over. Inevitably this system broke down at times. There were cases of shopkeepers joining a crowd that was invading a rival shop, and of the wealthy sending out cooks or servants to buy cheap goods when they heard a price-fixing riot was in town. The riots were well organized, so that their timing was known in advance. Maybe they had special 'January riots', when half of Paris would flock for the cheapest stuff of the year, behind a strange couple who'd queued for two nights in a sleeping bag because they'd heard a pair of fur coats was being looted at 70 per cent discount.

A theatre-ticket seller called Jacques-René Hébert produced his own paper, *Le Père Duchesne*, which tried to connect the daily movement to the revolution's higher ideals, and this paper regularly sold thousands of copies throughout the city. The paper supported a demonstration of 6,000 that marched to one market, everyone wearing the cap of liberty, inside which was a piece of oak bearing the slogan 'Long live the nation. Corn prices will come down.'

It was also from within the *sans-culottes* that the Society of Revolutionary Republican Women grew up. As well as helping to organize the raids on shops, this group arranged mass petitions to be handed into the Convention urging laws fixing maximum prices, and at one stage it organized a demonstration of the blind to take a petition. This type of action pressurized the Montagnards to stick to their pledges; to which the typical Montagnard deputy thought, 'Yes yes, I'm very grateful for all you've done, but if I give you a few bob, will you promise not to show me up again while I'm at the Convention?'

THE KING'S TRIAL

The King and his family, meanwhile, were still in the Temple prison. The King had access to a personal library of 1,500 books, he was allowed to look after his favourite dog and take it for walks round the grounds, and the family was provided with servants, though they complained they weren't the ones they wanted. The King could still order shoes from his usual cobbler, and he was granted protractors and a compass, though it's doubtful whether he recognized the irony in the fact that these objects had helped the rise of bourgeois thought in the first place. And, in a classically French touch, Marie Antoinette was allowed to order lingerie. All of which must have meant this was the only time left-wing people were screaming, 'Call that a prison? It's a bloody holiday camp!'

Adding to the royal comfort was the utter devotion of their former staff. The most striking example was that of Jean-Baptiste Cléry, the King's official hairdresser. During the battle at the Tuileries, he had escaped through a window and gone into hiding, but when he heard that the King had been arrested he went to see Pétion, the new Mayor of Paris, and pleaded to be put in the prison where he could attend to the ex-royal's hairdressing needs. For the next five months he barely left the King's side, grooming him to perfection each morning. Then three cooks who had worked for the royals got jobs in the prison kitchen so that they could smuggle in the finest meat and poultry for their imprisoned ex-bosses. Between them, the barber and cooks devised an elaborate code whereby they could transmit messages to the King and Queen about the progress of the Duke of Brunswick's army. Louis' sister, Madame Elisabeth, confirmed how these would work. For example: 'If the Austrians are successful on the Belgian frontier, place the second finger of the right hand on the right eye.'

It's hard to grasp how these characters must have coped with their former employers' predicament, for they literally worshipped them as if they were tending God himself. No amount of argument about rights or equality or men born free but everywhere in chains would have had the slightest impact, for they would simply retort, 'But he's the *King*.' When they saw the turnkey, having heard the King didn't like pipe-smoke, light up a pipe each morning just to blow smoke in the King's face, they weren't just horrified at the rudeness, to them it was an act of blasphemy. Either that or the barber was thinking, 'Bingo. When all this is finished the *Daily Mirror* will pay MILLIONS for this.' It was a sign of the times that the best-selling book in Paris became an account of the execution of Charles I.

Not all the King's ex-employees were so faithful, however. A locksmith called Gamain approached the Paris Commune with the information that he had installed, at the King's request, a secret iron cupboard in a wall at the Tuileries palace. The cupboard was for the secret correspondence between the King and his foreign allies and the Assembly members who were quietly on his side. The Commune sent Gamain and some witnesses to the palace, where the safe was jemmied out from the wall and, as predicted, found to be full of letters from Austria and Prussia detailing plans for royal restoration. Mirabeau and Lafayette were implicated, though by now one was dead and the other had fled to Austria. Had the King known the techniques of modern political spin, he'd have challenged the dates, announced that it wasn't illegal and merely involved a private business arrangement, blamed a secretary, denounced the tabloids and somehow persuaded the Convention to take no action except set up an inquiry that didn't publish a report for another eight years. But in these exceptional times, the safe ensured that his period of remand would soon be over, and his trial would begin.

The Convention debated the necessity and form of the trial, which gave rise to possibly the most powerful maiden parliamentary speech of all time. Making an impact in a legislative body now doesn't look easy, as experienced politicians know how to neutralize any speech, no matter how fiery, with polite decorum. If for example a politician waves his order paper and growls with fury, rising to a crescendo of 'This is nothing short of a national disgrace,' the camera pulls back to reveal nineteen people nodding vaguely, and the poor sod just looks like a nutcase. An MP could say, 'This proves the honourable gentleman could do with a cattle-prod up his arse,' and the response would be three 'Hear hear's, two 'Shame's and one 'Congratulations on a fine speech' from the MP it was directed against.

But Louis St-Just had finally achieved his ambition of being elected to the Convention, and he opened with a philosophical debate on the nature of the King's trial. The question was, he said, not whether Louis had been a criminal king, but whether he'd been a king at all. A republic, he explained, couldn't make distinctions between kings who'd been criminal and kings who hadn't, for their crime was denying their subjects' freedom by virtue of being king. St-Just had hit upon a certain logic. What legal framework could try a king in this revolution? To try him allowed the possibility that you could be a good and legal king. To make his point clear, St-Just went on, 'I do not see the possibility of any middle way: this man must either reign or he must die.'[2] This did make an impact. The flaw in the debate about monarchy had been to discuss the merits of Louis XVI as an individual. It's similar to today, when peculiar issues are thrown into the monarchy debate, such as 'They bring in a lot of tourists.' Which is a strange argument, as it seems to assume that Dublin and Paris have no tourists. Presumably when people go to the top of the Eiffel Tower they say, 'Hmm, well it's a nice view, but the lack of a monarch spoils it somehow.' In any case, *Starlight Express* brings in a lot of tourists but I hope no one would advocate making Andrew Lloyd-Webber head of state.

St-Just's argument showed how far the revolution had gone, even compared to the overthrow of the English monarchy. Charles I was tried as a bad king, his charge being that he'd 'led forces against parliament at York, Edgehill, Kineton Field, Brentford, Reading, Gloucester, Leicester, Cropredy Bridge, Cornwall, Newbury, Naseby, Kent, Sussex, Surrey, Essex and Middlesex', after which it must have been tempting to say, 'and all leading high-street stores!'

Ironically, St-Just's most lucid opponent was someone who agreed with his central point that kings were guilty for being kings, and that was Tom Paine. Paine wished for the royals to be deported to America and fade into obscurity, rather than executed. The trial was the first major example of the Montagnard thought process, as each practical question was debated as a philosophical problem. Deputies harangued each other with references to Rousseau and Voltaire and obscure points about justice and virtue, but the real point was whether keeping the King alive would help those who were trying to restore his rule. It was a grand version of modern arguments between activists, who fire quotes from Lenin back and forth in a debate about whether to go to the demonstration by train or by bus.

The trial did take place, and was decided in a dramatic fashion which would have delighted anyone with the TV rights, each deputy coming to the forum in turn to announce their verdict. To add to the tension, each was allowed to make a short speech explaining their decision. Robespierre made a joke by saying he was glad of this ruling, because 'You all know I can't stand making long speeches,' but apparently nobody laughed. It must have been acutely embarrassing, to have to clear his throat like a failed best man at a wedding and say, 'Right, well, anyway, to be serious for a moment . . . I vote for death.'

The most eagerly awaited vote was that of the Duc d'Orléans, Louis' cousin, who had been elected as a deputy, having retained an image of radicalism since allowing debates in the Palais-Royal.

He voted for death. This has been cited as an example of why the revolution can't be seen as a battle fought along class lines, as if the actions of one individual negate the movements of millions. It's like suggesting that because the English Lord Haw-Haw worked for the Nazis the Second World War was not fought between Britain and Germany.

For twenty-four hours this process continued, deputies sleeping across benches as they awaited the final verdict. Presumably someone was keeping score; they must have felt like a presenter of the *Eurovision Song Contest*, trying to stay alert and spritely through the counting procedure, saying, 'And now we come to the Minister for Marseille. Can you hear me? Are you enjoying the evening? Good, OK, can we have your score please?' Eventually the final score was announced and, by 387 votes to 334, the winner was death. The next day Lepelletier, one of the deputies, was approached in a street by a pedestrian who said, 'Aren't you Lepelletier?' He was probably slightly flattered, in the way a minor

Louis at dinner in prison.

celebrity is when recognized by the public, and agreed that he was. 'Didn't you vote for death?' said the stranger, and Lepelletier answered that he had. Then the pedestrian pulled out a sabre and stabbed him to death on the spot.

The King had been confined to his room for most of the trial, with only his barber for company. A crier came to the yard below his window to inform him of the verdict. The King asked for three days' respite, but this wasn't granted, though he was allowed a final evening with his family. Cléry the barber noted 'several minutes of silence interrupted only by sobbing'. This predicament would be tough enough for anyone, especially when his son asked to be allowed to accompany him the next morning, to plead with the crowd to let his father go. But the King had extra elements of turmoil to deal with. Here he was, in a more intimate moment than most of us can imagine, having to share it with the woman to whom he was wedded for reasons of political expedience. All he was ever able to offer her, in return for a life shared with a husband she had no affection for, was the trappings and duties of being Queen. Which might have been a reasonable deal, if she wasn't now in a prison bidding farewell to him on the eve of his execution. The people who, in his mind, he'd been put on the earth to rule were about to publicly chop off his head. Whatever rights and wrongs surrounded the matter, that had to go down as a failure.

At the end of their evening, the King assured his family he would see them all in the morning for a final embrace. His supper, Cléry informs us, was 'two chicken wings, vegetables, two glasses of wine, a sponge-finger and a little Malaga'. Then he slept in the same room as his barber, who woke him at five and helped conduct a Mass. The gates of Paris were closed. Eighty thousand armed guards patrolled the streets and no traffic was allowed to move. A steady drumbeat had been thudding through the city since 5 a.m. The King, now known as Citizen Louis Capet, decided he couldn't face a final meeting with his family, and was taken

The execution of the King at the *Place de la Révolution*.

outside to the cart for his journey to Place Louis XV, now renamed Place de la Révolution. As he climbed the scaffold, he turned to the crowd of 20,000 to make a speech that seemed to typify his life. For he got as far as 'I forgive my enemies' when an enormous drum-roll began and no one could hear a word he said. At which we can only hope that, if it were us, we would smile and say, 'I don't think today's going to be my day.'

Seconds later, sections of the crowd surged forward to dip their handkerchiefs in the blood of the now decapitated ex-King. Danton announced, 'The Kings of Europe threaten us. We hurl at their feet the head of a King.'

SLAVES ON THE MARCH

In normal times, normal people don't campaign on issues from the other side of the world. There are the odd exceptions, such as the middle-aged Christian couple from Somerset I met during the protests against the World Bank in Prague. The woman told me they'd been activists ever since her sister-in-law had given her a leaflet about international debt. She said, 'Since then we always take our holidays somewhere like this, because that way we can go to a museum in the morning and a demonstration in the afternoon.'

But often campaigns on international issues can seem to fall a little short of what's necessary to bring about the required change. You sometimes wonder whether, if you were being held in a damp basement by a Burmese torture squad, you'd think, 'Still, it's not all bad, at least they're holding a fund-raising awareness night in a Scout hut in Camden.'

Most of the time, to most people, these issues seem remote: either they feel assured their own government is acting in the best interests of fair play, or they don't feel there's anything they could do about it anyway. Just occasionally, a vast number will connect with the plight of people thousands of miles away, as happened during the years of apartheid South Africa, during the war against Vietnam or preceding the war against Iraq. Which may be why a colonist's agent living in France in 1792 wrote of the local attitude towards slavery, 'One spirit alone reigns here, it is horror for slavery and enthusiasm for liberty. It is a frenzy which wins all heads and grows every day.'[3]

In one sense it was practical for republicans to support freedom for the slaves, as a defeat for the colonists would be another blow to royal authority. But if their support was only a result of self-interest, that suggests a dreadfully clinical state of mind. It reminds me of the awful phrase sometimes used by the left that supporting anti-colonial movements is 'in the workers' interests'. As if you could ever persuade a bus driver to support the Palestinians on the grounds that he'll benefit personally. If that was the case, you could win people to the cause in the way you give people a horse-racing tip, whispering, 'Do yourself a favour and start running guns for the Hezbollah . . . Or if you *really* want to sort yourself out for the future, become a suicide bomber.'

One reason for the transformed attitudes towards slavery must have been that the poor Parisian could find it easy to feel comradeship towards other victims of the royal authorities. But mostly it was that the revolution had created the *possibility* of thinking about issues such as slavery. Before, most people were consumed with the ordeal of getting through each day, leaving no space in their mind to worry about the fate of those they would never meet. The revolution, by making them feel it *did* matter what they thought and felt about events in the world, that their opinions and actions *were* as important as those they used to think of as the élite, gave people the wherewithal to look outwards.

The slaves meanwhile were still pondering what to do with a ship that had been sent to San Domingo before the second revolution. It was under the authority of Sonthonax, a Girondin, with orders to prevent another slave uprising. Many of the troops on board were royalists, and the ship became a floating time warp, with arguments breaking out all day about whether a republic should be set up weeks after it already had been. Rows about the constitution became so heated that fights broke out over the tiniest issue. The most furious battle was over the issue of where the ship should land, and as soon as it did the two groups went their separate, armed, ways.

Soon after this, a local royalist landowner, Galbaud, announced he was taking control of the island. The slave owners rallied around him, as did the royalists on the ship. Sonthonax was left with a similar dilemma to that of the third estate before the storming of the Bastille. His only chance of defeating the royalists was to turn to the mass of the population. So the commander who'd been sent to disarm the slaves then armed them as thoroughly as he could, and an army of 10,000 blacks, many of them trained by Toussaint, stormed into Galbaud's area of Le Cap, forcing him to dive into the harbour. Galbaud was picked up by one of the many boats used by fleeing whites, who set sail for America. Where, it might be fun to suppose, they were met by crowds of people saying, 'You can't come in here, we've got no room. Don't come here trying to exploit our generous welfare system, what do you think we are, mugs?'

The same dynamic that sparked the revolution in France had pushed the slave owners into a harbour. And to complete the circle, the battle resulted in a fire that swept across the sugarfields, drastically reducing the supply of sugar to France and creating a sudden surge in the price, which led to another huge spate of demonstrations by Parisian women demanding the price rises were reversed. Little by little, it was becoming ever easier for *sans-culottes* and republicans in France to feel part of the same family as people thousands of miles away, whose names they would never know and whose faces they would never see.

10

. . . Complete Control

The bank notes of Europe
The Emperors and Kings
Curl in the Autumn as the burning of leaves

THE CALL-UP

By the time the King had been executed, every aspect of French life was up for reconsideration. Playing cards were redesigned, with the King, Queen and Jack replaced by cards depicting Liberté, Egalité and Fraternité. Anyone named Louis was entitled to give himself a new name. And in Bordeaux, clapping was prohibited as a form of applause appropriate only to a society built on social rank. This is an idea that seems to have returned, as a growing practice in radical youth movements today is 'twinkling', whereby if you agree with the speaker you hold your arms in front of your body and wiggle each hand. If these people ever see *The Black and White Minstrels* with the sound turned off, they'll think someone must be going down a storm. In the Bordeaux Jacobin Club, an agreement was reached that 'Expressions of joy and agreement should henceforth be made through the medium of the virile and republican word "Bravo".' The rules of draughts were changed, so that you couldn't crown a king. It's surprising Marat didn't demand keeping the crowning rule, but that if a King was taken, the

Revolutionary playing cards.

piece would be sawn in half, and shown to the crowd, who would dip handkerchiefs in the sawdust.

CIVIL WAR

Some distrust was felt towards the new government, simply because it was in Paris. This is a tension you can still sense between the capital and the rest of France, as Parisians are accused of a certain haughtiness towards their provincial countrymen. And on the wrong day they can be impressively surly. Ask them for directions and they'll nod vaguely. Ask for something more precise and they say, '*A gauche*' and you hope if there's a military coup, they're the ones with all the names because it would take a fair bit of torture even to get them to reveal the quickest way to the Métro. For example, I was looking for the Luxembourg Museum and, thinking I may have found it, had the following conversation with a security guard.

'Is this the Luxembourg Museum?'

'*Non.*'

'So where am I?'

'*Palais du Luxembourg.*'

'Where can I find the Luxembourg Museum?'

He nodded.

'Left or right?'

He gave a tiny nod, as if he was bidding at a prestigious auction. So I walked about four hundred yards in that direction and saw the Luxembourg Museum behind an enormous sign saying FERMÉ and a pair of padlocked gates. I went back to the security guard and said, 'You knew that museum was shut, didn't you?'

He looked straight ahead, completely expressionless, and said, '*Oui.*'

'All right, I'll come into the Palais du Luxembourg instead.'

'*Non.*'

'Why not?'

'*Fermé.*'

And all spoken without the slightest twitch of any muscle other than those essential for mouthing the words. Just above us on the wall in enormous letters was the slogan of the revolution itself, probably sculpted around the time of Robespierre and Danton. I said, 'You know what that slogan ought to say – "*Liberté, egalité, fermé.*"'

'Ahugh,' he said in a beautifully dismissive tone, and I felt charmed.

In 1793 the gap between Paris and the provinces must have been even more pronounced, and opponents of the Montagnards were able to exploit the sense of resentment towards what was seen as Parisian bullying. An issue that brought this resentment to the surface was recruitment to the army, upon which the survival of the republic depended.

The French Army faced a dilemma over what to do after it had chased the Austrians and Prussians away from their borders. Firstly it issued an appeal to the population of these countries to overthrow their royal families as they had done themselves. But they weren't sure whether the French Army should then cross the border to support the revolts it had called for. If it did, wasn't it just another invading army? But if it didn't, its calls for revolt were as useless as the advice my dad used to give me if I lost a fight at school: 'If someone hits you, then hit him back.' So they decided to march into Austria and Belgium, initially to instigate revolt, but in the process were indeed seen by many as just another invading army. Then, once they captured the Belgian port of Antwerp, every European government panicked. British Prime Minister Pitt expelled the French Ambassador and prepared for war, as did Spain, Tuscany, Naples and Venice. One deputy, Barer, announced with slightly suspect logic that 'each new enemy for France is another victory for liberty', an eighteenth-century version of the Millwall football song, 'No One Likes Us, We Don't Care'.

Within a few months Britain, Spain and almost every region of Italy joined the Austrians and Prussians in the war against the revolution. They formed a coalition, pledged to restore a monarchy in France and announced solemnly that God was on their side. Of course he was: God is always on your side in a war. There's no record, as far as I know, of a general saying to his men, 'Last night, in this our hour of need, I prayed to God for guidance. But unfortunately it seems he's backing the Turks on this one.'

A decree was passed to recruit 300,000 soldiers, the mayor of each district being responsible for providing a certain number and allowed to choose how to reach his tally. He could nominate recruits, which often led to fiasco as the mayors didn't want to upset anyone they knew. So in several areas the people sent were local beggars, and in one village, in Cantal, the Mayor selected thirteen cowherds who lived on a remote mountain and weren't aware the war had even started. Mayors could arrange a lottery of all able men, with lots drawn to see who went to the front. All of which must have been terrifying for the commanders, when they went to meet their new recruits and found them saying, 'Can you give me a *livre* so I can get home?', 'I'm here because I won the raffle,' and 'So which side are we on then?'

In the town of Cholet riots broke out in protest against conscription, and the whole region burst into civil war, led by a gamekeeper and a hairdresser. French troops were brought back from the front to deal with the rising. Vendéans slit the throats of anyone captured. Republicans developed a macabre respect for their opponents, one general writing, 'they only needed a better cause to possess all the characteristics of heroism'.

The problem for the Convention was that their demands for grain, resources and recruits to the army appeared to be exactly the same as the demands that used to come from the King. The resulting conflict involved the fiercest fighting of the war, and was full of stories such as that of Mme de Bonchamps, a noblewoman who was forced to flee with her two daughters after her husband was killed. Dressed as a peasant, she and a crowd of refugees ran on to a boat that came under gunfire, so everyone ran to the opposite side of the boat for safety, which made the boat tip up. Some drowned, but Madame and her daughters were rescued. They ran all day, to get to a farmhouse on part of her estate. The house was run by an old woman and, according to Mme de Bonchamps, 'I learnt from her own mouth that when the enemy had threatened to burn her house, she delivered to them my unfortunate servants who were all massacred.' The old woman was apparently matter-of-fact about this, and it wouldn't be surprising if she'd said to the troops, 'Could you wait twenty minutes so they can finish polishing the fireplace first?'[1]

Madame decided to keep running, but one child died of small-pox. Finally, the two survivors made it to the town of Nantes, where they were taken prisoner but told they would receive a pardon as long as they convinced the court they hadn't been part of the royalist revolt. Madame wrote that 'The judges found the child very attractive and one said he knew she had a voice which had charmed the other prisoners, and he would grant a pardon on condition she sang her prettiest song. The child wanted to please the court, and she thought the loudest of songs would be the best and the gathering would be delighted by the song she had heard so often. So, summoning all her strength, she sang fortissimo "Long live the King and down with the Republic."'[2]

BETRAYAL

In November 1792, Marat, with the panache of Muhammad Ali predicting the round in which he'd win a fight, announced that the leader of the French Army, General Dumouriez, would defect to the Austrians in March 1793. This was heresy, as Dumouriez was the heroic leader of the forces at Valmy. Now he was in the north, fighting the Belgians, along with the unlikely republican general Louis-Philippe, son of the Duc d'Orléans. Louis-Philippe, like his father, had continued to back the revolution, and the duke had even adopted the new name of Philippe Egalité. Louis-Philippe had led his men to a victory in the town of Jemappes, but now he and Dumouriez were growing to dislike the shape of the republic. Egalité playing cards and kingless draughts were possibly a step too far for a general of the nobility and someone who'd been fifth in line to the throne.

At the start of 1793 a new body was formed called the Committee of Public Safety, possibly the most innocuous-sounding body in all history, as if it would spend its time repairing cracked paving stones and advising people to wear suncream. Its most prominent member was Danton, and its first task was to deal with the noble officers whom it distrusted. So a rule was passed that generals must live at camp with their soldiers. Dumouriez responded with a letter to the Convention refusing to abide by any law it passed.

Danton was sent to persuade him to withdraw the letter. He sat up with the general until 3 a.m., after which he was supposed to return to Paris. But Danton didn't come back for four days, and nobody ever found out where he'd been. Given that he was one of the leaders of a government battling to avoid extermination, this is highly impressive. You couldn't imagine Jack Straw diverting from his prearranged schedule for ten minutes. Offering no explanation could only have been bettered if he'd stood at the Convention and said he'd met an old mate and thought, 'I haven't had a day off for two years so fuck it, I'm going on a bender.'

Wherever he'd been, his powers of persuasion failed to convert Dumouriez. Louis-Philippe wrote in his diary, 'General Dumouriez had decided to make highly secret overtures to the Prince of Coburg. He had communicated to him his plan to proclaim Louis XVI's son King, with the title Louis XVII.'[3] No wonder his army was being hammered: he was secretly supporting his opponent. He wrote another letter professing his wish to crush Robespierre and Marat, and on 5 April he and Louis-Philippe defected to the Austrians. At which point Marat must have thought, 'Bollocks – out by five days.'

ONE MORE SPLIT

Following the betrayal by the head of the army, the Girondins, who had wavered over the King's execution and planned to flee Paris before the battle of Valmy, began to lose every argument in the Convention. Hébert complained that the Girondins allowed into meetings 'bankers and sugar merchants, shaved and perfumed dandies and hosts of other undesirables who came to kill the Mountain'. *This* is what a parliamentary debate is supposed to sound like, with opponents calling each other perfumed dandies, not stuttering, 'The party opposite is unfit to govern,' to which the reply is 'Oooooh!' Then the Girondins were caught opening the Jacobins' mail. That always seals defeat in a row between two people in the same building. From then on, if ever a Jacobin was losing a debate, all they had to do was allow a brief pause and shout, 'Who the hell did you think you were, opening my mail?'

The Jacobins won a vote to introduce a law fixing a maximum price for each product, which made them more popular with the *sans-culottes*. St-Just proposed an elaborate constitution in which every public official would be elected, and to deal with public disorder local communes would elect six old men. In any disturbance, these old men, wearing tricolour scarves and white plumes in their hats, would arbitrate between the fighting groups until they dispersed. Anyone insulting the old men would lose their citizenship. What a fantastic image: a local hood standing in a pub car park with a broken bottle yelling, 'You're FUCKING dead' at a lad from a rival town, when a spectator calls, 'Scarper, here come the six old boys in fancy dress,' who arrive, look round at the debris and say, 'Now what did we come in here for?'

St-Just also proposed a prototype of the British Telecom 'Friends and Family' scheme, suggesting that 'Every man aged twenty-one is obliged to declare in the temple who are his friends. If a man gives up a friend, he is obliged to state the reasons before the people in the temple.' Murderers would be obliged to wear black for the rest of their lives, while 'Men who have lived blamelessly shall wear a white scarf from their sixtieth year' – which might not seem that much of an incentive. More radical was the proposal that all landowners had to till the soil between the ages of twenty-five and fifty, and that a soldier should never be allowed to return to his birthplace if he deserted or lost a weapon in battle. He added the note, 'One must frighten those who govern; one should never frighten the people.'

But before they could implement this sort of scheme, they had to deal with a Convention in which the Girondins still held many key posts. And the Girondins weren't going to give them up without a fight, which is why they aimed big, and arrested Marat.

THE TRIAL OF MARAT

In one sense the historians are right about Marat: he *was* the revolution's nutter. But every movement needs one. I remember that afternoon at the bridge in Prague, when the crowd was down to five hundred, opposite twenty lines of armed riot police, two hundred armoured vehicles, several water-cannon and a selection of snipers. And a Glaswegian with no front teeth stood on a bollard, wafted away a cloud of tear gas and yelled, 'One more push and we'll be through these bastards like FUCKING BUTTER.' Equally impressive was the student I knew who attended a meeting of over one thousand students at his campus, in the week that Freddie Mercury had died. It was announced there would be a one-minute silence in Freddie's name, but halfway through the minute this student yelled, 'The only good Tory is a dead Tory.'

Similarly, Jean Paul Marat sledge-hammered his way through the French Revolution. In one issue of *L'Ami du peuple* he wrote the statement that has been seized on ever since as proof of his crow-like, toad-like insanity, when he suggested that all it would take to cleanse France of all unhappiness was the execution of a selected 273,000 people. The chilling thing about this figure is its precision. If he'd said 100,000 or even a million, it could be written off as an outburst, in the way someone might say, 'To sort out America someone has to execute a million people' while watching an edition of *Jerry Springer*. But to get to 273,000 he must have worked it out carefully, sitting there with a pen and paper, saying, 'Priests, yes, definitely put them down, that's 8,000. Now, bank managers, hmm, tricky – baah, fuck it, put them down, that's another thousand. *Assistant* bank managers, no, they're not so bad, leave them. Maybe just do the worst fifty.'

Yet the more strident he was, the more popular he became. He was elected to the Convention after the September massacres, which he had accepted as a necessary strategy, and once a deputy he ranted in glorious fashion at the slightest provocation. When he was accused by a Girondin of wishing for a dictatorship he went berserk, but just as the room had cooled down he pulled out his pistol and put it to his own head, shouting that if the remark wasn't withdrawn he would blow his head off. Now *that's* how to get people watching Prime Minister's Questions.

One deputy said that after every speech from Marat it was 'necessary to have someone come in and purify the air'. Yet his irreverence, his predictions, his refusal to take part in pageantry and his obsession with keeping in contact with the *sans-culottes* through his newspaper made him, along with Danton, the most popular deputy outside parliament. One night, when he heard that a wealthy Girondin had attacked him in a speech, he went straight round to his house, wearing no shoes or socks, and invaded his dinner party. He stood before the guests, made a vitriolic speech denouncing their host, and left. *That* makes for a great parliamentary character, not Kenneth Clarke wearing slippers.

Camille Desmoulins said of Marat that he was two hundred years ahead of his time. Sure enough, in 1993 Kurt Cobain displayed a similar readiness with a pistol to Marat's exactly two hundred years earlier. When Marat signed a declaration urging the local sections to arm themselves in defence of Paris against the generals and the Girondins, that was the excuse the Girondins needed, and Marat was arrested. By going for their enemy's wild man, the Girondins must have hoped to take the heart out of the Montagnards, but they underestimated Marat's popularity. Thousands of supporters surrounded the courtroom, and made so much noise that Marat had to ask them to keep quiet so the case could be heard. Not only was Marat found not guilty, but as he was released a crowd tied him to a plank, placed flowers around his neck and paraded him through the streets to the Convention. There he was let down to make a speech – presumably untied from the plank – before being carried to his house, whose street had been decorated with torches down its length. The Girondins had proved themselves as distant from the mass of the population as a modern politician would if he said, 'I know what will make us popular – let's arrest David Beckham and that bloke with a burned face from the Falklands War.'

DECREE ABSOLUTE

The gap between most politicians and their electors has to be witnessed at first hand to be believed. Just prior to the 2001 general election in Britain, I was invited back to my old school to contribute to a debate with the three parliamentary candidates for the seat of Sevenoaks, plus myself for the Socialist Alliance. In came the Tory, a military-looking character, followed by a woman who was about thirty but dressed as if she was sixty. She wore a thick white blouse done up firmly to the top, a grey librarian's skirt and brown stockings. She was polite but passionless, slightly aloof, and if you were blind you'd have gone, 'Sniff, sniff – there's New Labour in the room.'

Seventy fifth-formers sat before us, texting each other from their mobiles, gazing at the ceiling and chewing. Then the Tory began: 'Labour is taking more in tax than ever before, and that means YOUR money,' which didn't entirely connect with a room full of fifteen-year-olds. He went on, 'And now it's handing our sovereignty to the bureaucrats of Brussels.' As if his audience would agree and call back, 'Yeah, man, like diss them Labour for mashing up our pound large-style.'

Then it was Labour's turn. She read out a speech she'd written entirely in biro, word-for-word off the page, with all the enthusiasm of Stephen Hawking's voice box. 'We – have – begun – to – succeed – in – many – areas – but – there – is – much – to – be [beat of two, three, four as she turns over the page] – done.' The kids chewed and texted and slouched until they were almost horizontal.

The Liberal was cool, a railwayman with a skew-whiff tie and a throaty south-London accent. I didn't do as well, though when I suggested the idea of raising tax rates on the richest in society, one girl shouted, 'Too right,' and I felt I was making contact. And then she carried on, 'Why should that bitch Jennifer Lopez get seventy thousand pounds an hour just for wiggling her arse?' The result of the vote was Liberal 43, Socialist Alliance 25, Conservative 2, Labour 0.

The Girondins were immeasurably closer to their electorate than modern politicians; they had, after all, helped lead a revolution. But the language, manner and lifestyle of Mme Roland, Louvet and most Girondins made them incapable of relating to people enforcing maximum prices and marching to war. Now it was their turn to declare that the revolution should go no further. Mayor Pétion published a letter to 'all those who own property', warning of the threat from *sans-culottes*: 'Your properties are threatened . . . conflicts are stirred between the haves and have-nots, snap out of your lethargy and chase these venomous creatures back to their lairs.'

On the opposite side, one Enragé, Varlet, appealed for a third insurrection. He arrived at his section and called for them to follow him immediately to the Convention, but unfortunately for him he did this at 11.30 p.m., when almost everyone had gone home.

The first stage of the Jacobins' plan for removing the twenty-two Girondins from their key government positions would be the arrest of M. Roland. The arrest began relatively politely. Roland refused to go, so the guards stayed outside his house waiting for further instructions from the Commune. His wife played for time by rushing to the Convention and demanding the right to speak in defence of her husband. But she ran into the sort of officialdom recognizable to anyone who tried to claim unemployment benefit in the 1980s. She was asked to fill in a form, was left in a room for an hour, then in another room for an hour more, and then told there was no one to hear her complaint for an hour and a half. Perhaps they should have had a waiting room with a sign saying IF YOU WISH TO ASK FOR A

PARDON FOR A FAMILY MEMBER FACING IMMINENT EXECUTION, TEAR OFF A TICKET FROM THE MACHINE AND WAIT FOR YOUR NUMBER TO BE CALLED.

Meanwhile M. Roland had climbed through to his landlord's part of the house, and hid there. At night the Council of the Commune still hadn't decided how to proceed, and M. Roland was able to escape. He fled from Paris and spent the next three weeks living in the Montmorency Forest.

The next day, 2 June, the Montagnards called an insurrection to surround the Convention and expel the twenty-two leading Girondins. Tens of thousands poured into the Convention to support this demand, and stayed even when the President of the Convention asked them to leave, which was as hopeless as lecturing those schoolkids about the European single currency. Not only did they not leave, but a *sans-culotte* called Hanriot made a speech unlikely ever to be paralleled inside a parliament building. It went, 'Tell your fucking President that he and his Assembly can go and fuck themselves, and if within the hour the twenty-two are not delivered, we will blow them all up.' If someone *did* say this in the British Parliament you'd expect it to be followed by, 'Order, order, the honourable gentleman is bringing the house into disrepute by suggesting it fucks itself.' The twenty-two were left with no choice and fled.

If this appears outrageously undemocratic, it must be remembered there was a real risk that the new nation would be overthrown by foreign armies and internal revolt, and this was the background to every decision taken.

One other incident that took place within the Convention that day was that Deputy Boissy d'Anglas had his scarf ruined, which he made a complaint about. There's a man who knew how to keep things in perspective. He must have got home that night and, when his wife asked if anything much had happened, answered, 'Yes it bloody did: look at that, torn to shreds!'

THE CONSTITUTION OF '93

The new Convention began by creating one of history's most radical documents, the 'Constitution of '93'. Land belonging to nobles who had fled was divided into small plots and sold to peasants, who had ten years to pay for it. All feudal dues were abolished, and municipal records burned so that they could never return. Every man between eighteen and forty would be armed for the defence of the Republic. A new Declaration of Rights was agreed, which declared, 'Society owes a living to the unfortunate among its citizens, either by finding them work or guaranteeing a means of subsistence.' It added, 'Education is a necessity for all,' and as far as I know Robespierre was not then caught sending his own kids to a private school in Hammersmith. Corporal punishment was declared illegal, and you almost wish the *Daily Mail* had been around then, as it would have been so confused about which issue to be most apoplectic about it would have spontaneously combusted in the newsagents.

More powers passed from the Convention to the Committee of Public Safety, which was now to be run by Robespierre, with his closest allies St-Just and the disabled Couthon, who travelled around in a remarkable early wooden wheelchair. All those who had emigrated were banished for ever and their land confiscated by the Republic. The law of maximum prices was enforced in every area, to ensure the enthusiastic support of *sans-culottes*. To prevent speculation, the Stock Exchange was closed.

The new constitution declared that 'Salvation depends on the people,' as well as 'Men of all nations are brothers and different people must help each other, as if they were citizens of the same state.' But the most remarkable clause of the constitution concerned the extension of democracy. This stated that every revolutionary measure would first be submitted to the forty-eight sections of the Paris Commune. Magistrates would be re-elected, every law would be voted on annually, and no politician could stay in office for more

Couthon's wheelchair.

than a year without having to stand for re-election. Voting was extended to every household, so 60 per cent of men had the vote.

Compare this to the changes brought about by New Labour, which prides itself on being constitutionally radical. Presented with this 200-year-old document, they would have said, 'It certainly works as a mission statement but we have to be realistic. So instead of abolishing hereditary posts, we propose to legislate for a phased withdrawal over several centuries. And the approach we've formulated on tithes is more radical than abolishing them, which is to keep them – but assure everyone we're operating an ethical-tithes policy.'

The number of Jacobin clubs grew to over one thousand, with an average of five hundred members in each. Children's sweets were wrapped in paper that had *The Rights of Man* printed on the side. If they'd been even more imaginative, they could have printed sets of Mountaineer-deputy cards you bought one at a time, so kids ran around playgrounds calling, 'Has anyone got a Danton I can swap for a St-Just?'

The entire Republic was dedicated to preserving the nation. Robespierre announced, 'Young men will go to war, married men manufacture arms and transport supplies, women make tents and uniforms, children turn rags into bandages, and old people repair to the public squares, stimulate the courage of the warriors and preach the hatred of kings.' It seems the old people came out best there. They must have been delighted to be told their role was to sit on park benches moaning that the young people weren't working hard enough and that foreigners are a bunch of bastards.

Prospects weren't so bright for the Girondins. Several followed Roland's example and escaped, including the man his wife had fallen in love with, Buzot. Buzot fled to Caen with Pétion, who must have felt that things had gone downhill since getting the come-on from the King's niece. But the others were arrested, including Mme Roland, who was locked in the Conciergerie to await trial. On arriving, prisoners were asked to hand over their belongings to an official, in much the same way as visitors to a modern police cell place their keys, inhalers and travelcards into one of those depressing little polythene bags. The Conciergerie was divided into two areas, one for prisoners who could afford to pay for their own room and one for the rest. Famous prisoners were granted a desk, books and writing equipment, which must have led to a certain amount of ego-based friction, as minor-celebrity prisoners yelled that they were as famous as him in the star cell, who hasn't done anything that's got a good review since 1784.

Mme Roland's complaint about the lack of facilities in her cell was met with the fairly damning retort that prisoners' allowances used to be five *livres*, but had been reduced to two *livres* a day by the last minister in charge of the place, who was her husband.

PARIS IN SPRINGTIME

Few of the films made about the French Revolution have been Hollywood blockbusters aiming at a mass market. *La Nuit de Varennes* featured Harvey Keitel, but even then his usual fans were probably disappointed, as at no point does he say, 'Danton, where the fuck you been for four days? Huh? HUH?'

But maybe someone ought to try one of those romantic feelgood movies that follow a group of mates who one by one get hitched to the woman of their dreams. There's Marat, with the odds stacked against him due to his resemblance to a series of exotic creatures, who none the less finds love and a hippy-ish marriage to Simonne, a Yoko Ono for her times. (Maybe they should have made a record together called 'Give Mass Execution a Chance'.) Marat's personal life prior to Simonne is difficult to decipher as he was so detested in certain circles he was subject of the wildest rumour. Mme Roland accused him of cavorting with a 'languishing sensualist in a luxury apartment', which hardly seems his style. But there is little question that he was devoted to Simonne. Defending his outbursts, she said they took place 'because his sensitive soul gave vent to just anathemas against public blood suckers and against the oppressors of the people'. God knows what a row between the pair of them must have been like. No simple 'Shut up!' 'Shut up yourself!' It was more likely to have been 'Your vile presence can be sanctified only with the necessary extraction of sufficient blood to appease the just and overdue demands of those who have suffered mercilessly at your decrepit hands.' 'All right then, *I'll* do the washing-up.'

Camille Desmoulins would provide the stable family figure, the one all decent types would be expected to aspire to. The exception to this would be that his newspaper carried such scurrilous attacks against the Royal Family that one royalist submitted to a magistrate that 'Camille should be declared insane . . . his ranting can only be the outcome of a feverish brain.' Despite this, he fell in love with Lucile Duplessis, whom he'd known since she was twelve. He declared his love for her when she was seventeen, but at that time she wrote in her diary, 'I'm not in love. But when shall I be? It's as if I'm made of marble.' Which is a wonderfully teenage-girl diary entry, and no doubt she felt it was immensely profound, the way a modern teenager does when they write something like 'My love for you is like a tumble-drier. It goes round and round.'

Lucile did eventually return his feelings, and they were married in December 1790 in the French Revolution's celeb wedding. His old schoolmate Robespierre was best man, and the witnesses were Brissot and Pétion, the Mayor of Paris. If *OK!* magazine had existed they'd have paid half a million for the photos. The couple moved into a flat close to Danton, but would still write each other letters, such as the one from Desmoulins that ended, 'Adieu, my good angel, my Lolotte, mother of the little lizard.'

They had a baby boy, Horace, and were the first parents to invoke the new law that parents had no obligation to impose a religion on their children, and they refused to have him christened.

For Desmoulins' friend and colleague Danton, domestic life was more turbulent. One deputy described Danton's typical evening as 'occupied with his pleasures ... always sitting down at table, surrounded by girls'. And he appears to have enchanted a trio of admirers: Mme de Genlis, Agnès de Buffon and Grace Elliot. The nature of his relationships is hard to determine, again because of the vitriol poured on him by so many historians. In one of the most respected biographies, Robert Christophe informs us that Grace Elliot may not have been his mistress because 'she had no desire to submit her satin-smooth skin to the embraces of this hairy and energetic monster'. What else – did his breath smell? Did he leave cigarette stubs in the bath, pick his toenails in the living room? He was a leader of the revolution, so he *must* have. And no maiden blessed with satin-smooth skin would fall for that, which is why he only seduced scaly women like Mme de Genlis and Agnès de

Buffon. Somehow this cobblers passes for history, when the authors ought to be getting rejection slips for being too crass from the *Sunday People*.

So it may be the image has been exaggerated, but we do know that Danton's wife Gabrielle bore four children, of whom the first died almost immediately. His letters to Gabrielle indicate an affectionate nature that contradicts his image. For example, he wrote to her, 'Give Antoine [a son] lots of kisses from me and tell him Daddy will try not to be away too long.' Once, en route to a diplomatic mission in Belgium, he insisted the coach took a detour via Arcis, delaying his meetings by a day so he could see his children. But shortly after the birth of the fourth child, when Danton was again away, a message was delivered to him that Gabrielle had died. The coachman returning him home reported 'incessant sobbing'. Desmoulins blamed the death on the attacks made on Danton by the Girondins, writing in his journal, 'His wife has received her mortal stroke from reading in the papers the invention that Danton pointed out the victims that should be assassinated in September. Those who know how much this woman loved Danton can form an idea of her sufferings.'

At the funeral, Danton ordered that the coffin was opened so he could take a last look at Gabrielle, at which point he hugged the dead body until he had to be prised away. His grief was, like all his emotions and actions, boundless. Robespierre wrote to him, 'If the certainty of having a tender and devoted friend could bring you any consolation, I offer that to you. From this time on I am one with you. I love you more than ever and will love you until death.' Oh, the French. If they'd both been English, they could have felt the same amount of affection and the letter would have been 'Right, well, cheers then, mate. Any time you fancy a drink, give us a call.'

After all this, Danton's colleagues were surprised when six months later he announced he was marrying Gabrielle's young friend, Louise Gely, who was fifteen. The unanswered question is how she approached this with her parents. Presumably she did it in three stages, each of which must have caused a major organ failure – (a) I'm getting married; (b) he's twice my age; (c) he's the revolutionary Minister for Justice. Danton continued to revel in shocking his colleagues, especially Robespierre. Robespierre was lecturing on the value of virtue, describing 'that magic virtue responsible for so many marvels in Greece and Rome; virtue is nothing other than the love of one's country and its laws', when Danton yelled, 'I'll tell you what virtue is – it's what I do every night to my wife.' If Robespierre ever did give way to sexual passion, you could imagine his post-coital chatter amounting to 'Yes, well, that was certainly fascinating, and one minute less than I'd allowed for, which is handy.'

He did however seem to establish a rapport with Elisabeth, one of the daughters in the Duplay household. He remarked that he'd implored her to believe in God by saying, 'You are still very young, Elisabeth; remember that it is the only consolation on earth.' Which might not sound much but in Robespierre's world was probably a direct come-on.

But Elisabeth's destiny lay elsewhere. One afternoon she came to the Convention with Robespierre's sister Charlotte, where she met Philippe Le Bas, a Jacobin deputy. She gave him an orange and they were instantly attracted to each other. Occasionally they met again at the Convention but were afraid of making their affections public, probably because it would have been like a sixth form, all the deputies jeering at the end of the day's business, 'Woo hoo, Le Bas, here she is. Has she got any fruit for you today?'

But suddenly Le Bas went missing. Elisabeth, not knowing where he lived, could only go each day to the Convention, throughout the period of the increasingly bitter split between the Mountaineers and Girondins, and as mayhem exploded with history in the balance, she would look forlornly round the hall for her Philippe. After two months he returned, took her for a walk in the gardens around the palace that was invaded a year earlier, and asked her to marry him. So, through the turmoil of revolution, Marat, Danton, Desmoulins and Le Bas all found true love, giving the film a delightful happy ending.

Except that all four would be dead within a year.

11

Year II

I fought the law

FRIEND OF THE PEOPLE

Amongst the disenchanted people of Caen was a young woman, Charlotte Corday, who like Robespierre had been an avid reader of Rousseau. However she supported the Girondins and despised the Montagnards. Watching the civil war flare around her home town, she coolly took the decision to travel to Paris and murder Marat. She planned to kill him in the Convention, but on arriving in Paris was dismayed to find he was ill. Marat suffered from psoriasis, which became progressively worse during his many months hiding in damp basements. By July 1793 it was so bad that the only relief he could find was to sit in a cool bath, which was where he spent much of his day, completing his work as one of the leaders of the government.

Corday booked into a hotel and bought a knife at a nearby market. A coachman told her where Marat lived, and she went round on the pretext of having information for him about the actions of counter-revolutionaries in Caen. At this point, we are informed by our old friend *Paris in the Terror*, his flat reeked of 'bad

Charlotte Corday

cooking, rancid grease and human sweat'. Of course it did. What else would it smell like, other than toad-like Maratty things? How the hell does anyone know what his flat smelled like, right down to the 'bad cooking'? How bad was this cooking? Was it too fatty, was the fish underdone, could the bolognese have done with a pinch of basil? This is the meaningless bias that passes for history. Imagine if a left-wing writer wrote a book claiming, 'Marat's house smelled lovely. There were always fresh flowers, and a pleasant aroma of nutmeg.'

What we do know is that Charlotte Corday was turned away from Marat's house by Simonne Evrard, but came back later to insist she had urgent news from Caen. Simonne was about to send her away again, but Marat heard her and called to send her up. It's worth stopping a moment to digest this. Here we have someone almost universally condemned by historians as an unspeakable tyrant, a bloodthirsty enemy of democracy, yet he's not only been elected, he's been paraded through the streets by thousands following his acquittal; *and*, despite being one of the leading figures of a country in a battle for survival, he calls out that a complete stranger should be allowed to visit him while he's in the bath. I can't know for certain, but I doubt that if you knocked at 10 Downing Street Tony would shout, 'Who is it, darling?' And when the answer came back, 'Someone with news from Halifax,' he'd say, 'I'm in the bath but send them up anyway.'

Once in the bathroom, they discussed the situation in Caen for around fifteen minutes. I'm aware this is a puerile thought in the circumstances, but it's amazing that no historian appears to have pondered the fine detail of this situation. A minister was discussing politics with a stranger while in his bath. Could she see his knob, or was it tastefully hidden by soapsuds, as if he was in a bubble-bath advert? Whichever was the case, she unveiled her knife and rammed it into his chest. Marat screamed; Simonne ran in, as did Laurent Bas,

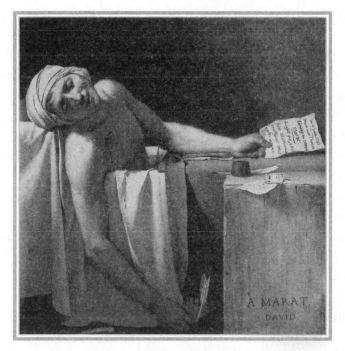

The Death of Marat

who was preparing an edition of *L'Ami du peuple*. Corday made no attempt to escape, but Laurent Bas detained her anyway, according to his statement by 'holding on to her breasts'.[1]

Charlotte Corday's breasts were also involved in the next part of the story, her examination by a deputy. In his statement he wrote that her hands were tied together while an interrogator snatched at a paper she was holding. 'She flung her shoulders back with such force, as if wishing to shield her breast with her bodice, that the pins and ribbons that held it together broke loose in such a way as to expose her bosom completely. She was acutely embarrassed.'[2] And she was trying to keep such a low profile that day. Maybe she wouldn't have minded, but felt this was gratuitous and not integral to the plot.

She proudly pleaded guilty, claiming that the death of this man would save the lives of thousands. Throughout her demeanour was what we might recognize from a suicide bomber: having made the mental leap to carry out the act, there was no hint of wavering, not a flicker of doubt to mar her ruthless efficiency. Within four days she was guillotined, but even in the act of losing her head she was the root of dissent within republican ranks. One of the executioner's assistants, Legros, held the head up for the crowd, then slapped it. This was considered a disgraceful breach of guillotine etiquette, and Legros was imprisoned for his outburst.

Marat, on the other hand, was embalmed, his skin disease cosmetically disguised, and laid out for thousands to mourn. Dozens of poems and songs were written in deference to him; cannon shots were fired; a hundred girls, their heads crowned with oak leaves, surrounded a chariot symbolizing purity to take Marat to his burial. Packed memorials took place all over France. Montmartre was renamed Mont-Marat. A square was named Place de l'Ami du Peuple. Thirty-seven towns across France renamed themselves Marat, which must have caused a lot of people to end up in the wrong place, and his heart was hung from the vaults of the Cordeliers Club. Here's another reason why a revolution such as this couldn't happen in

England. The biggest send-off anyone on the British left could hope for would involve a couple of choruses of the 'Red Flag' and some roses, and everyone would agree that 'Instead of hanging his heart, a nice photo of him speaking at an anti-war demo in Coventry would look best.' So condemn Marat if you like – and you certainly wouldn't trust anyone who glibly supported all his pronouncements without a great deal of anguish – but your condemnation has to be accompanied by an explanation for the extraordinary popularity of someone whose acclaim was built solely on what he wrote in his newspaper.

The greatest artist of the day, Jacques Louis David, was commissioned to paint a commemorative picture, which he named 'The Death of Marat', showing him martyred in his bath. But now, although the area that includes rue Danton and rue Cordeliers has many plaques noting the landmarks of the French Revolution, in the road where Marat lived and died, the rue de l'Ecole de Médécine, there are plaques commemorating matters to do with medicine but Marat is utterly forgotten, like an embarrassing relative whose photos are taken down after they've been arrested for an unsavoury incident in a public toilet.

In his will he left twenty-five *sous*, barely enough for two bags of sugar at the knockdown *sans-culotte* price.

WHERE IS DE SADE?

Left languishing in jail some time back in our story was the Marquis de Sade. While in the Bastille he'd become bigger and bigger until, according to his own letters, he was 'so fat I could hardly move'. He was also the victim of the most appalling bad luck. When he was eventually moved out of the Bastille for yelling at the passers-by, he wrote to his wife asking if she would pop into the prison office and collect the writings he'd penned while in jail. His wife agreed, but was in no rush. After all, it's not as if the Bastille was going anywhere, was it? So she made her way down there the following week, on the morning of 14 July 1789. No one knows whether, amidst the smoke and gunfire, one woman was yelling, 'Excuse me, could I just pick up my husband's poems?' And so somewhere in the Bastille as it became a battlefield, poor de Sade's work was lost in the rubble. There was very little chance that through the cannonfire someone would spot it and say, 'Oh hang on, we'd better hand this in.' The loss was the greatest disaster of his life, he said, causing 'tears of blood'.

The constitutional monarchy had agreed to free all prisoners jailed by a *lettre de cachet*, and de Sade was released. Launched into revolutionary Paris, this aristocrat felt liberated, and he became an active citizen in his Paris section. This required abandoning his noble status, so he became Louis Sade, working as a guard against traitors and as official recorder for the section. After the second revolution he was elected commissar for the cavalry. Then came a moment of pure Hollywood, when as president of his section he was asked to sign the death warrant for his hated in-laws, who had been directly responsible for his arrest, and whom he blamed for his years in the Bastille. A Hollywood director would make a huge slow-motion climax of the scene, involving endless shots of face, pen and death warrant. The reality may have been more mundane, and Louis Sade announced he was resigning as president since he couldn't possibly sanction their deaths. An argument ensued, at the end of which they were placed on a list of citizens to be spared.

Such was his revolutionary credibility that when Marat was murdered Sade was asked to deliver the oration at the funeral. But surely the Jacobins must have been a little worried that he might revert to his old ways and announce at the memorial, 'Anyway, I don't suppose there's anyone here who'd like to stab *me* in the bath and then fart in my face, is there? I've got plenty of aniseed.'

The Terror

It takes some imagination to comprehend the tension within Paris in the summer of 1793. Maybe if you imagine that al Qaeda is in control of France and Holland, preparing to set sail for an invasion of Britain, with Wiltshire, Norfolk and Hull already under Islamic law; then the British Home Secretary is murdered in his bath by a suicide bomber, and a jihad declares the aim is to destroy 'every last defender of London'.

As well as the anxiety caused by foreign armies, the other fear crackling through France and especially Paris was that of famine, as provincial farmers hoarded grain to sell it on the black market at a higher price. Paris was so short of food that the Luxembourg Park was ploughed up for crops. The response from the *sans-culottes* of the Commune was to demand a law threatening the guillotine for hoarders, and for anyone convicted of plotting against the revolution. The Commune issued a statement to the Montagnards: 'Have you outlawed speculation? No. Have you imposed the death sentence for hoarders? No. You have not done everything in your power to ensure the happiness of the people. The *sans-culottes* are ready with their pikes to enforce your decrees.' Armed demonstrations and riots backed up this text, and the Convention, partly in fear that the *sans-culottes* would carry out this act themselves, passed a law as requested, officially called the 'Law of Suspects', also known as the Terror. This is one of the many points during the revolution at which it's clear no one had quite mastered the art of political spin. Couldn't they have thought of a slightly more PR-friendly name than 'the Terror'? A modern government would have slipped it in as 'Section 24 of the Grain Redistribution Act (pike clause)' or something.

Farmers weren't so keen on the idea, complaining they were being forced to grow food at a loss. To modern British ears, this sounds somewhat familiar. Especially if you heard, as I did, a farmer on *Farming Today* complaining that the latest statistics on the numbers dying from CJD caught from beef were disastrous because 'this will continue to reduce the price of cattle'. I wondered whether they have a similar perspective on every news event. So if there was a plane crash, *Farmers Weekly* would report, 'Fortunately ten of the dead were vegetarians, so the impact on beef sales will not be as great as was originally feared.'

The Terror caused farmers more problems than any modern crisis, as the greatest change it brought about was the formation of a *sans-culotte* army, ready with pikes as promised. The Terror allowed this army to send a regiment to any farmer suspected of hoarding grain and force him to hand it over. It could use similar tactics to enforce the law of the maximum price, and requisition bread, meat, fish and wood for the bakers' ovens and arms manufacturers' furnaces. Robespierre boasted that 'You see how the rich have been stripped of their wealth to feed and clothe the poor.'

Under the Terror, a 'Revolutionary Tribunal' was formed, with the power to guillotine suspects convicted of hoarding or of aiding the foreign armies. It also backed the surreal law that aristocrats weren't allowed to live by the coast. Presumably this was to stop them escaping to join a foreign army, though it would have been interesting to see what the *Sun* would say if a couple of thousand aristocrats were plotting to sneak on to a cross-Channel ferry from a camp in Sangatte.

Mostly, the Terror was a device to help win the war. In Normandy, where the Republic was in full control of the area, no one was guillotined. In Lyon, which was torn apart by civil war, the Convention decreed that 'only the houses of the poor and the homes of good patriots shall be left standing'.[3] Which must have caused havoc with the property prices, estate agents advertising their most exquisite properties as 'poky little hovel, needs tons of work, miles from the shops'.

The first man to be guillotined under the Terror was called des Maulans, and the judge and jury burst into tears as the sentence was passed. But, as hit-men say, it got easier after the first one, and after a month there had been sixty-six victims. There were usually two or three executions per day, carried out in the Place de la Révolution, with refreshments available. Wouldn't that bring home to you the mundanity of life, to be mounting the scaffold and hear in the distance 'Do you want onions with that?'?

The launch of the Terror was presented by the Convention as part of the start of an entirely new era, so utterly new that it required a new calendar, with Year I deemed to have begun on the day the Republic was founded, 22 September 1792. On the site of the now-demolished Bastille, a statue to Nature was built, a woman with water spouting from her breasts. It was opened with each deputy of the Convention taking turns to drink a bowl of water that had spurted from the nipples. A statue of Liberty was erected next to the guillotine, and 3,000 birds let loose. This may all seem a tad over the top, even camp, but they *were* launching a new era in human society. In 2003 a performance like that would be put on to mark the launch of a new television production company. If a Terror and a new calendar were begun now the celebration would be at the Dorchester, with waiters in Roman togas wandering around with canapés while Lesley Joseph and the skinny hairdresser from *Coronation Street* posed for the paparazzi and three muscular blokes in thongs sent from a modelling agency were guillotined live while Martine McCutcheon mimed to her latest single.

The new era was deemed to be based above all on reason, as opposed to the mystical values of divinely ordained kings. So the new months were named for their scientific attributes. For example there was *frimaire*, meaning the month of frost; *thermidor* meant the month of heat; and *brumaire* was the month of mist. Again, this could only happen in French. In Britain we'd end up with months called 'Tut, the nights are drawing in' and 'Well at least it's keeping mild'. In any case it's doubtful whether such a change could ever take place in Britain, when you consider that the only time the calendar was altered, when it jumped ten days to the Gregorian system, there were demonstrations against the disappearance of these dates. It must have caused havoc with the chanting:

'What do we want?'

'Our ten days back!'

'When do we want them?'

'Ah, now there's a metaphysical conundrum . . .'

Each month was thirty days long, and five extra days were put by for festivals. A month consisted of three weeks of ten days, of which the tenth, the *decadi*, was the day of rest. The old system of weights and measures was replaced by the metric system. Most ambitious of all, plans were begun for moving to a metric time system, and a few decimal watches were made.

Theatres were required to show three times per week 'the tragedies of Brutus, William Tell and other plays which recall the glorious events of the Revolution'.[4] Which sounds a bit grim, like the plays put on by left-wing theatre groups in the '70s. A typical play would have begun:

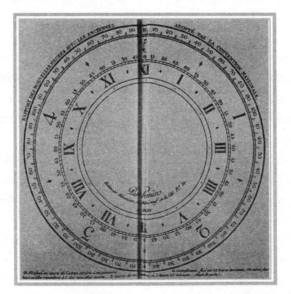

**Conversion chart from the old clock to the revolutionary
decimal clock. It would be worth the inconvenience just
to annoy Frederick Forsyth and Ann Widdecombe.**

[*Peasant carrying pitchfork approaches noble with a cushion up his jumper to make him look fat*]

PEASANT: It's a nice day today, isn't it?

NOBLE: For me it's always a nice day. For while we are just four per cent of the population, we own ninety-six per cent of non-clerical land. But tell me, I hear you have fallen in love. Is this true?

PEASANT: Indeed it is. I have fallen in love with liberty, for as long as the people yearn to be free we shall be richer than you, the Duke of Brunswick and all tyrants.

The Louvre, which had been a royal palace, became a museum. Civic banquets were encouraged in every district, in which the sparse amount of food would be shared out equally and diners had the pleasure of a succession of speeches to listen to during their meal. At one of these banquets, in the Section du Bonconseil in Paris, dinner had just been served when someone noticed the plates were all decorated with a feudal emblem. The publican was called and asked to replace the plates, but refused, arguing that if everyone was that sensitive they could eat off the table. So the diners did exactly that, but not before ceremonially smashing 180 plates, which they refused to pay for.

Another culinary consequence of the revolution came about when a *patissier*, who was suffering from the decline in sales of the formerly popular 'cake of kings', sparked a trend by renaming the same cake *'gâteau Marat'*. On the other hand, an American, Citizeness Mace, found herself in court for serving a cheese shaped like a white heart, which was described as a counter-revolutionary pudding. The *Daily Telegraph* should take note: *that* is political correctness gone mad.

The farmers of revolutionary France were less cynical, and had benefited from the abolition of feudal dues, but their enthusiasm for having their produce removed at gunpoint was limited. As well as food and wood, the *sans-culotte* armies raided the wealthier houses for clothing to be sent to the regular army, as if they were the military wing of a charity shop. This is why the Terror was often seen as the physical side of the 'economic radicalism' of Year II. And to be fair, this *was* economic radicalism, far more than the mundane policies of modern governments that claim economic radicalism. Certainly, more people would watch the discussion programmes after the Budget if the interviewer was saying, 'So, the main points of Gordon Brown's speech appear to be no change in the basic rate of tax, a two-billion-pound boost over three years for the public sector, and an army to be sent to the boards of multinationals to threaten execution if they continue to avoid tax through bureaucratic loopholes. Roy Hattersley, what do you make of all that?'

LOSING THEIR RELIGION

There's a contradiction at the heart of any religion, which I once saw graphically illustrated in a Pentecostal church I attended for the purposes of writing an article. Around eight hundred people leaped up to sing the opening number, which was clearly a favourite, as everyone cheered after the opening bar, the way a Barry Manilow audience would for 'Mandy'. The words came up on a screen, and the lyrics to this clappy sing-along began

> 'The Lord Reigns over us
> He burns all his enemies
> And the hills melt like wax
> La la la la la.'

The problem for religion is that, however strident and apocalyptic the spiritual message, in the end it has to conform to the reality of the material world. In a sixteenth-century village infested with the constant threat of plagues, war and bandits, it would seem perfectly in keeping with the environment that God should kill his enemies and melt the hills. But in modern Britain it seems a little extreme, so the words are sung but no one really means them, because when you really mean something you don't accompany it with a tambourine.

This process makes religion the most flexible of all ideologies. The Catholic Church that thought the idea of God itself was undermined by the discovery of Jupiter's moons now lives happily alongside modern physics and astronomy, having abandoned almost every notion that was once fundamental. The Anglican Church, having insisted that Darwin's theory of evolution was incompatible with Christianity, now readily accepts that God probably didn't make the universe in six days. In fact almost every priest, vicar and rabbi would agree that the Bible on which their whole system is based is not to be taken literally at all. It's as if a defendant charged with murder had their alibi disproved and stood up in court to exclaim, 'When I said I was at the cinema at seven-thirty, I didn't mean that literally! It was just a sort of metaphor.'

So a person's religion tells you very little about their beliefs. You can be a militarist Jew or a pacifist Jew, a Thatcherite Christian or a socialist Christian. Everyone will interpret their religion in a way that supports their ideas. To put this another way, religion isn't usually the problem. The conflict between Catholics and Protestants in Northern Ireland grew out of the issue of civil rights, not religion. When Catholic and Protestant kids get in a fight, the Catholics aren't thinking, 'We're going to keep chucking this rubble until you learn that that little wafer *is* the body of Christ.'

Similarly, I don't dislike the music of Cliff Richard for being religious, because so is the music of Bob Marley and Aretha Franklin. The problem with Cliff's music is he's sanctimonious, *Stars on Sunday Vicar of Dibley* teacake-parish-council Neighbourhood Watch religious. This is a mean-spirited, soulless religion, of which the highlight is the village Harvest Festival, as if a God that drowned almost the entire population can be palmed off with a tin of apricots.

The way in which a religion is interpreted reflects the lives of its followers. And in revolutionary France, the material world had changed. The Catholic Church was now despised for having been the main landowner until the revolution, and because most leading priests were refusing to sign an oath to the new constitution. Vast numbers of people were no longer content to accept the lowly place they'd been appointed to by the Church. So in place of Catholicism, a new religion emerged in the cities, which began as a worship of reason. Notre Dame was renamed the Temple of Reason. There was a new, *sans-culotte* version of the Lord's Prayer, which read:

> Our father who are in heaven, from whence you protect in such an admirable manner the French Republic and the Sans Culottes, your most ardent defenders.
> Give us today the daily bread which we eat despite the vain efforts of Pitt, Coburg and all the tyrants who unite to keep us hungry.
> Forgive us the faults which we have committed in supporting for so long the Tyrants from which we have purged France, as we forgive the Enslaved Nations, when they imitate us.
> Do not suffer them any longer to endure the fetters which restrain them and from which they are strenuously seeking to free themselves.
> But may they deliver themselves, as we have done, from Nobles, Priests and Kings. So be it.[5]

Who knows, maybe if there is a God he appreciated a bit of innovation, as he must be sick of the turgid version recited to him a billion times a week for thousands of years. It also became a common practice at funerals to send the deceased to 'eternal sleep'.

The problem for many of the leading practitioners of the new religion was that they couldn't accept why some people were still following the old religion, and thought they could legislate against it. So the newly formed *sans-culotte* army began a campaign for de-Christianization in the countryside. But in rural areas, life was still conditioned by the forces of nature as much as by any deliverance from tyranny; also, the clergy played a more important role in the community than they did in the cities. And the process of radicalization hadn't gone as far as in Paris, certainly not so far as to rewrite the Lord's Prayer. Most peasants were horrified by the new calendar, which had abolished the Sunday. This may seem confusing to anyone brought up in 1970s Britain, in which a Sunday creates images of deserted high streets, early pub-closing and *Sing Something Simple*, but even in modern Britain every attempt to modify a Sunday meets with a national furore until everyone is assured the special status of the day will be preserved. The revolutionary army made no such concessions, except to say that the rural communities wouldn't be needing their churches anyway as they were seizing all church bells and silver to melt down for ammunition.

When this army met resistance to its efforts at de-Christianization, it was shocked, like any new convert to a cause who can't comprehend why others can't see what looks so painfully clear. One pamphlet, written by a supporter of Hébert and distributed to villages, referred to priests as 'useless buggers who have not ceased deceiving husbands, seducing their wives and producing bastards'. As well as seizing metal, the armies destroyed crucifixes and staged ceremonies at the altar. One commissar, Vauquoy, insisted a whole village come to witness him in a ransacked church, drinking wine at the pulpit, where he announced, 'If there is a God, let him strike me down here and now, in front of you all.'

A commissar called Picot-Belloc entered a packed church with his regiment and marched to the pulpit, where he gave an instant sermon to the effect that there was no God, no Devil, no heaven or hell, that Jesus Christ had the pox and his mother was a whore, and that to liberate themselves the congregation must exterminate their priests and burn their saints. Which would make for a *Songs of Praise* worth watching.

Other regiments declared their aim as instilling the cult of reason into the rural people. One commissar announced he'd achieved this when 'I ordered all the priests to marry . . . some twenty promised to marry within two months, and I have authority to find wives for them.' They should have been thankful there was no television at the time, or this would have become a Channel 4 reality show, on once a year with every priest's move recorded as he undertook the challenge of getting married in two months or facing a line of *sans-culottes* with pitchforks.

Yet none of this gentle persuasion could prise the peasantry away from their allegiance to the Church. The attempt to destroy faith by destroying the Church was a disaster. In rural eighteenth-century France, superstition was the only force by which the peasants could give themselves any feeling of control. They were like football supporters who convince themselves their green socks are lucky to compensate for the truth that they have no influence on their team whatsoever. In addition to orthodox religion, most villages believed in local sorcerers, who could spread terror by predicting it. In a village in Vaucluse, the baker announced that every event in the revolution had been predicted by Nostradamus. At least he had the excuse of being a baker in the 1790s, unlike these twats today who shout, 'It's true, he said a man in the east with a beard would plot an evil act from a cave on the two giants of the West but you'd be all right if you were lower than the ninety-fourth floor' just because someone slapped it on the Internet.

The *sans-culotte* army was fairly successful in its economic aims. It instilled terror into anyone hoarding food or threatening to profiteer by selling it above the legal maximum price. And who can say, when they've been stitched up by emergency plumbers or those crooks who demand two hundred quid to tow your broken-down car into a garage, that they wouldn't have appreciated a visit from an army of the Terror to enforce a maximum price?

LIFE IN THE ARMY

As well as the *sans-culotte* army, during the Terror the regular army became unrecognizable from the royal army that had existed before. Thousands of volunteers marched alongside it, refusing pay and providing their own arms. Officers could be dismissed at any time by a soldiers' vote, and women were admitted, beating the British and American forces by around two hundred years.

Units comprised between fourteen and sixteen citizens, as this was deemed to create the greatest sense of camaraderie between soldiers. But discipline was harsher than it had been. One gunner wrote how six drummer-boys who'd been stuck for a week in their bivouac ran off to a nearby village, broke into a house and stole an old woman's jewellery; when they returned to the camp, they were spotted by a commander, who ordered the eldest two to be shot. The gunner wrote, 'The elder of the two died bravely enough, but the younger boy kept calling for his mother to come to his help. The tragic scene brought tears to the eyes of all the soldiers.'[6]

Political clubs were formed within battalions, and thousands of free newspapers were provided as speakers toured the front, attempting to inspire the soldiers. The most popular were Danton and St-Just. This is one of those points at which it's worth pausing to grasp how far this revolution had travelled. Five years earlier, it was almost impossible for anyone to attain status beyond their birth right. Now the entire army was inspired by a 25-year-old who'd been in gaol for burglaring his mum. Political puppet shows toured the camps. One performance, at Dunkerque, was described as 'puppets representing the kings and emperors being dragged in chains on an open cart, along the sides of which was inscribed the caption "crowned counterfeiters".'[7]

In August 1793 a conscription law was passed, and the defence of the Republic became the job of every citizen. One deputy announced, 'Let the job of every cartwright, joiner and wood-worker be to make rifle-butts, gun-carriages, powder-chests and wagons. Let locksmiths, blacksmiths, toolworkers and ironworkers be employed solely in the manufacture of guns.' Which makes you realize how vulnerable modern Britain could be in similar circumstances. Our leadership speech would be 'Let the coffee-shop workers produce tall lattes for the army, let the accountants work out how to carry part of the army's expenses into the following tax year, and let lap-dancers distract the enemy while production companies propose a docu-soap about the man who does the puppet show.'

The revolutionary nature of the army stunned the opposition. The Austrian Army, for example, couldn't understand why, as they marched through provincial areas, they were fired upon by most of the local inhabitants. The Austrians issued a notice to the people of Luxembourg declaring the French Army was 'duping you by the illusion of liberty and equality'. In an ironic touch they added, 'Up to now, we have always respected the peaceful dwellings of the inhabitants of a country which we are seeking to deliver from hateful slavery.' And they ended by announcing that, after any further attack from locals on their positions, 'we shall reply by burning ten villages in your country, and every place from which we are fired on . . . will be reduced to ashes'.

How many were won over to the royalist cause by this careful diplomacy isn't recorded. It reminds me of the newspaper columnist who, during the American bombing of Serbia, said she talked to a group of Serb protesters who opposed the US action. One of them, she said, suggested the Americans were bombing because they wanted to control the region. So 'I tried to tell them no one was interested in their dirty hate-filled blot on the landscape of Europe but they just wouldn't listen.'[8] Fancy, even that didn't win them over. Some people don't *want* to hear a reasoned argument, that's their trouble.

The case of Luxembourg was typical. A letter found on a dead

Prussian officer expressed the general frustration of the coalition's troops:

> The French *émigrés* have deceived our good king and all the foreigners in the most infamous fashion. They had assured us that the counter-revolution would take place as soon we showed our faces. They had also told us that the French troops were a collection of riff-raff and would take to their heels at the first shot fired . . . the French troops resembled in no way the picture drawn of them . . . we have seen them performing evolutions which have compelled the admiration of our generals.[9]

The civil war within France was also being won by the revolutionaries, following horror on such a scale that a common phrase was 'It's better to fight a year against the English than a month in the Vendée'.[10] At which the most aggrieved must have been the English, who probably put out a statement to both sides saying, 'What, are you calling us poofs?'

The slaughter on both sides in the civil war was utterly gruesome. Throughout France, around 40,000 people were sentenced to death during the Terror, over 70 per cent of executions taking place in the areas of civil war, which was finally won by the Republic. The war was being won by mass mobilization of the *sans-culottes*, the subordination of every corner of French society to a single purpose, and the Terror. The trouble was, like any habit, once you've started it's enormously difficult to stop.

ANOTHER ONE BITES THE DUST

Events in 1794, or Years I and II, had moved at such a pace, it's easy to forget certain figures who were prominent in earlier scenes but had slipped out of the main plot, as in a soap opera when a character no longer fuels interest and only pops up once a month. In the case of Marie Antoinette, it was as if the writers, having suddenly remembered she was still there, decided her only use would be to have a final flourish and be killed off. Her plight, bad enough already, became worse when a visitor gave her a carnation which fell on to the floor, spilling out a note outlining a plan for escape. Hébert responded by demanding her head, writing in his paper that if she wasn't executed soon he'd be happy to do it himself. Hébert seems to have been a left-wing taxi driver. He should have called his paper *Bloody aristocracy, they need stringing up – it's the only language they understand.*

Marie Antoinette was kept in the Conciergerie, which you can still visit, and a notice next to her old room informs you that 'She showed great firmness and dignity during her months in prison.' Not that you could blame her if she spent the whole time dribbling and singing rugby songs, but this statement is similar to the responses of Jennie Bond, the BBC's royal correspondent, who was sometimes asked to respond immediately to a broadcast by the Queen. She always said the Queen coped admirably and measured the situation perfectly and under the circumstances displayed great courage and warmth. But this could only be seen as an objective account if there was any possibility that Bond might have said, 'I couldn't make head nor tail of what she was on about. Cold, distant, pompous, unintelligible twaddle if you ask me. Back to you in the studio.'

At the time of the Queen's stay, Hébert was keen to make up his own stories, announcing he'd heard from the ex-Queen's jailer that she'd indulged in incest with her eight-year-old son. The main accusation against her at the trial was that she'd assisted foreign powers, though her son was called as witness against her and the incest charge added. After a sixteen-hour trial she was – inevitably – found guilty. The next day, as she set eyes on the cart prepared to take her to the scaffold, she expressed surprise at how tatty it was, though it probably didn't occur to her that, if she'd

**Drawing made from life by Jacques Louis David
of Marie Antoinette, on her way to the guillotine.**

tried to escape in one just as tatty three years earlier, she might not
be needing this one now.

After her execution she was taken to the gravediggers, who were
on their lunch break, so her head was left on the grass until they'd
finished. This gave the woman who was to become Madame
Tussaud enough time to sit next to it and sculpt a model out of
wax. So a final favour was done to her by whichever workmen had
agitated for a decent lunch break.

Her final act was to tread on the foot of Sanson the executioner,
then say, 'Monsieur, I beg your pardon, I did not do it on purpose.'[11]
Her defenders cite this as an example of her sturdy harmlessness,
civil and without malice to the end. I think they do her a disservice
and the feisty cow meant it.

HEADS BEGIN TO ROLL

Once the Law of Suspects had been passed, the future also looked bleak for the twenty-one leaders of the Girondins who had escaped after their expulsion from the Convention. Within days of Marie Antoinette's demise they were brought to trial, and within a week, against the wishes of Robespierre, they were found guilty. Camille Desmoulins, tortured by self-doubt, called out, 'Oh my God, it is I who have killed them,' and fainted. Some of the defendants screamed, especially one called Valaze. Brissot leaned across to stiffen his colleague's resolve and tell him not to be afraid, to which Valaze replied that he was screaming because he'd stabbed himself with a hidden dagger. This was the greatest problem caused by any of the defendants, and the court dealt with it by acting as if nothing had happened. The dead Valaze was taken down to the cells along with his live co-defendants, then dragged back to the dock and sentenced to death, despite being dead. The live Girondins spent their last night discussing philosophy before being taken to the guillotine the next morning, standing in their carts singing a rousing 'Marseillaise'.

This was a new stage in the revolution. Now the victims of the Convention were not just aristocrats and royalty but those who had helped spark the revolution. Bailly the astronomer, Barnave the writer and the rest took their turns, and the dead Valaze was left till last, which must have been a bit of an anti-climax for the crowd.

Mme Roland was tried separately, and allowed one last visitor, a disguised Sophie Grandchamp, her ex-lover. Mme Roland asked Sophie to be present at her execution, 'in order to bear witness of what happened'.[12] Given the large crowd that was sure to turn out for such a mass celebrity guillotining, they had to agree on an exact spot for Sophie to stand, at one edge of the Pont-Neuf bridge, so that Mme Roland could see her. They managed to exchange a last look, and Sophie wrote, 'I read in her eyes the pleasure she felt at seeing me at this final and unforgettable appointment.' The accounts of her last moments are conflicting, though they all insist she won her final battle. Beside her at the scaffold was a man accused of laundering money, who was trembling with fear. According to some reports, seeing his discomfort she insisted on going first to 'show him how to die', whereas one biography claims she insisted she went second, saying, 'I wish to spare you the grief of seeing my head fall.'[13] It's a sad thought that if you make a grand departing gesture, your last thought is probably 'I bet the bloody journalists report that wrong.'

M. Roland was still in hiding in the countryside when he heard the news that his wife had been sentenced to be executed. He walked several miles to the village of Bourg-Baudouin and sat on a bank. Maybe he thought of the extended battle he'd fought with Mme Roland's father over his wish to marry his daughter, and the pedestrian life they may have lived had this revolution not intervened; or how events had brought out abilities in her that otherwise would never have been discovered. It must have crossed his mind that if she'd been content to be the wife of a clerk she wouldn't be enduring her last hours before having her head cut off. Whatever it was, we'll never know for certain because he pierced himself with a sword three times and lay down to die.

Every other escaped Girondin was caught and executed except for the transvestite Louvet, who got back to Paris and out again in safety. Buzot and Pétion were hunted for months, Buzot sinking into the greatest despair when he heard of the plight of Mme Roland. Eventually, convinced they were about to be caught, they lay in a field and shot themselves in the head. In Buzot's pocket was a book called *Satan Is Sitting in Marat's Armchair* and a diamond-studded picture of Mme Roland.

ABOLITION

It's one of the quirks of history that the British praised themselves as the nation that abolished modern slavery. The only reason they could abolish it was because they were doing it in the first place. It would be like if Harold Shipman had stopped his career half-way through, then was hailed as a hero for abolishing the practice of murdering old women. But even when it came, abolition was driven by a desire to out-manoeuvre the French. The British colonies were more profitable using free labour, whereas the sugar plantations of the French territories yielded a greater profit from slavery, which is why, if the British took control of San Domingo, they had every intention of reintroducing it.

Amongst those with a more genuine claim to have abolished slavery was Sonthonax, the Girondin sent to San Domingo to disarm the slaves, who then armed them in order to fight off a royalist coup. When the Spanish and British saw an opportunity to capture the island and re-establish slavery, Sonthonax pledged to fight them, saying, 'Yes, let us perish a thousand times rather than permit the people of San Domingo to fall again into enslavement.'[14]

Against the foreign armies would have been 100,000 slaves, led not just by Sonthonax but also by Toussaint L'Ouverture, who had trained an army of 5,000 under his command. Once the deputies of the Mountain had expelled the Girondins, the slave leaders sought their backing. Three delegates – an ex-slave, a mulatto and a white man – were sent from San Domingo to join the Convention in Paris. On their first day, the President of the Convention officially embraced them, and the next day the ex-slave, Bellay, spoke of the need to officially abolish slavery, and fight the foreign armies eager to restore it. A motion was moved that 'when drawing up the constitution we paid no attention to the unhappy negroes. Let us repair the wrong. Let us proclaim the liberty of the negroes.'[15] The black and mulatto delegates embraced each other on the tribune, and slavery was officially abolished. This, you might assume, was a crucial and poignant moment in the French Revolution, if not in history. But apparently you'd be wrong. Amidst all the tales of horror and gore inflicted by revolutionary France, many of which were indeed horrible and gory, how often is the abolition of slavery given the slightest mention? Simon Schama, in nine hundred pages, doesn't find room for a single syllable on the matter. Fortunately, at least one detail of the impact it had at the time is known, because a deputy rose to announce an incident amongst the spectators: 'A citizeness of colour who regularly attends the sittings of the Convention has just felt so keen a joy at seeing us give liberty to her brethren that she has fainted. I demand that this fact be recorded in the minutes.'[16]

12

It's All Going Wrong

I believe in this, and it's been tested by research,
That he who fucks nuns will later join the church

FALLING OUT

An incident shortly after the abolition of slavery showed how fragile the republican government was, in spite of its victories in the war. An address was sent by the maritime businessmen to the Convention, which they called 'On the Occasion of the Enfranchisement of Negroes'. It began, 'Bravo! This is the cry with which all our places of business resound when the public press brings us details of your great operations. Certainly, we have all the time to read them at our leisure since we no longer have any work to do. There is no longer any shipbuilding, still less any construction of boats. Thanks to your decree, three hundred thousand workers have no other occupation than to talk about the rights of man and the constitution.'[1]

Arms dealers, fox hunters, is there anyone in the world who doesn't defend indefensible behaviour on the grounds that it 'creates jobs'? You can imagine hit-men in a TV discussion yelling, 'But what about the jobs we create? Without us there'd be fewer undertakers, less of a demand for striped sticky tape and chalk, plus, everyone we kill who was working, that takes someone off the dole.' Similarly, it seems the shipyard owners of republican France could have looked a freed slave in the face and said, 'Oh *you're* happy now you won't get gunpowder exploded up your arse, but I've had to lay off another four blokes this week.'

This one letter illustrates the attitude of the wealthiest of the bourgeoisie when faced with the radicalism of Year II. They were fully behind the idea of a transfer of power away from the King and nobility, but they had no time for the stuff about equality, free education, smashing feudal plates or abolishing slavery. They were willing to let it go on because it was obvious the government of the Mountain, with its special relationship with the *sans-culottes*, was the only force that could win the war. They were a pragmatic bunch, and if Terror and radicalism were necessary to preserve the Republic, they were prepared to tolerate them for the time being. But they were still going to shriek, 'Abolishing slavery? Huh, it's political correctness gone mad.'

It also meant the revolution was still divided, despite the demise of the Girondins. The group around Hébert, and the Enragés, passionately believed in the radicalism and embraced the Terror. One of Hébert's followers announced, 'When a detachment of the Revolutionary Army comes to a village, it must enquire whether the local farmer is rich. If he is, he must be guillotined at once.'[2] If Hébert had the technology, he'd have set up a call centre from which Geordies could ring farmers on Sunday mornings and say, 'You've got a lot of money in your account. Can you tell us how you intend to get rid of it? We need to see it all gone by the twenty-fifth or we'll have to chop your head off. Sorry, Mr Giles, but that it is our customary procedure.'

Danton, Desmoulins and their supporters warned that the Terror was spiralling out of control – Danton was in such turmoil during the trial of the Girondins that he disappeared for another month, claiming he'd left through 'ill health'. The faction led by Robespierre was somewhere in the middle. Despite this difference of opinion, the government continued passing extraordinary new laws, such as establishing the right of every child to free primary school education and allowing illegitimate offspring a claim on their parents' will.

Robespierre felt his next move should be against the Enragés, who were taking control of some areas of society out of the government's hands. He attacked the *sans-culotte* movement for being 'obsessed' with the issue of maximum prices, and turned in particular against the Society for Revolutionary Women. The society was demanding stricter enforcement of the maximum-price laws, and the rehabilitation of prostitutes into society. The Convention declared the society illegal. Then the deputies also declared their opposition to the de-Christianization programme.

Part of the problem for the leaders of the revolution was that they represented a bourgeoisie who were a minority of the population. The Montagnards were a minority within that minority. Now even that minority was fragmenting, so each faction became gradually aware that, for an even smaller minority to impose its will, it would need to eliminate the other factions decisively. Hébert began plotting a further insurrection, and he and his close associates were arrested, tried and guillotined. It was all going horribly wrong.

'NEXT!'

The left can be bafflingly puritanical at times. I once heard a lecture entitled 'Will There Be Sport Under Socialism?'. The speaker informed us there wouldn't be any desire for sport in a socialist society, as everyone would seek more fulfilling desires, such as hill-walking. So all the struggle through the centuries will be worthwhile in the end, when our prize is to spend all day up the Cotswolds with a thermos and a fucking haversack.

This was the sort of thing I imagine frustrated Danton about his colleagues, as he became more ostentatious as the revolution went on. But this difference in outlook became a minor issue compared to the more fundamental rift that was brewing. Following his warning that the Terror should be slowed down, Danton was removed from the Committee of Public Safety, after Robespierre had become an official member in July 1793. In December Desmoulins began publishing a newspaper called *Old Cordeliers* with Danton's support, which called for an end to the growing power of the Committee for Public Safety. The third copy of the paper demanded 'Open the Prisons,' and sold 50,000 copies. But the most enthusiastic readers were those who wanted to end the Terror in order to return to a monarchy. This was the trap the leaders of the revolution found themselves in. Either they defended the revolution with increasingly widespread terror, or relaxed the Terror and reinvigorated the forces hoping to bring down the Republic altogether. Desmoulins seemed aware of this logic, which is why he also proposed a peace treaty with the British and Prussians. Robespierre ordered a public burning of issue 3 of the *Old Cordeliers*, to which Desmoulins, knowing that Robespierre knew Rousseau's quote, replied, 'Burning is not the answer.'

St-Just and others on the Committee demanded Danton's arrest, saying, 'If not, he will arrest us.' When Danton heard that Robespierre may be about to arrest him, he retorted, 'If I thought that were so, I would eat his bowels out.'

Now the two major factions in the Convention revolved around these two erstwhile friends. Yet this wasn't just a personal power battle driven by ambition, a sort of eighteenth-century Brown/Blair tussle. Both men had been on a remarkable journey, from obscure normality, via the legal profession, to directing a vast human experiment. Robespierre continued to approach every problem with a dedicated and methodical desire to save the Republic. Danton expressed his wish to save the Republic and its panache so that he could retire to his country home with his teenage bride. Robespierre could see that Danton, if he succeeded in deposing the Committee of Public Safety, would remove the bodies preventing the Girondins from returning to power. But whom could Robespierre turn to for support? The *sans-culotte* militants? Unlikely, as he'd just chopped off their leader's head. The wealthy? They despised all he stood for.

If the problem had been a maths puzzle, the answer would have been easy enough – he had no choice but to arrest his friend. But it was a human puzzle, so he hesitated, and then arrested his friend.

DANTON'S DEMISE

Danton was aware this was coming, and his friends pleaded with him to leave, but he refused. He claimed he was happier to be the guillotined than the guillotiner, though that hardly fitted with his conduct of the previous three years. Maybe part of his insistence on seeing through this final battle was the opportunity it would give him to bow out with a spectacular final flourish. But also, he may have been exhausted in a sense that few of us could begin to comprehend. Life must get tiring when no discussion can take place on any subject without it developing into tub-thumping oratory, when the emotional limits are stretched in all directions on an hourly basis.

Each day, for four years, Danton had experienced peaks and troughs that for most people would stand out as life-defining episodes. He'd been at the decision-making heart of every major event through the revolution, toured the frontline of a makeshift army in a ferocious war, lost his wife and child, could see the whole project spiralling into unstoppable chaos, and now his former friend wanted to chop off his head. I think a bit of Danton thought, 'Do you know, I've had enough.'

A few days before the arrest he met Robespierre, who begged him to withdraw his criticisms of the Terror. It's rumoured that during this meeting Robespierre drank a glass of champagne that made him dizzy, but no agreement was reached, and they ended with a brief embrace, the sort that says, 'I know one of us is about to kill the other, but that doesn't mean we weren't close.'

Danton's arrest was orchestrated to deny him his opportunity for a performance. He was arrested along with Desmoulins, three of his supporters and a batch of characters charged with theft, to make his faction seem like common criminals.

Danton was accused of taking bribes, and there was evidence that he had used his position to broker arms deals between manufacturers and the army. He'd also indulged in a spot of insider dealing to make money on the stock market. But it was his support for Desmoulins' proposals to end the Terror and the war that Robespierre's supporters couldn't accept. Danton was charged with having served the King, having helped to set up the shooting at the Champ de Mars and enriching himself at the people's expense. A fixed jury was put in place and the courtroom was packed for the trial. Desmoulins was nervous and deemed to be a disappointment, though he must have felt like the support band at a gig, with only part of the audience watching, a cluster of his fans at the front and most people milling about outside discussing 'What do you reckon Danton will start with?' Throughout the trial, Danton seems to have exuded the egomania that any comedian who's made a speech on a serious subject would recognize. You make your point, but afterwards are plagued by thoughts such as 'I expected the joke about the cruise missile and the Afghan village to get a bigger laugh than that.'

Danton was fighting, with little hope, for his life, but revelled in performing on the centre stage of history. He improvised a speech that lasted for hours, including lines such as 'There will soon, as far as I can see, be only one man left on his feet – the executioner; and with no one left to guillotine, he'll guillotine himself out of sheer desperation.' His oratory was crammed with such wit that the Committee for Public Safety became concerned he was winning the fixed jury round. So St-Just announced the trial to be at an end, and Danton was sentenced to the guillotine, to which he replied, 'What does it matter if I die? I've caroused, spent lots of money, and loved women. Now it's time to sleep.' He added that 'If I leave my legs to Couthon and my testicles to Robespierre, the revolution could last a while yet.'

Desmoulins was tortured in two ways as he awaited his fate. He wrote in a last letter that 'I could bear execution from Pitt, but not from my colleagues.' But this letter, to Lucile, ended, 'Goodbye, my life, my soul, my divinity on earth. I still see Lucile. My crossed arms embrace you, my bound hands clasp you, my severed head reposes on your breast. A tear falls from my eyes for you. I fall asleep in the calm of innocence.' As he mounted the scaffold he added the glorious line, 'At thirty-three, I am the same age as the *sans-culotte* Jesus.'

Lucile had been hysterical throughout the trial, and had asked to leave the courtroom. After the conviction she arranged to stand at an arranged spot on the route the cart would use to take him and Danton to the guillotine. As the cart passed she held up their baby and screamed as the family exchanged looks for the last time. When they arrived, Danton handed the driver a few coins as a tip. His last words were to the executioner: 'Don't forget to show them my head, it's worth it.'

Danton has secured his place in official history. Along from the Odéon theatre in Paris is a fine statue of the man, bearing an inscription of his statement that 'After bread, the next thing man needs is education.' Nearby is Le Bar Danton, in which you can buy a *'sandwich Danton'*, a wholesome feast including ham, cheese and a fried egg. He's become the acceptable face of the revolution, in schools, in art and in savoury snacks. Partly this is because he can be portrayed as a liberal victim of the revolution's excesses. A popular play, *The Death of Danton*, performed at the Odéon in Paris in 2002 took this stance, as did the magnificently charismatic film *Danton*, in which he is played by Gerard Depardieu.

But Danton wasn't a put-upon liberal trying to create a cosy revolution and keep it away from the nutters. He was more responsible than anyone for the second revolution and overthrow of the King. As Minister of Justice he virtually sanctioned the September massacres. He was a lobbyist for the King's execution, a crucial player in organizing the revolutionary army and an advocate of almost every revolutionary measure up until the events leading to his arrest. Any character to emerge today proposing anything half as radical would be called a 'mad-dog Marxist anarchist Taliban-supporting fanatic'. He was arrested because he proposed dismantling the bodies that could save the radical programme of Year II, whereas Robespierre insisted on maintaining these bodies, which were sure to lead to the collapse of the radical programme of Year II.

The other reason why Danton is fêted where Robespierre is vilified is probably that he doesn't fit the revolutionary stereotype. But the stereotype is only partly true. Movements and campaigns do tend to have their Robespierres, stern and humourless, but they also usually have their Dantons, rolling up two hours late with the placards and an empty bottle of whisky. Any movement worth following must surely celebrate the value of both, for once they start chopping off each other's heads it's in trouble.

MME DEFARGE HAS HER DAY

Danton's execution accelerated the carnage. As Robespierre and the Committee of Public Safety lost their support throughout the country, they came under more attacks from a variety of groups in the Convention. So they responded with more terror, until they introduced a special law called the Great Terror, with similar logic to the launching of a new chocolate bar as 'all the terror you've always loved, but bigger and brighter than ever before'. Which is why a contender for the all-time award for cheek has to be Sanson, the official Chief Executioner, who complained that with all the extra work he was doing, he deserved a pay rise. His letter outlining his grievance said:

> As I, personally, cannot be everywhere at once, I must have trustworthy helpers, for the public insists on decency. It is I who pay them. Last Saturday they warned me that if I did not raise their wages, they could not continue to work for me. Circumstances obliged me to pay this increase. Besides, I have to pay a huge rent . . . indeed I am substantially in debt. I cannot go on borrowing money. I beg you to order the payment of money due to me. As the situation is urgent, I beg you, to enquire into the truth of this.[3]

To give him his due, as you read this you find yourself thinking he's got a good point, until you remember, HOLD ON – YOUR EXTRA PRODUCTIVITY WAS CUTTING MORE PEOPLE'S HEADS OFF, YOU PSYCHO.

The Great Terror was indeed a busy time for Sanson. The only evidence required for conviction was 'moral proof', and this led to batches of up to forty executions per day, a total of 1,376 in about seven weeks. Lucile Desmoulins was arrested and sentenced to the guillotine, as was the widow of Hébert; the two shared a cell, where they became friends in the days before their executions.

If the Committee for Public Safety deemed someone worthy of execution, within a day their hands would be tied, their head shorn and their collar ripped, and they would be summoned by Sanson, standing at the top of the ten steps leading out of the Conciergerie. Then the victims would be loaded into a cart, Sanson checking the prisoners against the list on his document, a crowd would shout, '*Vive la République,*' and they'd be on their way. Except for one morning when, in an incident anticipating the crucifixion scene in *The Life of Brian*, a man called Gossin called after the cart, 'Take me too, I have been condemned.' Sanson asked his name, checked his list and tried to send him away. But Gossin ran after the cart and clambered on board; as soon as he was there, he began screaming, 'Oh my wife and children!'[4] A performance artist, perhaps.

Amongst the spectators of the victims' final moments were the patrons of a restaurant on the terrace of the Tuileries gardens called La Guillotine, where the names of those to be executed that day were printed on the backs of the menus. But our image of the period remains to some extent a myth. Far from crowds of *sans-culottes* relishing the deaths of long lines of aristocrats, most of the people executed during this prolific stage of the Terror were themselves poor, accused of plotting against the ruling faction. There *were* crowds for each day's executions, but one of the most tragic aspects of this must have been that some days the numbers were less than others. What would that do for the ego, if you got a small turnout, and the last thing you ever heard was a conversation between the officials that went 'Not many in today.' 'No, still, it's a sunny day, a lot will have gone to the fair.' 'Well, it might mean we get off early'?

For many people, life carried on as normal. Throughout the Terror in Paris, twenty-three theatres and sixty dancing clubs stayed open. And one of the results of the steady drip of death must have been that people became blasé. Far from the macabre enthusiasm of *A Tale of Two Cities*, the crowd became weary of the guillotine, not necessarily from fear or lack of enthusiasm for the Republic, but because the rate of heads, and the kind of people losing them, were signs that the virtuous nation they'd fought so hard for was slipping away.

For political victims it became a matter of the utmost importance to know how to die well. Mme Roland enhanced her reputation greatly with her unfaltering death, whereas Hébert was said to have 'died with no balls'. If someone had thought of it, they could have organized a 'death of the month' competition, in which contestants tried to match the three finest deaths with a panel of experts, in reverse order on a postcard.

THE CULT OF THE SUPREME BEING

In his time of crisis, Robespierre behaved as many other people have, and turned to religion. Except that, this being the French Revolution, he made up one of his own: 'the Cult of the Supreme Being'. Although deeply opposed to the Catholic religion, because of the Church's role in the old regime, he abhorred atheism, and used it as a charge against enemies in the Convention.

Granting citizenship to Protestants and Jews was a very modern stance, similar to that in most secular schools, in which children participate in Christmas, Hanukkah, Eid and Diwali, and the only belief not celebrated is atheism. No school would dare put on an atheist Nativity play, for which the precocious kid runs home yelping, 'Mummy, Daddy, I've been picked to play the chimpanzee!'

The Supreme Being, on the other hand, was declared by Robespierre to be 'a constant reminder of justice . . . it is both socially valuable and Republican'. How does an eternal omnipotent being behave as a republican, I wonder. Does he have to stand for election every million years? When his son is sent to Earth, does he claim that the reason he can do miracles is nothing to do with his family line, just coincidence, and any man can walk on water if he receives the will of the people? Whatever, it was all to be heralded at a vast extravaganza in June 1794 called the Festival of the Supreme Being, which would have impressed as the opening ceremony of a modern Olympics. A choir of 2,400 children sang a 'hymn to the Supreme Being', followed by a regiment of blind children singing a 'hymn to divinity'. A monumental effigy of Atheism was set on fire, revealing a monument to Wisdom inside. Then a procession, estimated at 300,000 people, marched to the Champ de Mars, where a fifty-foot-high statue of Hercules made by David out of *papier mâché* was revealed. It must have been an overwhelming display, but sadly six weeks later the whole religion came to an end. So if that *was* the only religion in history to have been praising the right god, when it collapsed after one festival he must have been fucking furious.

FLEURUS

Whatever its official religion, the Republic still had to defend itself against characters such as Pitt, who declared his wish to 'wipe the Republic off the face of the Earth'. St-Just was sent to the northern front, to help lead a battle in the Belgian village of Fleurus. This was the first time a military campaign included an airborne division, when the French General Jordan was sent up in a balloon. It's easy to underestimate the difference a balloon could make, when we're used to warfare between armies of absurdly disparate means, one side with an incalculable mass of laser-guided hardware, the other a poverty-stricken collection of desert people whose annual military parade probably involves their defence secretary announcing, 'Look what I've found, everybody,' before unveiling a really huge stone.

The French won decisively, and from there marched through Belgium with little resistance. Combined with victories in Spain and Austria, the Battle of Fleurus removed the short-term possibility of France's enemies reaching Paris and reimposing a monarchy. St-Just returned to the capital to make the announcement but, asked to give his personal account of the triumph, he said, 'I like it when victories are announced, but do not wish them to become pretexts for personal vanity.'[5] Which must make him the most mature twenty-six-year-old of all time. Most blokes of that age would have stood at the Convention and said, 'So I've nutted Brunswick, and he's run off back to Prussia, ain't he? – bottled it.'

ENOUGH IS ENOUGH

Traditional history suggests that nations rise or fall because a king is strong, a queen is weak, Thatcher is tough or Mandela is brave. Powerful military regimes are usually explained as the product of a decisive leader, who could make stirring, combative speeches. Yet at the beginning of the twenty-first century, the nation which can dictate its will to virtually the entire planet is led by someone who opens a war by looking blank for several seconds and then saying, 'We will get tough with the suicide bombers.' Which, apart from anything else, suggests he hasn't quite grasped one of the central points about suicide bombing.

Nations, empires and movements boom or collapse according to greater forces than the personal traits of their leaders. Most accounts of Louis XVI deride him as weak, or, as Carlyle suggests, 'taciturn and irresolute'. But was he really, any more than Louis XV? We'll never know, because Louis XV was never faced with a movement of millions of people dedicated to removing him from power. Louis XVI's hopelessness reached its peaks during the greatest points of mass revolt, fussing about the leaves in the midst of his overthrow, and writing '*Rien*' in his diary after the storming of the Bastille. Trotsky, in his history of the Russian Revolution, compares this to the diaries of the Russian Tsar. On the day he dissolved parliament, the Tsar wrote, 'The Duma was closed today. Was quietly busy until dinner. Went paddling in a canoe.' On the day he was overthrown he wrote, 'Dmitri came to dinner. Nothing happened today.' The explanation for the similarities between Louis and the Tsar, said Trotsky, was that 'to a tickle we all behave differently, but to a red-hot iron alike'.[6] Revolution requires more than millions of people opposing the old order; it depends on them *actively* opposing it. No news broadcast ever said, 'The President of Indonesia was forced to resign today when millions of people throughout the country thought, "Tut, isn't he dreadful?"' Only when that thought becomes an action, when vast numbers feel motivated to argue and debate, to form new organizations, to defend them from attack, to run to the carpenter for a plank of wood and climb on a perfume shop to cut the drawbridge chains, does sullen resentment become revolution. Equally, when that enthusiasm wanes, when the hope and belief that a new society is possible comes back into question, the revolution will falter and stumble.

And by July 1794, or Thermidor Year II, despite the victories on the war front, the people who had made the French Revolution were losing their enthusiasm. One reason was that the link between the Jacobins and the *sans-culottes* was being broken. The law of the maximum was now being applied more vigorously to wages than it was to prices. Shopkeepers were finding inventive ways to get round the maximum price code; for example, butchers took to selling pork only after it was cooked because the regulations didn't apply to cooked meat.

The proportion that, had they been asked in a poll, would have said they supported the revolution may have been as high as ever, but if you said, 'A thousand people are needed immediately to defend the gates of the city,' many who would once have eagerly grabbed their pike would now hesitate. Parisians were thinking the equivalent of 'I would, but my exam is the day after/I'm taking the dog to the vet/Crystal Palace are playing at home.'

Robespierre appears to have noticed this during the Festival of the Supreme Being, when he heard mocking calls as he marched in the procession. A Swiss man who helped to organize the festival described Robespierre that day: 'he never looked one in the face and was continually blinking his eyes in a painful manner. He told me that he was as shy as a child, and that he trembled whenever he went up on the rostrum.' Robespierre had done as much as anyone to turn the King from a powerful figure into a historical weakling. Now Robespierre too had lost his support, and was transformed from a figure vilified by history as cold, clinical and ruthless to a gibbering fool who hurt when he blinked.

And the Jacobins had another problem. Following the Battle of Fleurus and other military victories, there was no immediate danger to the Republic. Many of the wealthier businessmen who had never supported the Terror had none the less tolerated it because they were aware the Republic couldn't be saved without it. The laws against hoarders and speculators were essential if the army was to remain supplied and the *sans-culottes* were to be kept lively. But now they had no need to put up with it. So for Robespierre and his colleagues, every day brought fears of a new conspiracy. An assassination attempt was made on Collot d'Herbois, a leading Jacobin. Robespierre retorted by having Fouché, an opponent, followed, to the extent that Fouché didn't dare visit his dying daughter in case Robespierre's men were waiting for him. In such a way were these once-great figures, who had previously spent their time plotting the course of a new world, reduced to sweatily plotting their own survival by conspiring to shoot their ex-allies, like the coked-up gangsters in the last scenes of *GoodFellas*.

THE END OF ROBESPIERRE

Robespierre decided to unleash a new attack. He said in the Convention, 'People! You should be informed that there exists within your bosom a league of scoundrels who are at war with public virtue.' But he wasn't going to say who they were. He appears to have followed that smug politician's ploy of telling interviewers, 'All will be revealed in the full statement tomorrow.' The trouble was, by not saying who was on the list, everyone in the room worried it might be them. Then one deputy arose to say, 'One man paralyses the Convention. That man is Robespierre.'

Robespierre returned home to M. Duplay the carpenter, where he was apparently in good spirits. But the next day Fouché moved in for the kill. One deputy demanded the arrest of Robespierre, and the President agreed to put his arrest to the vote. You can only imagine what graphics would be on show if the BBC had been around to record this moment, Peter Snow howling, 'There's the guillotine, and there's Robespierre's head, and each deputy can vote to lower the blade just a *bit* further, and if Fouché can win aalll these deputies here, then, let's see if it works, there it goes, into the basket!'

The Convention voted to arrest Robespierre, his brother Augustin, St-Just and Couthon, the paralysed Jacobin, wrecking the heart of the Committee of Public Safety. But Robespierre's friend Philippe Le Bas, not long married to Elisabeth Duplay, who had waited for him each day at the Convention, stood up and said, 'What about me? I demand to be arrested along with my colleagues.'[7] An act of immense courage, principle and inspiration – but what a twat.

The prisoners' last hope now was a rising of the *sans-culottes*. There were demonstrations, possibly of several thousands, in opposition to the arrests, but nowhere near sufficient to reverse the decision. One supporter of Robespierre, Hanriot, made an attempt of sorts to turn the demonstrations into an armed rescue, but he'd been drinking since three in the morning, so he rode on horseback to the meeting of the Commune with his sabre in his hand and shouted, 'Kill all policemen. Kill! Kill!'[8] Hanriot's attempt at writing the first ever gangsta-rap lyrics failed when he was arrested himself, then jumped out of the prison window into a pile of horse manure and lay there for several hours before being discovered and rearrested.

The arrested Jacobins were held in the Luxembourg Prison by an armed policeman who described later how the detained Robespierre was sitting in an armchair when, 'I leapt on him pointing my sword at his heart and cried, "Surrender, traitor." He said, "It is you who are the traitor." At these words I took hold of one of my pistols and fired. I meant to shoot him in the chest, but struck him in the chin and smashed his jaw.'[9] Refreshingly honest, compared to a modern police report which, after such an incident, would claim the wound was caused when Robespierre gouged a hole in the inside of his own mouth. But the shot sparked off possibly the most farcical demise of any government ever. In panic at the gunfire, Robespierre's brother jumped out of the window, whereupon his fall was broken by an old man passing by. Augustin was rearrested as he lay in an agonized heap, and the poor sod he'd landed on was crippled for life. Le Bas shot himself successfully and died instantly, at which point the disabled Couthon slid out of his chair and tried to escape by crawling down a corridor. A sympathizer picked Couthon up and the policeman gave chase, when, according to his own account, 'I fired at random, missing Couthon,

**The arrest of Robespierre, or an eighteenth-century
South London night club.**

but hitting the man who was carrying him in the leg.'[10] They don't change, do they?

A surgeon was called to treat Robespierre's jaw, extracting his teeth with no anaesthetic. The next day the surviving prisoners were taken to the guillotine. Couthon was the first up, but because he was paralysed he had to be tied to a plank, a process that took fifteen minutes while a huddle of helpers tried to put him in place. When Robespierre was taken on to the scaffold his bandages were removed and 'pints of blood' poured from his mouth. Luckily for him, he was unaware of one final set of arrests that had been made the previous evening. M. and Mme Duplay had been taken to prison, where, by the time Robespierre made his way to the scaffold, Mme Duplay had hung herself from the bars in her cell window. And there, as Robespierre was shuffled into place under the blade, was Sanson, the man who had carried out so many of Robespierre's orders. So I wonder whether the last words Robespierre ever heard were, 'Just before I do this, you couldn't sign this chit for me, could you, to say I'm still owed a week's dosh and expenses for that overtime back in the winter?'

PAINE IN JAIL

The overthrow of the Montagnards completed a remarkable journey through the revolution for Tom Paine. He'd arrived in France as a hero, fleeing the English government for having inspired the popu-lation with his book defending their cause. On his arrival he was attracted towards the Girondins, partly perhaps because, tending to come from wealthy backgrounds with better education, more of them could speak English. And Paine steadfastly refused to learn French. So in that respect he was typically English. It's unclear how he managed to be a deputy in the Convention without understand-ing the language, but maybe he even tried to get round that in an English way, by shouting slowly. His first speech was probably

'What we need to do with the King – I SAID THE KING . . . the KING, DEAR, the ONE – WITH – THE – CROWN.' This can't have been his only motive for falling into the Girondin camp. Unlike anyone else in the Convention, Paine was a revolutionary before the revolution. But the reality posed harsher questions than he could have anticipated when he wrote *Common Sense* or *The Rights of Man*. In the middle of the revolution, the Terror presented itself as a solution to the immediate problem of farmers withholding grain. To Paine, it was a negation of the much more peaceful revolution he'd advocated. Whatever the reason, the Terror led to him being jailed in the Luxembourg Prison. As the Terror went berserk, Paine's name was marked down for the guillotine.

Each morning a turnkey would walk round the prison with a list of the prisoners due to be executed later that day. When he came to the cell of a condemned prisoner, he'd chalk a cross on the door, and later that day someone would come round to collect the condemned and take away anyone in a cell marked with the deadly chalk. But Paine had developed a fever, which almost killed him, so the prison Governor allowed him to have the cell door open for fresh air. One morning the turnkey arrived at Paine's cell, stopped at the door and marked it with a cross – but because the door was open, he marked the inside. After he went, Paine shut the door. That night the porters arrived to take the next day's victims, but as they couldn't see the cross on Paine's door they left him alone. The nearest I can imagine to how he felt, as the porter hovered outside, is the sensation of being sat on a bus with no ticket and no money, while the conductor walks slowly by, then stops for a moment, and your heart's pounding while you're thinking, 'Just walk past, just walk past.' Despite this, if I ever meet anyone who's had the experience Paine had, I'll try not to say, 'I know exactly what you went through.'

But Paine was doubly lucky, because two days after this incident came the overthrow of Robespierre, with the result that the list of pending executions was withdrawn, and Paine was released. It's to be hoped that at some point someone passed him in the street and thought, 'Hang on, I put a chalk mark on his door in the prison once,' and spent the rest of the day shivering under a blanket.

DE SADE IN JAIL

A similar trauma was experienced by the artist formerly known as the Marquis de Sade. He had published his most atheist work of all, declaring that 'Religion is a phantom invented by infamy, which has no other goal but to deceive them [the people] or to arm them against one another.' But this came out as Robespierre was attacking the de-Christianization campaign, and Sade was arrested and jailed. On 8 Thermidor Year II, the prosecutor drew up a list of twenty-eight prisoners to be guillotined the next day, and Sade was one. For some reason, the next morning when the days' victims were piled into the cart Sade was marked as 'absent'. He didn't know himself that he'd been put down for the guillotine and afterwards attributed his escape to a friendly deputy from his home town.

The next day, the Jacobins were overthrown. Sade was released, but being broke he had to lodge in someone's attic, his only income as a prompter in a theatre. Who on earth trusted him with that job? The urge to whisper to an actor, 'This is where you wank into a chalice' must have been overpowering. He continued to write; and the new regime, apparently aware that putting him in jail had been tried by both royalists and republicans and didn't make any difference, decided instead to commit him to an asylum.

He was taken in by François Coulmier, a hunchback and former priest who rejected the prevailing attitudes towards madness. A surgeon called Pinel won a battle to release most of the patients from the city's asylums, and Coulmier, instead of punishing sufferers, sought psychological cures, and insisted patients were treated in comfort. Sade was given one of the best rooms in the asylum, with a four-poster bed and a room from where he could host dinner parties.

Then Coulmier and Sade built a theatre within the asylum, which put on two shows a month, a play and an opera, with one professional actor and the rest of the parts played by the patients.

THERMIDOR

If television news had existed in 1794, the world would have been treated to pictures of dancing Frenchmen celebrating the liberation of Paris from Jacobin terror. Maybe it would have been similar to the week following the liberation of Kabul by the Northern Alliance. But these displays of supposed mass delight are not always to be trusted. On that occasion I saw one TV reporter being asked how people felt about the fact that General Dostum, head of the liberating army, had run a series of sex-slave camps the last time he'd been in charge of Kabul. And the reporter replied, 'Yes, but everyone's got their dirt if you look for it.' Which I suppose is true. Some of us have had affairs that we tried to keep quiet, and some of us have run sex-slave camps – we're none of us squeaky clean, are we?

So the first fact that contradicts the notion that the fall of the Jacobins represented a move from terror to peace is that the execution of Robespierre and seventy of his allies amounted to the biggest batch of guillotining on a single day in Paris throughout the revolution. Some Jacobin deputies were spared, for example Billaud-Varenne, who was exiled instead to Guyana, where he took up breeding parrots. But over the next few months mass executions of Jacobin supporters took place, including three hundred in Lyon, who were enclosed in a shed which was set on fire. The remains of Marat were removed from the Panthéon. The Commune was deprived of its functions, and the voting system was altered to exclude the poorer sections of the electorate. The maximum price on food was removed, helping to cause a famine, of which one paper that supported the new regime said, 'One only meets in the streets pallid and emaciated countenances, on which are depicted pain, weariness, hunger and distress.'[11] Following a further failed uprising of *sans-culottes* demanding a return to the maximum-price laws, there were further massacres of Jacobin supporters. One deputy said, 'Wherever you look there is throat-cutting.' In Tarascon, Jacobins were hurled into the river, to the applause of the local nobility. The traditional dress of the *sans-culottes* was banned.

There was a craze in victims' balls, to which only those who had lost a relative to the guillotine were admitted, and everyone had to wear a shirt with an open neck and a red silk ribbon around their throat to symbolize a victim of the guillotine.

A writer who was hostile to the revolution, Michelet, wrote in the 1840s of an incident at this time, 'A man alive today who was then ten years old was taken to the theatre by his parents. After the show, men in shirt-sleeves asked the spectators as they came out, "A carriage, *master*?" The child did not understand this expression, and when he asked for an explanation, he was told simply that there had been a great deal of change since the death of Robespierre.'

SOMETHING WENT WRONG

As well as becoming victims of the guillotine, in the aftermath of their overthrow the Jacobins were turned by history into subjects of 'selective grieving syndrome', a condition that causes the sufferer to feel a deep sense of horror at certain atrocities, while remaining strangely unmoved by equal atrocities elsewhere. This seemed to reach epidemic proportions following the attacks on New York on 11 September 2001, when many of the politicians and journalists who appeared most distraught about the World Trade Center were those who had composed themselves more sturdily during the slaughter of 50,000 civilians in Chechnya, or tens of thousands in Nicaragua, or 1,800 in Lebanese camps, for which Ariel Sharon was judged to be 'largely responsible'.

A similar conundrum occurs throughout history, and the terror of the French Revolution is a classic example. Historians, film-makers, writers of schoolbooks weep for the victims of Robespierre, yet those killed by royalist armies or by the regime that overthrew the Jacobins are rarely even given their own footnote, let alone whole novels or films.

The other consideration often strangely forgotten is that the Terror took place in a country under siege. It was part of the war. And not a modern war, in which people feel they're participating in the midst of battle because they watch the TV discussions, or write newspaper columns about it. This was a war in which every person in France was a participant, because the royalist armies had declared their intention to treat anyone who didn't help restore the monarchy as an enemy. It became a test to ask each other in France, 'If the Duke of Brunswick arrived, what would you have done to deserve execution?'

The Terror was part of this war. Yet from Carry On film to professional academic, the war of which the Terror was one part is ignored, leaving the image of a handful of maniacs bent on blood-lust and vengeance. It's as if a history of the British suggested we all went insane around 1944, blacking out windows at night, sleeping in underground stations and sailing across to Normandy to shoot thousands on the beach for no apparent reason.

In addition, the revolutionaries were caught in a trap. As events unfolded they were faced with a continual choice, whether to defend the Republic, or surrender. Surrender would have involved widespread carnage, but the defence involved terror, and that in turn became savage and a great deal of it was indefensible. Many historians lament the lack of 'men of greater stature', a Mandela or Gandhi, perhaps, who could have found a more enlightened way out. But the revolution *did* throw up men of stature. Lafayette had played a crucial role in the American War of Independence. Paine, Mirabeau, Danton and Desmoulins were remarkable figures. But none of them could escape the choice: internal terror or external and greater terror.

The quandary of those who chose to defend the revolution was that each event threw up a more grisly choice. So you might condemn them and the path they chose, but at what point should they have given up? Should they have refused right from the beginning to oppose the injustices of the King's absolute power, on the grounds it might lead to an unseemly revolution? Should they have backed down when the King sent his army to crush the third estate, or when he tried to escape?

Even those who label the Jacobin experiment a shameful disaster must acknowledge that Robespierre wasn't trying to build a personal empire but to eradicate the vast chasms of inequality, material and philosophical, that had infested the whole of society for centuries. It was Robespierre who insisted on removing property qualifications so that every man should have the vote. And he, more than any other deputy, eradicated discrimination against Protestants and Jews. Asked about his attitude to property, he said, 'Ask that merchant in human flesh what property is. He will tell you, pointing to men he has herded and shackled, "Those are my property."' It was the right of every citizen, he insisted, to own a small amount of property, by which he meant a small business. This web of small businesses, none of them ever becoming big businesses, may appear utopian, especially to Marxists, who propose a collective ownership of property, with production aiming at human need rather than profit. None the less, Robespierre was aiming to liberate humanity, a task riddled with difficulties at the best of times.

Once the Terror was ended, it became much harder to supply grain to the cities. One writer described how, in the famine that followed, 'The mothers of Caen were allaying the cries of their new-born children with rags dipped in water – that way they did not take long to die. Better than watching one's children grow too feeble to cry.' There was plenty that was diabolical about the Terror, but before condemning it, you should imagine living under the daily fear of an army committed to destroying 'every defender of Paris'.

And wonder whether, as you waged a daily battle for grain that was only being won since the Terror began, you would watch a hoarder of bread being taken to the guillotine and think, 'This is going to go down very badly on *Blue Peter* in two hundred years' time.'

13

Napoleon and the
End of Radicalism

You think it's funny
Turning rebellion into money

THE DIRECTORY

The new government, following the Thermidor coup, was called the Directory. It was made up of a council of five hundred deputies, still elected but with stricter property qualifications to exclude the poor from the electorate.

There was still a financial crisis, which at one point became so serious the government pawned the Crown Jewels. The Directory was committed to destroying the radicalism of Year II, but it aspired to the ethics of the original leaders of the third estate. So in 1795, or Year III, when a group of royalists attempted an uprising the Directory mobilized the National Guard to put them down, and the commander given the job of ensuring this was done effectively was Napoleon Bonaparte. He impressed his employers with his military acumen, but then went missing for two hours after the battle. One story is that the army chiefs eventually found him in bed with a blonde called Suzanne, which is probably a bit too James Bond to be true, as if he ran straight from leading a victorious battle, opened a bottle of champagne, fought off one last royalist who had a metal claw for a hand and then said, 'Now, Suzanne, I think it's time to attend to *another* uprising.'

If the crushing of the royalists indicated one side of the Directory's nature, the other was shown by the way it crushed another attempted rising, by a radical group called the Conspiracy of Equals, led by Gracchus Babeuf in 1796. One problem with putting down Babeuf's revolt was that one of its leaders was Drouet, the postman who'd captured the King at Varennes, and who was still a national hero. After becoming a deputy on the back of his famous escapade, he fought in the army and was captured by the Austrians, tried to escape from the Spielberg fortress in a hand-made parachute and broke both his legs. During a lull in the war with Austria, Drouet was released and returned to France, where he began campaigning for the idea that the most practical method for sorting out the problems of the Republic was for the entire population to leave the country with all their possessions and settle on the land of France's enemies. Did he honestly imagine this would work? Maybe it was part of a plot, so he could return to the post office at Ste-Ménéhould with a spectacularly easy round. But what a fantastic career. If anyone hadn't kept up with him for a while, and asked what he'd been up to, what would they have thought when he answered, 'I captured a king, jumped out of a fortress with a parachute made out of tissues and tried to relocate the entire population'? After Babeuf's plot, Drouet again escaped from prison, this time without breaking his legs, but he was unable to do anything for Babeuf, who was guillotined.

Throughout these crises, the Directory still had to conduct a war. Following the victory at Fleurus, the Republic was no longer in immediate danger of invasion, but it still faced steady hostility on every border. Lurking in the army, so far only a minor player in events, was the man who would take command of that situation to become the best-known character of the entire revolution.

NAPOLEON

The view that history turns on the personalities of a few individuals holds a special place for Napoleon. If only he hadn't been so small, he wouldn't have been so cross, then he wouldn't have tried to rule the world. All those soldiers who froze in the Russian winter might have been spared, if only someone had persuaded him to see a psychotherapist. 'Is it really Pitt and Wellington that make you angry, Napoleon? I want you to explore what makes you uncomfortable with *yourself*.' The first flaw with the theory that Napoleon's antics can be explained by his height is that he was five feet, six and a half inches – small today, but at the time this was the average height of Frenchmen. So a 'Napoleonic complex' must have entailed him thinking, 'I'm fed up of not being able to reach where top cupboards will be in two hundred years' time. That's it, I'm invading Belgium.'

Napoleon had been brought up in Corsica and went to military school in France. He emerged as a second lieutenant, though his ambition at this point was to become a writer. You can't help thinking that some people in history who wanted to become writers or artists, like Napoleon and Hitler, should just have been allowed to get on with it. Put it another way: imagine the damage Frederick Forsyth might have done if he'd taken up something that really mattered. We'd now be living in a post-nuclear heap of rubble, saying, 'He wanted to be a writer apparently.'

Napoleon supported the revolution, joining the Jacobins after the King's escape to Varennes. He played an impressive role during the war, especially in resisting a counter-revolutionary army in Toulon in the south of France.

One week after putting down the royalist uprising, a French general retired, and Napoleon was named as his successor. But it's debatable whether his next life-changing experience was as lucky. Later that year he met Rose de Beauharnais, whom he decided to call Joséphine. Shortly after meeting her, Napoleon wrote a letter to a friend, saying, 'She has the prettiest little cunt in the world. The three islets of Martinique are there.'[1] Which I have to confess to not quite understanding, but he was obviously very much in love. (It makes you want to go and check out a map of Martinique though.) The couple were married a few months later, but it all started to go wrong on the honeymoon, when Joséphine insisted on taking her dog Fortune and letting it sleep in bed with them. On their wedding night it bit Napoleon.

Straight after the honeymoon Napoleon left to command a French army in Italy, with the aim of turning the Italian states into republics, run along similar lines to France. Napoleon enjoyed rapid success, partly because his army was playing by the rules of the new order. He chose his generals on merit, and stated that every soldier could become an officer. He rewarded all ranks with the promise of wealth, paid for by mass looting of whichever area they were invading. He didn't leave himself out of this equation, awarding himself several houses, an estate in Belgium and a park.

During the campaign, however, he arranged to meet his wife in Milan. She didn't turn up, because she'd started an affair with a lieutenant called Hippolyte Charles. Napoleon wrote the most desperate letters, often two or three in a day, but Joséphine never replied and usually didn't even open them, until Napoleon wrote to the Directory saying he was coming back to Paris to get her. The government thought it wasn't best for the leader of an army in the middle of a war to abandon the battle, come home and confront his cheating wife, so they begged Joséphine to go out to Italy and keep him happy. She agreed on condition she could take Hippolyte and the dog with her and take eighteen days to get there.

Napoleon was placated by Joséphine's arrival, and proceeded to set up republics across Italy. But the French war was moving further away from the revolutionary spirit that had originally inspired it. Napoleon's next expedition was to Egypt, driven mostly by the chance to plunder. To fund the trip, he had to raise 9 million francs, for which he approached his friend Brune, who had robbed so much from the Italians that the bottom of his carriage collapsed under the weight of the gold he'd nicked.

THE UNITED IRISHMEN

Despite the internal upheavals, the revolution still provided inspiration to its supporters around the world. Partly this is because most of the world was a year behind events, there being no *Sky News* or CNN. If there was, the guillotinings would probably have come in bursts of three followed by a gap, to fit in with the commercial breaks, and incidents such as the storming of the Bastille would have been shown from every conceivable angle, maybe with a special camera inserted into the end of a pike.

But the revolution had also broken down the biggest barrier to social change, which is the belief that social change isn't possible. The idea that provides the greatest protection to the injustices of the modern world is not that these injustices are right, but that they're inevitable – 'There will always be rich and poor, it's human nature,' or 'There will always be some race that gets picked on.' I'm sure in Ancient Rome people said, 'You'll never stop crowds paying to watch people spear each other to death, it's human nature. I mean, you'll never have a society that entertains itself by watching twelve puerile people wander aimlessly round a house for ten weeks, will you?'

The revolution made change seem possible for the first time, as illustrated by the response in Ireland. This is a nation subject to possibly more stereotypes than any other. Even now the global view of the Irish as a quaint backward people seems to be encapsulated in nonsense like *Riverdance*, as if the Irish really move like that. Dublin is a major modern European city: they couldn't have built that without moving their arms. And the most popular view of the problems of Ireland is that the Protestants and Catholics have never got on, so a solution depends on finding a way of keeping them apart and accepting each other's space. But this wasn't the case after the French Revolution.

As in France, the country was dominated by an ideology that restricted trade, science and personal ambition while inflicting poverty on the peasants. The difference was that this ideology was inflicted on them from outside, by the British, who imposed import controls, duties and arbitrary laws such as the one banning Irish companies from processing Irish wool. Which ironically is the sort of peculiarity that, two hundred years later became thought of as 'Irish'.

After the storming of the Bastille, the Irish opposition looked to France. The prison for peasants who had fought against English landlords became known as the Irish Bastille. And on the first anniversary of the revolution Belfast held a carnival, complete with fireworks, at which 6,000 people listened to an address to the French nation, and to another to the Irish urging them to copy their example. As in France, many of the founders of this movement were frustrated businessmen, including Henry Jackson, who owned a foundry that he used to make pikes for distribution to rebellious supporters.

The most influential leader was a trainee lawyer called Wolfe Tone, who had already carried off an impressive feat by being the National Secretary of the Catholic Committee, despite being a Protestant. At first this could seem strange, as if perhaps it was the one thing they forgot to ask at the interview. But Tone was sympathetic to the plight of Catholics, saying, 'they have been stripped of all land, the bulk are in the lowest degree of misery, they seldom taste bread, live in wretched hovels and labour incessantly'.[2] His mission was to unite the Catholic peasants with the Protestants, and many of his most committed followers were Presbyterians. His mission statement was the cry 'Our freedom must be had at all hazards. If the men of no property will not help us they must fall; we will free ourselves by the aid of that large and respectable class – the men of no property.'[3] This began a great tradition of defiant Irish speeches, which continued through the Famine, the Easter Rising, the war of independence and up to Roy Keane's 'You're fucking useless, stick it up yer bollocks,' before storming out of the World Cup.

Tone's plan was to persuade the French to send an army that would back an uprising against the aristocracy. He went to Paris to propose his plan, but had to wait three months before getting an appointment to see the leaders of the Directory, as if he was an unknown writer who'd arrived in Hollywood and was trying to meet producers to sell his screenplay. He found this frustrating, though to be fair there can't be many governments that would respond immediately when told, 'There's an Irish bloke at the door says he wants you to send a fleet of fifty ships to invade his country.' But Tone's logic was appealing: the English would be severely weakened if they were thrown out of Ireland and replaced by the French. The Directory agreed to send a fleet under one of their leading generals, Hoche, with Tone as a commander. Tone was eager to leave immediately, and kept asking almost every day why they couldn't go straight away, like a kid eager to get to the seaside. He seems eventually to have lost his temper on the day he wrote in his diary, 'The excuse now is that we are waiting for some charts or plans which must be washed in water-colours – a worthy subject for delay in the present stage of business!'[4] They finally set off in December 1796, but as they were approaching Cork a freak hurricane in Bantry Bay meant the entire fleet had to turn back.

Tone's followers were waiting and waiting for the French fleet, so that they could begin the uprising. But the English spotted the ships in Bantry Bay, and the Chief Secretary for Ireland, Lord Pelham, wrote, 'Nothing but terror will keep them in order.' Anyone suspected of supporting Tone was flogged, villages were burned, and one English officer complained of 'the smoke and flames of burning houses and the dead bodies of boys and men slain by the Britons, though no opposition had been given'.[5]

Despite the failure, the population of Ireland seemed impressed that the French had sent anyone at all. Tone's organization, the

United Irishmen, grew in membership until there were 120,000 across Ulster, and Tone, undaunted, set about persuading the French to try again. Apart from the growing ferment in Ireland there was another reason why he was convinced they would win this time: the Royal Navy was on the point of mutiny.

English sailors hadn't had a pay rise for 150 years, and were aware of their importance in the war against the French. Many of them had sympathized with the revolution from the beginning, and thousands were Irish, so after the brutality inflicted against their countrymen they were less inclined than ever to support the navy for which they worked. At Spithead, near Portsmouth, this poem became popular amongst seamen:

> Is this your proof of British rights?
> Is this rewarding bravery?
> Oh! Shame to boast your tar's exploits
> Then doom these tars to slavery.[6]

Statements from the sailors began, 'The Age of Reason has at length revolved.' The navy responded by making concessions to most of the demands, but another mutiny broke out in Sheerness, where the sailors blockaded the Thames. The scale of the crisis was such that *The Oxford Book of the War Speeches of William Pitt* includes a note with this episode, that 'had the French been able to land in Ireland in the summer of 1797, they would have found its occupation an easy task, and the end of the British Empire would have been at hand'.

This wasn't how events unfolded, partly because by the time of the second attempted invasion, the French Revolution had become a more conservative affair. Its army sought wealth and markets for the bourgeois tradesmen, rather than liberation for the population, so mutinies and calls to end oppression held less interest for the revolution than would have been the case in its early stages. The second uprising in Ireland was supported by a much smaller French force than the last time, though this time they did actually land. The British Army, recovering from its low point, crushed this rebellion with floggings, burnings and hangings more brutal than before, especially by Orange lodges, specially set up by the English to encourage the Protestants to recover a sense of loyalty to the Crown as a creed above Catholicism.

Wolfe Tone was captured on board a French ship and sentenced to execution. On the night before, he decided to cheat the executioner and cut his own throat. A jailer discovered him, not quite dead. A surgeon was called in order to keep him alive long enough to be hanged, and Tone's only words to the surgeon were, 'I am sorry I have been so bad an anatomist.'[7] That's the Protestant work ethic for you.

PAINE LEAVES FRANCE

Almost inevitably, Napoleon worked for a while with Tom Paine. Paine agreed to assist Napoleon with his knowledge of British geography for a potential invasion, but when Napoleon sought a longer-term relationship, Paine rejected the offer. Paine was still enthusiastic for revolutionary ideas, despite going through an experience that might have left the keenest of us cynical. So, rather than attain an official military position in Napoleon's army, he persisted with his next book, which he'd begun while languishing in jail. This one was called *The Age of Reason* and outraged the authorities of every country, who all concurred that Paine was 'preaching atheism'. But how does anyone 'preach atheism'? Do you wander down roads on Sunday mornings, knocking on the doors of religious people and saying, 'Good morning, have you heard the bad news?'

The aim of his book was to place reason above mysticism, because 'To argue with a man who has renounced the authority of reason is like administering medicine to the dead.' Christians, he said, tell us to 'worship a God who sent his only son to die. What sort of an example is that?' Questioning the logic of the New Testament, he asked why, if Jesus was to make all things known to all nations, he could only speak one language. After he was released from jail he pondered why, if the first five books of the Old Testament were by Moses, three of them were written in the third person, including the passage in Numbers Chapter 12 that says, 'Moses was very meek, above all the men which were upon the face of the Earth.' If he really wrote this, said Paine, that would make him the most *arrogant* man on Earth.

Once again the book sold in vast numbers. But Paine could sense that France was sliding towards dictatorship, and wanted to leave for America. The trouble was, he'd been angry with George Washington for not doing enough to get him released from prison, so he'd sent him a letter saying, 'As to you, sir, the world will be puzzled as to whether you have abandoned your principles, or whether you had any'[8] – which was pretty unequivocal. It's surprising he didn't finish it off with 'PS: You owe me fifty cents for that cheese.' Paine was sneaked back into America by Thomas Jefferson, but *The Age of Reason* had turned American society against him. The *Gazette of the United States* wrote, 'Paine is the infamous scavenger of all the filth which could be raked from the paths which have hitherto been trodden by all the revilers of Christianity.' Another editor wrote, 'What! Invite to the United States that lying, drunken, brutal infidel!'[9] Because the Americans wanted to establish from the outset that you'd never be able to rise to a position of influence there if you practised lying or infidelity.

THE COUP

While in Egypt, Napoleon had some respect for the place he was invading. He turned the deck of his ship into a floating seminar for his army to debate matters of Egyptian culture. And he stole the

Rosetta Stone, which revealed the workings of hieroglyphics, though the British stole it back off him later and kept it for themselves. But at this point comes the incident which does what you might have thought was impossible, and makes you feel sorry for Napoleon. Just as he was about to launch the Battle of the Nile against the Royal Navy, his friend Junot told him that Joséphine was spending every available moment with Hippolyte Charles. This in itself must have been a blow to Napoleon's ego, but on hearing this he wrote letters to friends, and to Joséphine, detailing his torment at the news, only to find the ship carrying the letters intercepted by the British, who then published them in the *Morning Chronicle*.

Could anything be more humiliating? It would be like the *Daily Mirror* 3 a.m. girls publishing photos of Saddam Hussein's wife in the Groucho Club snogging Jamie Theakston.

The distraught Napoleon continued his military adventures, and clearly fell in love with Egypt, announcing, 'I saw myself founding a new religion, riding an elephant and in my hand a new Koran that I had composed to suit my needs.'[10] Isn't that cheating? I suppose whenever he got to a bit he didn't fancy, he'd say something like, 'What's this? No bacon? Scratch that bit out.' And the rewritten version would be full of passages such as 'And God said that every year on that day a grapefruit would be shoved up the arse of all men called Hippolyte.'

Napoleon was summoned back from Egypt in 1799 by leading members of the Directory, who were panicking at the disarray the government had fallen into. Every leading figure was embroiled in corruption. To pay for the army they'd had to raise taxes, so the middle classes turned against them; the royalists were plotting another coup; and the Jacobins were recovering their popularity. One clique resolved that in order to stop either of these groups from coming back to power the army should stage its own coup and end the instability of the Directory. They asked General Joubert to carry out the coup, and he accepted. But Joubert was killed in battle the next day. So the Abbé Sieyès asked General Moreau, who declined but suggested Napoleon.

Far from Napoleon's rule springing from ruthless efficiency, it began with chaos. Napoleon marched into the parliament and announced he was taking power, at which point someone scratched his face and he ran out of the building. Napoleon's brother Lucien went out with him and returned on a horse. Could you imagine any modern MP doing anything a fraction as interesting as riding into the House of Commons on a horse? Even if they did, current politicians would just look blank and say, 'I refer the honourable horse to the answer I gave some moments ago.'

At this second attempt, the Bonapartes won enough deputies to complete the coup, and established a three-man ruling committee of Napoleon, Sieyès and Roger Ducos. A placard proclaiming the new government was posted in Paris, saying, FRANCE WANTS SOME-THING GREAT AND LONG-LASTING. SHE HAS NO DESIRE FOR A MONARCHY. SHE WANTS PEACEABLE CONSERVATIVES, NOT UNRULY INNOVATORS. His rule was ratified with a referendum, though this might not have been all that accurate. For example 500,000 'yes' votes were counted from the army, although no one in the army was polled because, announced Lucien, 'The army *must* be in favour of Napoleon.'

None of this solved Napoleon's personal crisis. Over the next year Joséphine did her best to emulate Marie Antoinette, buying nine hundred dresses and a thousand pairs of gloves, while Napoleon started going out with an actress. Everyone in Paris knew except Joséphine, but then she announced she wished to see the play in which the leading lady happened to be Napoleon's mistress. At one point the actress had to say the line 'I shall seduce many more,' and the entire audience rose to face Joséphine, laughing and applauding.[11]

One night Napoleon was with the actress in their palace at St-Cloud, while Joséphine was in the grounds. Suddenly the actress let out a scream so piercing it could be heard throughout the grounds.

Joséphine and the valets rushed up to the room and found Napoleon lying on the floor, having had an epileptic seizure, whilst the actress stood by the bed, naked, yelling because she thought he was dead. That's just what you want when you've had a seizure, isn't it?, your wife bursting in to find a yelling naked actress while you're barely able to move or speak, as you splutter, 'I . . . knooow thiiiis loooooks baaad.'

The nature of Napoleon's rule has been debated ever since. My first experience of this took place when I joined the actors' union Equity in 1984, and I was asked to attend a meeting of activists in someone's front room on a Sunday afternoon. For three hours I sat there,

Napoleon I – just the odd compromise with the ideals of the revolution.

listening to a group of seven people debating how at a forthcoming regional conference we should counter the argument put forward by the Workers' Revolutionary Party that Margaret Thatcher's government was a Bonapartist dictatorship. I suppose it was the failure to get that issue cleared up that allowed her to stay in power for eleven years.

Napoleon Bonaparte's dictatorship was clearly a Bonapartist dictatorship. He established a bourgeois regime, with bourgeois values, while eradicating the radicalism that had accompanied them in the days of the revolution. A national legal code, the Code Napoléon, was introduced. The French language became dominant in every region. A national bank was established and a national education system was set up, with science prevailing over religion

Napoleon in his smart-casual gear.

as its central aim. An arrangement was made with the Pope to revive the Catholic Church in France, as long as it accepted that it would never recapture its old role as part of the state. The reopening of the churches was carried out with great ceremony; Napoleon ordered all his generals to attend, but none of them knew the procedure and all stood up or knelt down at the wrong times.

France had become a modern bourgeois nation. No tithes, no natural positions of authority for those born into them, no bizarre hunting laws, no 'building roads on a Sunday' rule, no compulsory swishing of frogs. And no unruly innovators.

To ratify his rule, Napoleon held another referendum, this time to make him leader of France for life. One soldier wrote in his memoirs, 'We were summoned by our General who said "Comrades, you are free to hold your own opinion. Nevertheless, I warn you that the first man not to vote for Napoleon will be shot."'[12] The marvellous thing is that someone could come up with a similar rule now about having to vote Conservative, and there'd still only be a 2 per cent swing.

THE JACOBIN BUG

One of the contradictions of Napoleon's army was that, whilst it imposed the dictator's values on its vanquished territory, the soldiers themselves were still motivated by the radicalism of the revolution. Wherever the army travelled, they took Jacobin ideas with them. Pitt announced his fear that, 'the messengers of Jacobinism' had ventured into India to 'form Jacobin clubs, which they succeeded in establishing. They were required to swear in one breath, "hatred to tyranny, the love of liberty, and the destruction of all kings and sovereigns".'[13]

He may have been referring to Tipu Sultan, an Indian soldier who was one of fifty-nine people to form a Jacobin club in the Indian province of Srirangapatna in 1797. Tipu planted a tree of liberty, wore the French liberty cap and proclaimed the object of the club as bringing the ideals of the revolution to India. As part of this campaign he assembled a library to educate his followers and the local peasantry. More worryingly for Pitt, he persuaded his army to drive the British out of his province. When it was eventually recaptured, Tipu was defeated and killed, and the British systematically burned every book in the library.

Another foreigner inspired by the revolution was Francisco de Miranda, a Venezuelan who came to France to take part in the revolution. He was appointed as brigadier by Danton, and fought at Valmy with such success that he became a general. When he eventually returned to South America he fought with Bolívar for Venezuelan independence, and was killed on Bastille Day. Since then, every Bastille Day, Venezuela has sent an official delegate to the tiny village of Valmy, where there's a statue of Miranda, a pig farm and the remains of the replacement windmill that eventually blew over in a hurricane.

The revolution's influence also spread to Iceland, which at the time was ruled by Denmark. In 1809 a British soap merchant arrived there with a Danish interpreter. The Danish Governor of Iceland refused to allow the soap man to sell his goods, so the trader arrested him and placed the interpreter, Jorgen Jorgensen, in charge of the country. As a supporter of the French Revolution, Jorgensen announced a new constitution, with an end to monarchy, universal male suffrage and stating, 'The poor and common have the same rights as the rich and powerful.'[14] He only stayed in power for two months, until the Royal Navy arrived and deposed him, but he must remain one of the few world leaders of the nineteenth century who could ask you to buy soap in a variety of languages.

NAPOLEON AND TOUSSAINT

Of all the international repercussions of the revolution, the greatest must have been in San Domingo. Toussaint's army, along with their

ally Sonthonax, had fought off the Spanish. Sonthonax then established an education system for ex-slaves, in which they were taught
Greek and Roman history. During the rule of the Directory, Toussaint
insisted the island was part of the French Republic, 'one and indivisible', meaning its inhabitants must be free. But he was aware that
the Directory was fragile, and a more hostile government might try
to restore slavery, so he made a speech aimed at anyone considering
such an attempt: 'Do they think that men who have been able to
enjoy the blessing of liberty will calmly see it snatched away? They
supported their chains only so long as they did not know any condition of life more happy than that of slavery. But today when they
have left it, if they had a thousand lives they would sacrifice them all
rather than be forced into slavery again.'[15]

After Napoleon's coup, Toussaint's army took over the Spanish
half of the island, to strengthen their position against a possible
attack. Then it became known that Joséphine's mother owned a
plantation there, which had gone to ruin as a result of the wars. The
notion that Napoleon might be up the pub saying to his mates, 'Now
I've got her mother giving it that about her bloody plantation,'
appears to have alarmed Toussaint. He wrote twenty letters to
Joséphine assuring her the plantation had been restored to prime
condition, and when no reply came back, he felt certain her old man
was preparing an invasion.

He was right. Napoleon sent an expedition under General Leclerc,
with orders to disarm the population and deport the generals before
imposing 'special laws'. In total, Leclerc was in command of 34,000
troops, who started by reducing a village of 2,000 houses to 59.
Toussaint's army launched a ferocious guerrilla resistance, and by
the time Leclerc died there were only 10,000 of his men left alive,
8000 of whom were in hospital. The remaining generals tricked
Toussaint into coming with his family to a meeting, at which they
were all arrested, bound and sent on a boat to France. It was
recorded that as Toussaint left he said, 'In overthrowing me, you
have cut down in San Domingo only the trunk of the tree of liberty.

It will spring up again by the roots for they are numerous and deep.'[16] He was kept in a jail in the mountains, where he died within two years.

Much as he predicted, after Toussaint's death, Napoleon lost a further 25,000 men before giving up and awarding the island its independence. This was never a separate battle from the revolution, but an integral part of it, the fate of the battle in each country bound up with the fate of the other.

14

The Revolution in the Mind

With music . . . Exchanging slaves for majesties
Modern waves of tragedy

BLISS WAS IT

As well as the political impact it had across the world, the revolution transformed culture, creating the atmosphere that produced revolutions in music, poetry, science and philosophy, of which the following are just some of the examples.

Poetry

William Blake is mostly known as an eccentric who drew his visions of angels and demons, in rare lucid moments writing about tigers burning bright and England's green and pleasant land. But just as a connection can usually be found between real life and the weirdest dreams, Blake's visions were linked with his times. He wrote a poem called, unimaginatively for him, 'The French Revolution', in which he described the attitude of France's religious leaders:

I love hanging and drawing and quartering
Every bit as well as war and slaughtering
Damn prayer and singing
Unless they will bring in
The blood of ten thousand by fighting or swinging.

The revolution appears to have given him a sense of community with the peasants of France and the slaves of the Caribbean, and it was as part of the *Songs of Experience*, published in 1794, that he wrote:

Tyger Tyger, burning bright,
In the forests of the night:
What immortal hand or eye,
Could frame thy fearful symmetry?

The exact meaning of every word is open to question, though it seems clear the tyger represents the revolution, and the question is about the nature of a god that can have created it. Or perhaps for some reason in the 1790s while he was obsessed with the progress of the revolution, he thought, 'Sod it, I'm going to have a break from France and write a poem about a tiger with 'tiger' spelled wrong.'

Blake was among the earliest of the Romantic poets, who supported the revolution and backed the triumph of reason but rejected the functional philosophy sweeping Britain at the start of the Industrial Revolution, in which there was no role for imagination. Equally strident in his support for revolution and imagination was Lord Byron, whose poetry and rakish lifestyle made him possibly the greatest celebrity in Europe. At parties and balls, it was said, his poetry would literally make women swoon. This is something difficult to imagine in our day, when the nearest we get to romantic poetry is on birthday cards that have verses such as:

Here's to say I love you in my own sweet loving way,
On this very very very very very special day.

He was popular with the wealthy he lampooned, partly because he
represented a spontaneity that they had to suppress, with their curt-
seying and passing the port in the right direction. But when he
declared Napoleon to be 'freedom's son', he was forced to leave Britain,
which he did in a replica of Napoleon's carriage. With a flamboyance
reminiscent of Danton, he caroused and campaigned, wrote, inspired
and debauched himself. Eventually he perished at the same age as
Danton, with a similar exhaustion, having spent his fortune on raising
an army to fight on the side of the Greeks in their war of independence.

The impact on poets was almost universal, so that whether they
considered themselves political, satirical, romantic or visionary they
were defined by their attitude towards the revolution. Wordsworth's
was the most explicit, with his famous 'Bliss it was in that dawn to
be alive,/But to be young was very heaven!' Later he recoiled from
his youthful enthusiasm, which is not an unusual path to take,
though it is fairly spectacular to go from 'Revolution is bliss' to 'On
second thoughts, I prefer daffodils.'

Music

Beethoven, whose life and work was inspired by the events of
the French Revolution, made one of the greatest statements to sum-
marise its aims. His main employer, Prince Lichnowsky, asked him
to play for the amusement of the Prince's guests and Beethoven
refused. The Prince went beserk, so Beethoven broke off relations
with a letter saying . . .

Prince, what you are, you are by circumstance and birth.
What I am, I am through myself; there are, and always will
be, thousands of princes, but there is only one Beethoven.

For Beethoven, the revolution represented a triumph for individuality, and he was ecstatic when the French Ambassador to Austria suggested his Third Symphony should be dedicated to Napoleon. The result was the grandest symphony up to that point, the first to aim at telling a story, with its depiction of military victories and funeral marches celebrating the death of old values. Yet the impact of the revolution on Beethoven is often ignored. One typical biography claims that he only dedicated a symphony to Napoleon because he was 'drawn towards powerful figures'. So it could have been anyone – Marie Antoinette, Arnold Schwarzenegger, Sven Goran Eriksson – Napoleon was just the first to spring to mind. It's as if in two hundred years' time someone said, 'The Specials weren't really bothered about Nelson Mandela, they were just attracted to people in jail. And it scanned well. If they'd left it a few years it would have gone "Free-ee Jonathon Aitken."'

But the symphony was composed, printed and about to be taken to the printers, when a friend ran in and announced that Napoleon had abandoned republicanism to make himself Emperor. Once Beethoven had taken this in, he went into a rage, ripped out the dedication and scratched out the word 'Bonaparte' with such anger that he ripped the paper to bits. Which you would do, if your republican hero made himself King. It would be a bit feeble if you went, 'Oh dear' and gently erased it with the rubber on the end of your pencil.

Philosophy

It's hard to imagine how excruciating it must have been for sup-porters of the revolution to come to terms with the fact that Napoleon no longer represented the early spirit of the revolution. It was particularly awkward for the philosopher Friedrich Hegel. As a supporter of the revolution and of Napoleon's armies, when Napoleon marched through his home town of Jena, Hegel rushed out excitedly to welcome his hero. When he got home, however, he discovered that Napoleon's army had burned his house down.

Hegel saw his mission as explaining how, in the aftermath of the revolution, change in society came about. The motor for change, he said, was conflict between ideas. Any idea, he said, is in constant conflict with other ideas, and the outcome of this conflict is a new set of ideas leading to new conflicts, and so on, and he called this system 'dialectics'.

In effect Hegel was saying that everything, no matter how constant it seems, is in a state of change. This change takes place continuously, although most of the time it's invisible. For example, if you look behind the surface of a major social upheaval, you'll almost certainly find a gradual building of tension, whereas if you see the same event undialectically you see only the sudden outburst, the pamphlet, the speech, the head on the pike, the shadowy crowd crying, 'Down with ze Queen!'

So this period gave us Blake, Coleridge, Burns, Southey, Kant, Schelling, Hegel, Beethoven, Wilkinson the ironmaster, Schubert, Mendelssohn, Chopin, Liszt, Rossini, Turner, Constable and the romantic poets. Whereas two hundred years from now, I doubt people will say, 'The late twentieth century was amazing, giving rise to Halliwell, Davidson, Davro, Lloyd-Webber and Hurley.'

EMPEROR

By 1804, Napoleon was no longer even pretending to adhere to the set of principles that drove the revolution. He pronounced himself Emperor, crowned by the Pope, so that his offspring would succeed him. Which, as sell-outs go, has to be pretty much admired. He reintroduced Catholicism as the official religion, declaring, 'How can a state be well governed without the aid of religion? When a man dies of hunger next to another who is gorged, he can not accept that disparity without someone in authority saying, "God has decreed there must be rich and poor, but in the afterlife for eternity it will be the other way about."'[1]

In one sense Napoleon was even more powerful than most monarchs, because he declared that his brothers couldn't take their place in line to the throne unless they left their wives, whom Napoleon didn't like.

Now as he strode across Europe there was no suggestion that this was for the liberation of men who were born free but were everywhere in chains; it was to make France, and especially himself, stronger. Sadly, it seems to have driven him mad. He developed a twitch in his shoulder, which would run amok as he was dictating letters. He took to scratching his face until it bled, and became terrified of open doors. And he introduced a new element to his military strategy, insisting that he had to have a wank immediately before a battle. He developed a dislike for Fridays, convinced they were unlucky. And he was unable to make any decision without first looking at the sky to see his two lucky stars – which must have made daytime decision-making impossible. But mostly he took his advice from a little red genie. He said he'd made a ten-year pact with the genie just before a battle in Egypt, in which the spirit would protect him as long as he introduced a universal republic. If Napoleon reneged on the deal, the genie would give him three formal warnings before abandoning him to his enemies. So it was that the revolution that began as a cry for reason against mysticism ended up in the hands of a little red genie.

From the coronation onwards, whenever he established power in a new province, he tarnished the republican message by making one of his relatives King. His whole family was used to build his power base, so he wrote to his cousin Eugene: 'I have arranged a marriage for you with Princess Augusta, daughter of the elector of Bavaria. She is very pretty. I am sending you her portrait on a cup.'[2]

When he invaded Italy a second time he was excommunicated by the Pope, so he arrested him. I don't agree with the concept of emperor as such, but I suppose if you are one you might as well do stuff like arrest the Pope.

He did a deal with Poland, that he would support their independence from Russia if they granted him 40,000 soldiers. When he visited Poland, his carriage was surrounded by supporters, including an eighteen-year-old called Marie-Louise Walewska. He arranged to meet her, and she turned out to be a countess, married to a 77-year-old with whom she'd had a child. Napoleon told the Polish government he wouldn't attend their ball unless Marie-Louise danced with him, so the old man was ordered to do his duty and stay at home. Then Napoleon insisted that, to cement the deal, Marie-Louise had to marry him. The Poles agreed (except for her husband), but the next problem was that the only person who could annul his marriage to Joséphine was the Pope, and he'd had him arrested. If only *Jerry Springer* had been on at the time.

Napoleon did the deal he had to do with the Pope, releasing him so he could permit the Emperor to remarry. But he probably incurred the Pope's wrath again with his next trick, which was rewriting the Catechism that has to be learned by children in Catholic countries. The new question/answer recital began

> We owe to Napoleon the first, our Emperor, love, respect, obedience, loyalty, military service, the dues laid down for the defence of the empire and its throne . . .
> Are there not particular reasons which should attach us to our Emperor?
> According to the Apostle Paul, those who don't, render themselves worthy of eternal damnation.[3]

Which is pretty clever, to take Catholicism and make it madder, a feat not equalled until Puff Daddy covered a Sting song and made it worse.

Napoleon eventually over-reached himself in spectacular fashion with his bid to invade Russia, in 1812. He later said his plan was so flawed that his red genie was advising against it – but he ignored even *him*. That's real megalomania, to invent an imaginary advisory genie and then tell him to piss off as well.

Even when his troops were winning, the Russian escapade was a disaster. Any soldier who injured a limb had to have it amputated to avoid gangrene. After one battle, a surgeon got through two hundred limbs in twelve hours. Of 450,000 troops that set out, only 160,000 were capable of fighting by the time he got to Moscow, and once he arrived there, the Russian Army fled, so Napoleon couldn't complete his aim of massacring it. Stuck in the cold, Napoleon was forced to retreat, but as his troops tried to loot villages for supplies they were captured by peasants who carried out the most imaginative tortures. A whole village would turn out to beat a soldier to death with hoes. And they probably justified it by saying, 'All we're doing is exercising our traditional way of life. These soldiers are pests, and if we stop doing this, we could lose up to four million jobs in the hoe-making industry.' Compassionate Russian officers would shoot captured French soldiers rather than let the peasants get to them. And the famine was so bad that soldiers would eat their own fingers after they had dropped off from gangrene. To keep warm at night some would disembowel a dead horse and climb inside.

As the army dissolved, the revolution sank officially to its beleaguered end. Almost every power in Europe supported an invasion of France, until Napoleon was forced to abdicate, and the King's brother, titled King Louis XVIII, took over. In spite of all the betrayals of the revolution that Napoleon had enacted, his defeat devastated radicals around Europe. Hegel wrote, 'It is a frightful spectacle to see a great genius destroy himself. The entire mass of mediocrity has brought down the highest to the same level as itself.'[4] Byron retreated into a room alone for four days. In his diary he wrote, 'Today I boxed an hour, wrote an ode to Napoleon and ate six biscuits.'

Napoleon was exiled to the island of Elba but, like the Terminator, the revolution kept re-emerging after each supposed death. Napoleon escaped from Elba with 1,000 supporters, and Louis XVIII immediately fled. Napoleon made his way to Waterloo in Belgium, where he was met by the Duke of Wellington and a Prussian army that defeated him for the last time. As he returned to Paris, he was still surrounded by supporters, but his statement to them summarized the difference between his attitudes and those that sparked the revolution when he said, 'I could not, I will not be King of the mob.'[5]

CONCLUSION

You can be a hero in an age of none

'We need a revolution,' said the lad, no more than nineteen, in the packed meeting at the University of Warwick where I was speaking about the French Revolution. 'And we, I mean us here, can begin to make that revolution right after this meeting, by . . .' He paused. What would he say? By mobilizing the peasantry of the Coventry area? By going on a Long March to Leicester? 'By smiling,' he said. "Cos you smile and, like, someone has to smile back – even, like, a capitalist, and you make, like, ripples.'

The strange thing was, this didn't seem as mad as it might have done. Because at least there was an element of belief that, like the peasants and postmen of France, we can try to change society through our own actions. Don't get me wrong, I feel his strategy is flawed, not least because there would be all the usual splits. A militant wing would break away to laugh, then as they went around bellowing, 'Haaa haaa,' another group would complain that the laughers were turning public opinion against the movement and we could win over some important people if we made do with a slight grin.

One of the most famous quotes on the French Revolution is that of Zhou Enlai, one of Mao Zedong's ministers, who was asked what he thought the effects of the revolution were and replied, 'It's too early to tell.' And he had a point, because the battle over what it was all about is still being fought. It certainly rippled beyond its first century, because Lloyd George, when rejecting mounting a full-scale invasion of Russia after the Bolshevik Revolution, gave as his reason the failure of the Duke of Brunswick to crush the French Revolution with similar tactics. For today's establishment, the French Revolution provides proof of the mayhem that reigns when those who talk of equality get their way. Which is why I get the impression we're not supposed to like it very much. I wouldn't go so far as to suggest a CIA mole in the scriptwriting team at *Blue Peter*, but every reference to the revolution as nothing but carnage is a warning – leave things as they are, these people who ask you to protest about things might seem well-intentioned, but if they get their way it will be heads on pikes in the Arndale Centre.

For the establishment relies on passivity, the very opposite of revolution. For a kaleidoscope of reasons, most people most of the time choose not to confront the injustices on the planet. Even when they do, their suggestion is invariably that a different president, or chairman of the World Bank, would possibly be fairer. The last group that any one considers should run society is themselves. But for five years in France, that wasn't the case.

Whatever conclusions you draw from it, an episode which draws millions into activity they never would have believed possible, as the French Revolution did, creates the most spectacular human stories, of hope, defiance, comedy and tragedy. The revolution created dozens of magnificent characters, but it destroyed nearly all of them as well. Hundreds of years of fame were bought for a price of youthful death. Robespierre, Danton, Desmoulins, Marat, St-Just, Brissot, the Rolands, Babeuf, Le Bas, Couthon, almost every major player perished in the drama they were writing. Even Tom Paine, who scraped his way back to America, was a pariah, penniless in Philadelphia. A friend described his condition: 'His shirt was in tatters, and he gave off the most disagreeable smell possible. I got a tub of warm water and soap, and washed him from head to foot, taking three times before I could get him clean. His toe-nails were like bird claws.'[1] When he died, the Quakers refused to bury him in their ground. William Cobbett tried to bring his body home to England, but the bones got lost on the way. Almost the only character who seems to have made it through unscathed as a significant character from beginning to end was Sanson, the official guillotiner.

The royalist victims were equally tragic. The Royal Family was all guillotined. And Count Fersen, following the execution of Marie Antoinette, was an emotional wreck for the rest of his life. Then in 1810 the word went round that he was responsible for poisoning Prince Christian, heir to the throne of Denmark. Whether this was true or not isn't clear, but either way the crowd at Christian's funeral procession thought it was, so when they spotted Count Fersen they tore him to death in the street.

Maybe the reason the leaders of the revolution are so despised is that they did something so rare in our own times: having set their sights on a more just society, they did all they could to see it through. Instead of turning swiftly from radical spokesmen to respectably suited local politicians shaking hands with businessmen on regional television, they responded to every attack by resisting their enemies with the full force of an armed population.

For the millions whose names we will never know the grandest questions were united with the tiniest. The matter of how they could secure food for the next month was tied up with the question of how the world should be run, what rights we are born with and whether there's a god. Those citizens prepared to lead their neighbours into occupying the stores to demand price reduction were the ones most likely to produce a pamphlet suggesting a programme for the rights of women. Those who stood firm at Valmy, or tried to calm their breathing and their furiously pumping hearts as they approached the Versailles Palace to retrieve the royals, were the ones most likely to sit up all night discussing the role of astronomy, the most efficient method of farming and whether there should be sport after the revolution.

And this is possibly the revolution's most enduring impact. To give one example, by the 1840s the heroes of the revolution were becoming heroes of the early labour movement. A book about the history of Merthyr Tydfil, written in the 1860s, says, 'A few who thought highly of *The Rights of Man* and *The Age of Reason* assembled in secret places on the mountains and, taking the works from under a concealed boulder, read them with great unction.'[2] I wonder if anyone has ever read anything by a modern British politician with *any* unction, let alone great unction. Can you imagine a group sneaking up a mountain with a torch, finding a boulder and going, 'Hnnnnn, *push*, just a bit more, here we are, the speeches of John Prescott'?

Perhaps the most concise summary of the outlook of the mainstream politician of the early twenty-first century was given by Tony Blair, when an interviewer asked him what he dreamed about. His reply was, 'These days I don't have much time for sleep, let alone dreams.'[3] As if it's a matter of pride to be unable to dream. Besides which, this makes no sense, as sleep doesn't take any longer if you have a dream. If you have a ten-minute dream you don't wake up ten minutes late shrieking, 'Oh no, now I've missed my train because of that poxy dream.'

The French Revolution shaped millions of minds into looking in the opposite direction. It created a world of boundless possibilities. It allowed millions of people to see all matters, whether personal, political, grand or minute, as connected and depending on each other; it allowed every concept to be open to question. The imagination could rule, and the full potential of human creativity was unleashed. The French Revolution created that sense across continents, across the world of slavery and into every corner that could receive the news. It asks the question of everyone who comes across it – 'So what will *you* do to combat the slave-owners, the gabelle officers, the Dukes of Brunswick of your own time? You can let history pass you by, or find the Drouet or Demoulins that's in all of us. The French Revolution was the polar opposite of a society ruled by those who have forgotten how to dream.

The revolution, for all the gore and horror it contained, has continued to provide inspiration for people who object to the unequal way that society is organized, in which the richest 360 people on the planet own the same amount as the poorest 2 billion. It provides the evidence that peasants, slaves, postmen and washerwomen can change the world, and change themselves as they do so. Because there are more of them than there are nobles, priests and kings. Because, when you think about it, if all the 2 billion got together and smiled at the 360, that would look pretty spooky.

However, the revolution had one other astonishing long-term impact, in that it made life inconsolably miserable for the people of Hartlepool. During the Napoleonic Wars, the French were depicted in the English press as monkeys. So, when a shipwrecked boat crashed into the coast of Hartlepool with no one on board except a monkey, the local population took the monkey for a Frenchman, tried it in court and hanged it. And that's all that anyone knows about Hartlepool. You mention Hartlepool to anyone, especially in the north-east, and they'll just say, 'That's where they hanged that monkey.' Which proves Zhou Enlai right: as a result of the French Revolution, there could one day be a scientist from Hartlepool who discovers a cure for all known diseases, and as he's about to announce this at a press conference someone will shout, 'Oy, Hartlepool boy, you hung that bloody monkey.'

NOTES

Introduction

1. Carlyle, *The French Revolution* (London, 1989), p.96
2. Ibid., p.74
3. Shama, *Citizens* (London, 1989), p.732
4. Hobsbawm, *Echoes of the Marseillaise* (London/New York, 1990), p.103

1: The Ancien Régime

1. Fraser, *Marie Antoinette* (London, 2001), p.144
2. Warwick, *Danton and the French Revolution* (London, 1909), p.27
3. De Tocqueville, *The Ancien Regime and the French Revolution* (Manchester, 1955), p.152
4. Shama, *Citizens*, p.12
5. Sebastien-Mercier, *The Waiting City* (London, 1933), various
6. James, *The Black Jacobins* (London, 1938), p.12

3: The Enlightenment

1. Darnton, *Forbidden Best-Sellers of Pre-Revolutionary France* (London/New York, 1996), p.164
2. Rousseau, *A Discourse on Equality* (London, 1984), p.42
3. Rousseau, *The Social Contract* (London, 1968), p.184
4. Rousseau, *Confessions* (Oxford, 2000), p.370
5. Darnton, *Forbidden Best-Sellers of Pre-Revolutionary France*, p. 96
6. du Plessix Gray, *At Home with the Marquis de Sade* (London, 1998), p.24
7. Ibid., p.65

4: The Crisis

1. Sebastien-Mercier, *The Waiting City*, p.108
2. These three references from Huet, *Mourning Glory* (Pennsylvania, 1997), p.152
3. Sieburg, *The Incorruptible* (New York, 1938)
4. Huet, *Mourning Glory*, p.152
5. Roland Bowen, *Cricket: A History of its Growth and Development Throughout the World* (London, 1970)
6. Godechot, *The Taking of the Bastille* (London, 1970), p.59

5: On to the Bastille

1. Godechot, *The Taking of the Bastille*, p.162
2. Roger Price (ed.), *Documents of the French Revolution of 1848* (London, 1996), p.20
3. Morris, *A diary of the French Revolution* (London, 1939), p.149
4. *Documents of the French Revolution*, p.54
5. Bowen, *Cricket* (London, 1970), p.67

6: Taking Sides

1. Gottschalk, *Lafayette and the French Revolution* (London, 1973), p.14
2. *Documents of the French Revolution*, p.62
3. Surely you've heard of this without me having to tell you where it's from
4. Rudé, *The Crowd in the French Revolution* (Oxford, 1967), p.57
5. Carlyle, *The French Revolution*, p.251
6. Willert, *Mirabeau* (London, 1898), p.74
7. James, *The Black Jacobins*, p.51
8. Ibid., p.72

7: The King Reacts

1. Keane, *Thomas Paine* (London, 1995), p.223
2. Ibid., p.331
3. Ibid.
4. Ibid., p.307
5. Renier, *Robespierre* (London, 1972), p.59
6. Whaley, *Radicals* (Gloucestershire, 2000), p.32

7. *Documents of the French Revolution*, p.87
8. Schama, *Citizens*, p.554
9. *Documents of the French Revolution*, p.90
10. Schama, *Citizens*, p.558
11. Levy, Applewhite and Johnson, *Women in Revolutionary Paris* (Chicago, 1979), p.19
12. Ibid., p.108
13. This and the immediately following references are to *The Life of Madame Roland* by Jeanette Eaton (London/New York/Toronto, 1930)
14. J.B. Morton, *St-Just* (London, 1939), p.9
15. *Documents of the French Revolution*, p.110
16. Ibid., p.114
17. Soboul, *Understanding the French Revolution* (New York, 1982), p.236
18. Cloomis, *Paris in the Terror* (London, 1965), p.75
19. James, *The Black Jacobins*, p.91

8: The Second Revolution

1. Allen, *Threshold of Terror* (Gloucestershire, 1999), p.65
2. Ibid., p.80
3. Ibid., p.112
4. Warwick, *Danton and the French Revolution*, p. 247
5. Schama, *Citizens*, p.720
6. Maton's account is from *Documents* p.146
7. *Documents of the French Revolution*, p.158
8. Warwick, *Danton and the French Revolution*, p. 267
9. Belfort Bax, *The French Revolution* (New York, 1902), p.42
10. *Documents of the French Revolution*, p.162
11. Brown, *The French Revolution in English History* (Edinburgh, 1918), p.64
12. R. Coupland (ed.), *The War Speeches of William Pitt* (Oxford, 1916), pp.65–6
13. Brown, *The French Revolution in English History*, p.115

9: The Republic

1. *The Life of Madame Roland*, p.234
2. Soboul, p.282
3. James, *The Black Jacobins*, p.98

10: . . . Complete Control

1. *Documents of the French Revolution*, p.311
2. Ibid., p.317
3. *Memoirs of Louis-Philippe* (New York, 1973), p.394

11: Year II

1. Pernoud and Flaissier, *The French Revolution – History in the Making*, p.223, (London, 1960)
2. Ibid., p.226
3. Soboul, *The French Revolution*, p.342
4. Ibid., p.569
5. McGarr, *Marxism and the Great French Revolution* (London, 1993), p.68
6. *Documents of the French Revolution*, p.289
7. Forrest, *Soldiers of the French Revolution* (Durham, USA, 1990), p.110
8. Polly Toynbee, *Guardian*, May 1999
9. *Documents of the French Revolution*, p.296
10. Ibid., p.299
11. Fraser, *Marie Antoinette*, p.412
12. Eaton, *The Life of Madame Roland*, p.312
13. Ibid., p.322
14. James, *The Black Jacobins*, p.111
15. Ibid., p.114
16. Ibid.

12: It's All Going Wrong

1. James, *The Black Jacobins*, p.115
2. Renier, *Robespierre* (London, 1972), p.134
3. *Documents of the French Revolution*, p.279
4. Sieburg, *Incorruptible*, p.191
5. Soboul, *The French Revolution*, p.405
6. Trotsky, *The History of the Russian Revolution*, p.114
7. McGarr, *Marxism and the Great French Revolution*, p.76
8. Cloomis, *Paris in the Terror*, p.395
9. *Documents of the French Revolution*, p.331
10. Ibid., p.332
11. Soboul, *The French Revolution*, p.443

13: Napoleon and the End of Radicalism

1. McLynn, *Napoleon* (London, 1997), p.104
2. Connolly, *Labour in Irish History* (Dublin, 1983), p.43
3. Liam Ó Réagáin, *The Best of Tone* (Cork, 1972), p.108
4. Ibid., p.144
5. Newsinger, *United Irishmen: the autobiography of James Hope* (London, 2001), p.21
6. Brown, *The French Revolution in English History*, p.157
7. Liam Ó Réagáin, *The Best of Tone*, p.192
8. Keane, *Thomas Paine*, p.431
9. Hawke, *Thomas Paine* (New York, 1974), p.344
10. McLynn, *Napoleon*, p.225
11. Ibid.
12. Ibid., p.254
13. R. Coupland (ed.), *The War Speeches of William Pitt*, p.260
14. *Saga* (Icelandic Journal), Issue 37, p.138. Impressive, ay? Is anyone really going to check that up?
15. James, *The Black Jacobins*, p.160
16. Ibid., p.271

14: The Revolution in the Mind

1. R. M. Johnston and Philip Haythornwaite (eds), *In the Words of Napoleon* (London, 2002), p.110
2. Ibid., p.161
3. McLynn, *Napoleon*, p.352
4. Rees, *The Algebra of Revolution* (London, 1998), p.34
5. R. M. Johnston (ed.), Philip Haythornwaite (ed.), *In the Words of Napoleon*, p.317

Conclusion

1. Hawke, *Thomas Paine*, p.382
2. Thompson, *The Making of the English Working Class*, p.544
3. Interview in the *Independent*, October 2000

BIBLIOGRAPHY

I've never been entirely sure of the purpose of bibliographies. What's the point of telling the reader there is a more detailed account of the obscure battle obliquely referred to in Chapter 23, in a pile of documents only available if arranged by prior appointment with the National Crop-Rotation Museum in Budapest? So the books in this bibliography are mentioned for one of two specific purposes: either they are available and offer the reader a more detailed account of the issues I've covered, or they allow me to show off.

Despite what I've said about Simon Schama's *Citizens* (London, 1989) it is an entertaining read, with plenty of gripping stories in its 900 pages. The problem is, because he has such contempt for the revolution he misses out the millions of human stories that revolve around the mass of humanity that supported it.

Diametrically opposite to *Citizens* is *Marxism and the Great French Revolution* (London, 1993); a 100-page synopsis of the whole event from start to end by Paul McGarr. This is a splendidly thorough and readable account; an ideal introduction for anyone who can't manage the 300 pages of *this* book.

Somewhere in the middle (in size and style but not politically) is *The French Revolution* by Albert Soboul (London, 1989), 600 pages, full of analysis, devoid of pomposity, but could do with just a smidgen of humour to lighten up the dryness. Still, Soboul was a Communist Party member, and 'lightness of touch' wasn't always the first phrase to come to mind for your average Stalinist.

The Crowd in the French Revolution by George Rudé (Oxford, 1967) is full of remarkable and fascinating details about who was involved in each of the main uprisings. The trouble is it's out of print, so I'm buggered if I know where you'd get hold of a copy.

But the book worth pursuing most of all is *The French Revolution – History in the Making* (London, 1960). Compiled by Georges Pernoud and Sabine Flaissier, it contains excerpts of contemporary documents, from a watchmaker who helped storm the Bastille, the King's barber, Drouet, Sanson the executioner and dozens more – compelling from start to finish.

Of the books that deal with one aspect of the revolution, the most essential is *The Black Jacobins* by C.L.R. James (London, 1938). Through exhaustive research, James uncovered the full story of the slave rebellion and linked it beautifully to the events in France. All that and he loved cricket.

The most entertaining book I found on the Renaissance was Michael White's biography of Leonardo, *The First Scientist* (London, 2000). For the English Civil War, start with the splendidly concise pamphlet *The English Revolution 1640* (London, 1940) by Christopher Hill. After that the subject is plagued with books that leave you thinking, 'I'm sure that was fascinating but what actually happened?' This can be dealt with by John Buchan's biography of Cromwell, *Oliver Cromwell* (London, 1934).

Robert Darnton's *Forbidden Best-Sellers of Pre-Revolutionary France* (New York/London, 1996) gives a lucid and explicit account of the alliance between philosophy and pornography before the revolution. Expect to see this serialized on Channel 5 if they ever got told to cover history. *The Taking of the Bastille* by Jacques Godechot (London, 1970) is wonderfully detailed and personal about the early stages of the revolution. *The French Revolution in English History* by Philip Anthony Brown (Edinburgh, 1918) does a similar job for the impact in Britain. And *At Home with the Marquis de Sade* by Francine du Plessix Gray (London, 1998) tells that character's staggering story with the aplomb he deserves. *Rights of Man* by Tom Paine (London, 1791/2) remains as glorious and inspiring as ever, and should be compulsory reading for every living creature. The biographies of Paine by John Keane

(London, 1995) and David Freeman Hawke (New York, 1974) capture the essence of the bloke's amazing life. *The Waiting City* (London, 1933) is a fascinating collection of articles written about Paris by Louis-Sebastien-Mercier between 1782 and 1788. Frank McLynn's biography, *Napoleon* (London, 1998) is a wonderful account, with remarkably few of the tedious maps and arrows that plague most Napoleon literature. And *A Place of Greater Safety* by Hilary Mantel (London, 1992) *almost* manages to tell the whole story of the revolution as a novel.

Then there are the books I used as sources for material on the main players, almost all of which are hopelessly out of print. For Robespierre, there's *The Incorruptible* (New York, 1938) by Friedrich Sieburg, *Robespierre* (Edinburgh, 1936) by G.J. Renier, *Robespierre* (London, 1972) by John Laurence Carr, and the imaginatively titled *Robespierre* (Glasgow, 1975) by the wonderful George Rudé. For Danton there's *Danton* (Paris, 1964) by Robert Christophe, *Georges Jacques Danton* (New York, 1928), which is part of a series called 'Voices of Revolt', and by far the best, *Danton and the French Revolution* (London, 1909) by Charles F. Warwick. Jean Paul Marat is so despised it seems hardly anyone dares write a biography, best to keep him locked away with no one referring to him, the way Victorians did with their mad grannies. The one exception I could find was *Jean-Paul Marat* (London, 1927) by Louis Gottschalk.

Amidst the countless piles of glossy bonkers about Marie Antoinette, the most palatable account may well be Antonia Fraser's *Marie Antoinette* (London, 2001). (I may be a little soft there as a consequence of her having such a magnificent husband.) The book that so enraged Pamela Oldury and her pencil was Jeanette Eaton's *The Life of Madame Roland* (London/New York/Toronto, 1930).

On the cultural impact of the revolution, I must recommend the splendidly passionate biography of Lord Byron, *The Politics of Paradise* (London, 1988) by Michael Foot. What a wonderful irony that the finest book about this spectacularly suave, handsome, glowing sex god should be written by the man known as the scruffiest old sod of the twentieth century.

The details of other subjects connected, if slightly peripheral, to the revolution, are best found in . . .

Labour in Irish History, James Connolly (Dublin, 1983); *The Best of Tone*, Liam Ó Réagáin (Cork, 1972); *Blake's Collected Works* (Penguin edn, London, 1977); *The Life of Beethoven*, David Wyn Jones (Cambridge, 1998); *The Algebra of Revolution*, John Rees (London, 1998); *The Making of the English Working Class*, E.P. Thompson (Penguin edn, London, 1981).

Now for books that come clearly in the second category – an excuse to show off. On the changing philosophy of pre-revolutionary times, it may be worth reading a bit about Descartes. The *Descartes for Beginners* book (Cambridge, 1998) by Dave Robinson and Chris Garratt is an excellent introduction, especially when it informs you that Descartes never got up before eleven and sometimes spent all day sitting in an oven. Similarly *Introducing Rousseau* by Dave Robinson and Oscar Zarate (Cambridge, 2001) does a fine job. Rousseau's *The Social Contract* (Penguin edn, London, 1968) and *A Discourse on Inequality* (Penguin edn, London, 1984) are much easier to read than you would imagine philosophy could be. So is his *Confessions* (Oxford, 2000) but to be honest it does go on a bit. The other enjoyable Enlightenment text is Voltaire's *Candide* (Penguin edn, London, 1947).

Revolutions and the Revolutionary Tradition in the West 1560–1991 edited by David Parker (London, 2000) is an academic account of European revolutions, though from the title it's fairly obvious it's not full of cartoons and pop-up features. And *Revolutionary Europe* (London, 1964) by George Rudé covers a similar topic over a shorter period.

The build-up to the revolution is covered in *The Coming of the French Revolution* (Princeton, 1947), by Georges Lefebvre, *Origins of the French Revolution* (New York, 1980) by William Doyle and *The Ancien Regime and the French Revolution* (Manchester, 1955) by Alexis de Tocqueville. Amongst other books called *The French Revolution* are those by Belfort Bax (London, 1902), George Lefebvre (London, 1964), A. Goodwin (London, 1953), Christopher Hibbert (London, 1980) and a series of articles edited by Ronald Schechter (2001). *The Great French Revolution* (London, 1909) by Kropotkin is possibly the only work supporting every action of the *sans-culottes* written by an anarchist prince.

More selected writings are in *The French and their Revolution* (London, 1998) edited by Richard Cobb. *Understanding the French Revolution* (New York, 1982) is a collection of articles by Albert Soboul: fascinating – but probably only if you're as unhealthily obsessed by the subject as I am. Another series of articles, including the lightning story, are in *Mourning Glory* (Pennsylvania, 1997) by Marie-Hélène Huet. And there is *Echoes of the Marseillaise* (London/New York, 1990) by Eric Hobsbawm.

A Social History of the French Revolution (London, 1963) was written by Norman Hampson, but to be honest I can't remember a single thing about it. *Women in Revolutionary Paris* (Chicago, 1979) by Levy, Applewhite and Johnson contains some great documents. On a similar subject is *Women of the French Revolution* (London, 1987) by Linda Kelly. *Radicals* (Gloucestershire, 2000) by Leigh Whaley starts off well but gets bogged down in detail. *A Cultural History of the French Revolution* (New York, 1989) by Emmet Kennedy covers culture, just as *Soldiers of the French Revolution* (Durham, USA, 1990) by Alan Forrest covers soldiers. *Provincial Politics in the French Revolution – a study of Caen and Limoges from 1789-1794* (Louisiana, 1989) by Paul Hanson was probably never, to be fair, aiming at a mass audience. *The Permanent Revolution* (London, 1988) edited by Geoffrey Best is bollocks. And *The Masses Arise* (London, 1989) by founder of the Militant, Peter Taafe, stops just short of telling us the *sans-culottes* would have solved everything if they'd built a Marxist faction inside the Labour Party and that slavery was abolished by the San Domingo branch of the Militant.

The Incidents of the French Revolution in Brittany (year unknown) by G. Lenotre, cost me 50 pence in a second-hand bookshop and I was thoroughly ripped off. *The British Monarchy and the French Revolution* (New York, 1998) is by Marilyn Morris, and *The Angel of the Assassination* (London, 1935) is a soppily sympathetic biography of Charlotte Corday by J. Bowen Shearing. The only biography of Mirabeau I could find is *Mirabeau* (London, 1898) by P.F. Willert, M.A. (no less).

There is of course the most famous attack on the revolution, *Reflections on the Revolution in France* (Penguin edn, London, 1973) which is good for a giggle, especially the rabid introduction by Conor Cruise O'Brien. *Paris and its Provinces* (London/New York/Toronto, 1975) by Richard Cobb gets interesting and then goes into several pages of French. And it keeps doing this. Presumably he must have sat in his publisher's office and insisted, 'If people can't be bothered to become fluent in a foreign language to read my book, they don't *deserve* to know about Paris and its provinces.'

Artisans and Sans-culottes (London, 1981) by Gwyn Williams has some excellent quotes on the nature of the mass movement. Rodney Allen's *Threshold of Terror* (Gloucestershire, 2001) is an amazingly detailed account of the August 10th revolution, as if you're reading the following week's Sunday papers.

Two highly detailed accounts from characters who supported the early stages of the revolution are *Memoirs of Louis-Philippe* (New York, 1973), and *A Diary of the French Revolution* (London, 1939) by Gouverneur Morris. But reading these is a matter of searching through piles of tedious nonsense for the occasional nugget. The same is true for *Lafayette and the French Revolution* (London, 1973) by Louis Gottschalk. The prize for detail probably goes to Richard Cobb, whose *The People's Armies* (New York, 1987) runs to 700 pages – quite big pages with small type – just on the issue of the *sans-culotte* armies of 1793/4. And there's not one picture.

Dealing with the other side of the Terror *Last Letters* (London, 1987) by Olivier Blanc covers the last letters of prisoners about to be guillotined. An ideal cheery gift for Christmas perhaps. Also dealing with the Terror is, as the observant will have noticed, *Paris in the Terror* by Stanley Cloomis (London, 1965). And this was a BOOK SOCIETY CHOICE.

The latter stages of the revolution are covered in *The Directory* (1946) by Georges Lefebvre. And the really keen could search out *The*

War Speeches of William Pitt chosen by R. Coupland (Oxford, 1916). Possibly the only available study of the fascinating Gracchus Babeuf is *The Spectre of Babeuf* (London, 1997) by Ian Birchall. And a splendidly inspiring account of the turmoil in the British navy at the time is *The Cutlass and the Lash – Mutiny and Discipline in Nelson's Navy* (London, 1985) by Jonathon Neale. Equally fascinating is *The autobiography of James Hope* (London, 2001) by John Newsinger, about a stalwart of the United Irishmen.

The Peter Weiss play *Marat/Sade* (London, 1965) is one of the few attempts to rescue Marat, who manages to have a lower place in history than Sade. And another novel covering all the major characters in the revolution is *City of Darkness, City of Light* (London, 1997) by Marge Piercy.

Trillions of books have been written about Napoleon, so this is only the scantest glance, but apart from McLynn's biography (*Napoleon*, London, 1997) the best I'm aware of is *In the Words of Napoleon* edited by R.M. Johnston and P. Haythornwaite (London, 2002), revealing the most absorbing of the general's diaries and letters. Also interesting is *The Diary of a Napoleonic Foot Soldier* (Windrush, 1991), by Jakob Walter, one of the few who made it back from Moscow. Unfortunately most books on the Napoleonic era are more like the huge biographies by Robert Asprey. I'd have spent my money more wisely if I'd used it to buy crack.

Finally, *The French Revolution* by Thomas Carlyle, available for about a fiver, is excellent value. It's utterly hostile to the revolution, but in such flowery prose (eg 'o squalidest horse-leech') you can forgive him. It's more poignant when you know he wrote it in 1834, and after eighteen months work left it to John Stuart Mill. Mill came round the following week to inform Carlyle his servant had accidentally set fire to it and destroyed the whole thing, and Carlyle had to start all over again. Thank God we now live in an age of computers and no one can ever lose a huge chunk of work like that. You see, just because one attempt at a major work ends in ruins, doesn't mean you won't ever get it right in the end.

PICTURE CREDITS

Page 6: Portrait of Marat, Joseph Boze. Musée de la Ville de Paris, Musée Carnavalet, Paris, France/Bridgeman Art Library (GIR21164)

Page 53: Maximilien de Robespierre, Louis Leopold Boilly. Musée des Beaux-Arts, Lille France/Bridgeman Art Library (LIL16762)

Page 57: Portrait of Georges Danton, French School (18th century). Musée de la Ville de Paris, Musée Carnavalet, Paris, France/Bridgeman Art Library (GIR28337)

Page 70: 'The Oath of the Tennis Court', Jacques Louis David. Chateau de Versailles, France/Bridgeman Art Library (GIR34107)

Page 92: 'À Versailles, À Versailles', French School (18th century). Musée de la Ville de Paris, Musée Carnavalet, Paris, France/Bridgeman Art Library (GIR28334)

Page 112: Portrait of Thomas Paine, English School (19th century). Private Collection/Bridgeman Art Library (BAL137442)

Page 137: Portrait of Toussaint L'Ouverture, Joseph Julien Guillaume Dulompre. Bibliothèque Nationale, Paris, France/Bridgeman Art Library(GIR80795)

Page 162: Female Sans-Culotte, French School (18th century) Bibliothèque Nationale, Paris, France/Bridgeman Art Library (GIR161092)

Page 170: 'The Day of 21st January 1793: The Death of Louis XVI', Isidore Stanislas Helman. Bibliothèque Nationale, Paris, France/ Bridgeman Art Library (GIR173921)

Page 197: 'The Death of Marat', Jacques Louis David Musée Lambinet, Versailles, France/Bridgeman Art Library (GIR177550)

Page 215: Queen Marie Antoinette on the way to her execution, Jacques Louis David. Private Collection/Bridgeman Art Library (TPG115382)

Page 235: 'The Arrest of Robespierre', Jean Joseph Francois Tassaert. Musée de la Ville de Paris, Musée Carnavalet, Paris, France/Bridgeman Art Library (GIR18488)

Page 256: Napoleon I on the Imperial Throne, Jean Auguste Dominique Ingres. Musée de l'Armee, Paris, France/Bridgeman Art Library (GIR28464)

Page 257: Napoleon after his abdication, Hippolyte Delaroche (Paul). Musée de l'Armee, Paris, France/Bridgeman Art Library (GIR157912)

INDEX

(page numbers in italic type refer to illustrations)

Scribner

Also available in Scribner

Reasons to be Cheerful
Mark Steel

From punk to New Labour through the eyes of a dedicated trouble maker.

'Anyone who has ever taken part in a demo — or just wishes they had – will devour Mark Steel's book in one sitting' **Ken Loach**

'A unique political chronicle of the last twenty-five years that manages that tricky win-double of being both intellectually rewarding and hilariously funny' *Time Out*

'Hysterically funny in his demolition of the inelegant nuttiness of far-left verbiage, Mark Steel makes intelligent people laugh hopefully, a job of extraordinary value' *Independent*

ISBN 0 7432 0804 8
£6.99